Fodor's

LOS CABOS

Welcome to Los Cabos

With coastline that stretches from the Sea of Cortez to the Pacific Ocean, and 350 sunny days a year, Los Cabos is Mexico's ultimate seaside escape. The sister towns of Cabo San Lucas and San José del Cabo offer endless summer and distinct experiences that range from all-night bar crawls to Thursday-night art walks. Between them the Corridor presents all-inclusive resorts with everything for the perfect vacation. As you plan your upcoming travels to Los Cabos, please confirm that places are still open and let us know when we need to make updates by writing to us at this address: corrections@fodors.com.

TOP REASONS TO GO

★ **Beaches:** More than 80 km (50 miles) of gorgeous strands with towering rock formations.

★ **Golf:** Spectacular views from greens designed by the world's best course architects.

★ **Nightlife:** Cabo's after-dark, into-the-dawn party scene draws a loud, festive crowd.

★ **Sportfishing:** Beginners and pros drop a line in the "Marlin Capital of the World."

★ **Whale-Watching:** The gentle giants that migrate here swim right next to the boats.

★ **Spas:** Desert healing treatments in sumptuous resort wellness centers.

Contents

MAPS

Fodor's Features

Chapter 1

EXPERIENCE LOS CABOS

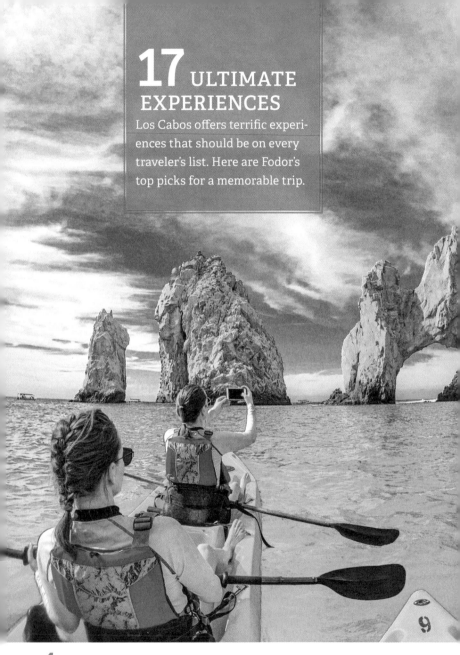

17 ULTIMATE EXPERIENCES

Los Cabos offers terrific experiences that should be on every traveler's list. Here are Fodor's top picks for a memorable trip.

1 El Arco At Land's End

These towering granite formations let you know you've arrived at the tip of the Baja Peninsula where the Pacific meets the Sea of Cortez. Accessible only by boat, El Arco ("the Arch") has become the region's emblem. *(Ch. 3)*

2 Todos Santos

This típico town on the West Cape is a perfect day trip and home to a growing expat community, cozy lodgings, and great eateries. *(Ch. 6)*

3 Whale-Watching

Gray whales migrate to Los Cabos every year from December through April, down Baja's coast and up to the east, making for a memorable viewing. *(Ch. 3, 6, 7)*

4 Shopping

Stock up on hand-painted tiles, pottery, cigars, tequila or mezcal, pure vanilla, straw hats, embroidered clothing, hand-blown glass, silver jewelry, and fire opals, plus beaded crafts of the Huichol people.

5 Sailing

Find sailboats docked at the Cabo San Lucas Marina and take a tour along the region's ultrablue waters. *(Ch. 3)*

6 Marina Golden Zone

Peruse upscale shops at Luxury Avenue and enjoy fine dining at Cabo's downtown marina. Stroll along the boardwalk for stunning sea views and dine in a traditional Mexican-style cantina. *(Ch. 3)*

7 Nightlife

A major spring break destination, downtown Cabo is known as a party zone, but you can also opt for low-key outings in San José del Cabo. *(Ch. 3, 5)*

8 Desert Excursions

Venture through the Baja desert atop a friendly camel, sail across the canyon on a zipline, cruise the sandy basin on a mountain bike, or take a thrilling ATV tour among desert and cacti.

9 Cabo Pulmo National Marine Park

Stretching 5 miles from Pulmo Point south to Los Frailes, this national park encompasses the only living hard coral reef in North America. *(Ch. 6)*

10 Seafood

Cabo is famous for its seafood, especially dishes like chocolate clams, fish tacos, smoked marlin, and lobster.

11 Sportfishing

Cabo San Lucas is nicknamed "the Marlin Mecca," but there are over 800 species of fish here. Sportfishing remains one of the area's most popular pastimes.

12 Beaches

In Los Cabos, soft, sandy beaches stretch for about 50 miles beside the turquoise and navy waters of the Pacific Ocean and the Sea of Cortez.

13 Golfing

One of the world's top golf destinations, Los Cabos has courses throughout the area by big-name designers like Jack Nicklaus and Tom Weiskopf.

14 Surfing

Los Cabos, with its warm seas, offers both intense and gentle waves, focused in the Pacific coast, the East Cape, and the Cabo Corridor.

15 Gallery Hopping

Stroll the charming cobblestone streets of San José del Cabo where colorful banners hang over a historic downtown that is home to high-end art galleries and a weekly Art Walk, November to June. *(Ch. 5)*

16 Spas

Get pampered at one of the many resorts with spas offering scenic outlooks and extensive body and beauty treatments.

17 Farm-to-Table Dining

In Ánimas Bajas, trendy organic restaurants like Flora Farms, Los Tamarindos, and Acre offer the chance to dine right on the picturesque farm where your food was grown. *(Ch. 5)*

WHAT'S WHERE

1 Cabo San Lucas.
Cabo has always been the more gregarious, outspoken of the sister cities. The sportfishing fleet is anchored here, and cruise ships anchored off the marina tender passengers into town. Restaurants and bars line the streets and massive hotels have risen all along the beachfront. Here you'll find the towering Land's End Rocks, and the famed landmark, El Arco.

2 The Corridor. Along this stretch of road, which connects San José to Cabo San Lucas, exclusive, guard-gated resort complexes have taken over much of the waterfront with their sprawling villas, golf courses, and upscale shopping centers.

3 San José del Cabo. The smaller, quieter, and more traditional area of Los Cabos has colonial architecture, an artsy vibe, and quality restaurants. Just minutes away are golf courses, boutique hotels, and luxury resorts, plus the community of Ánimas Bajas where organic farms are producing extraordinary dining experiences.

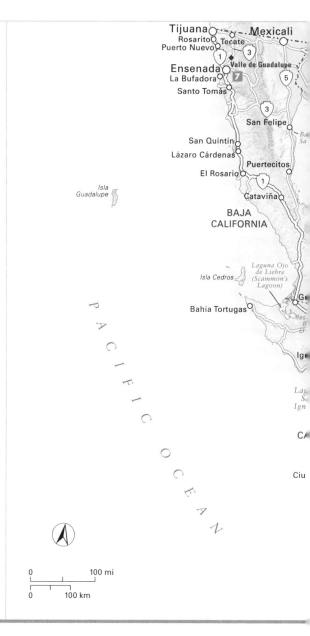

4 Todos Santos. Only an hour north of Cabo San Lucas, Todos Santos lies close enough to be part of Los Cabos experience—but still be that proverbial world away. This *típico* town on the West Cape is home to a growing expat community, as well as some cozy lodgings and restaurants.

5 La Paz. The capital of southern Baja is a "big little" city, one of the most authentic on the peninsula. La Paz is a laid-back community with excellent scuba diving and whale-watching. Its lovely oceanfront *malecón* features a number of good restaurants and hotels.

6 East Cape. One of the last undeveloped stretches of sandy serenity in the area lies east of San José del Cabo along the Sea of Cortez, to north of Punta Pescadero, Los Barriles, and Rancho Buena Vista and is home to the beautiful Cabo Pulmo National Park.

7 Baja California. The beaches and seafood of Rosarito, Ensenada, and Puerto Nuevo in the northern stretches of the Baja peninsula, close to the U.S. border, draw surfers, RV'ers, and the spring break crowd; the Valle de Guadalupe provides respite and fantastic vineyards.

Best Beaches in Los Cabos

PLAYA DEL AMOR (LOVER'S BEACH)
Water taxis, glass-bottom boats, kayaks, and Jet Skis all make the short trip out from Playa El Médano to this frequently photographed patch of sand, which is backed by cliffs and Cabo's most iconic landmark: El Arco. *(Ch. 3)*

PLAYA EL MÉDANO
Cabo San Lucas' main swimming beach is also one of its most popular. Known as a party beach, it's much like a daylong parade route fueled by buckets of beer, powerful margaritas, and that carefree feeling of being on vacation. *(Ch. 3)*

LA RIBERA
Off the beaten path, this white-sand beach on the East Cape is perfect for kayaking, paddleboarding, swimming, and snorkeling away from the crowds. It's also known for its fishing tournaments and proximity to Cabo Pulmo. *(Ch. 6)*

BAHÍA CHILENO
Halfway between San José and Cabo San Lucas, Chileno is easy to find thanks to well-marked signs. It skirts a small, crescent-shape cove with aquamarine waters perfect for swimming and a reef where you can snorkel among colorful fish or explore tide pools to the east. It is consistently ranked one of the cleanest beaches in Mexico. *(Ch. 4)*

PLAYA COSTA AZUL
Cabo's best surfing beach runs 3 km (2 miles) south from San José's hotel zone along the Corridor and connects to neighboring Playa Acapulquito in front of Cabo Surf Hotel. Surfers usually congregate in summer when waves tend to be the largest. Swimming is not advised due to strong currents and rocks. *(Ch. 4)*

PLAYA BUENOS AIRES
This wide, lengthy, and accessible stretch of beach is one of the longest along Cabo's Corridor. Much of it is unswimmable, but it's a great spot for quiet runs or walks. You can also rent water-sports equipment here and sometimes spot whales breaching from January to March. *(Ch. 4)*

PLAYA LAS VIUDAS
Just west of Bahía Santa María along the Corridor, the small "Widow's Beach" has tide pools, a shallow reef, and rock outcroppings that create private areas and natural tabletops in the sand for beach picnics. *(Ch. 4)*

Bahía Santa María

BAHÍA SANTA MARÍA
Part of an underwater reserve and protected fish sanctuary, this broad, horseshoe-shape beach has placid waters that are ideal for snorkeling. The cove is surrounded by rocky, cactus-covered cliffs but there's no shade, so you might want to bring an umbrella and your own supplies. *(Ch. 4)*

PLAYA MONUMENTOS
At eastern end of Playa El Médano, this point break popular with surfers is best viewed from Sunset Monalisa restaurant perched on the cliff. (True to the restaurant's name, it's a great place to be when the sun goes down.) The powerful waves mean it's not a good swimming beach. *(Ch. 4)*

PLAYA ESTERO
At the mouth of San José del Cabo's lush estuary that starts at the north end of Hotel Zone, this beach is home to more than 350 species of wildlife and vegetation and can be explored on foot or via kayak. *(Ch. 5)*

PLAYA LOS CERRITOS
If you're visiting Todos Santos, the best beach nearby is Playa Los Cerritos, famous for its surfing. It's great for beginners thanks to consistent but not overly powerful waves, and wading is possible near shore. The beach conveniently has a restaurant, bathrooms, and surf shops, but can get a little congested on weekends. *(Ch. 6)*

PLAYA PALMILLA
Multimillion-dollar villas and the ritzy One&Only Palmilla resort line this serene beach, protected by a rocky point that makes for calm water and the best swimming near San José. It attracts surfers to the offshore Punta Palmilla farther out to sea. *(Ch. 4)*

What to Eat and Drink in Los Cabos

MEZCAL, TEQUILA, AND DAMIANA

A locally made liqueur is the herbaceous damiana made from the dried leaves and stems of the damiana herb. You'll also find mezcal and tequila tastings easily at top restaurants and resorts. Although there are at least five "local" Cabo tequilas, most of the good stuff hails from Jalisco.

FARM-TO-TABLE MEALS

Just outside San José, you'll find farms producing fresh, beautifully green organic produce. Acre, Flora Farms, and Los Tamarindos are top farms in Ánimas Bajas, where you can enjoy Baja Sur's magical garden bounty. If you're near Todos Santos, check out Jazamango.

CHILAQUILES

Whatever you do, don't call these breakfast nachos. This traditional Mexican brunch favorite consists of fried tortilla chips smothered in salsa verde, crumbly cotija cheese, and eggs.

GUEMES TAMALES

While tamales may be known across Mexico, the *guemes* variety are specific to the Baja Peninsula. Made with pork or chicken, olives, and raisins, the steam-cooked corn wrappers are similar to the Cabo version called "fadados" prepared with stewed chicken, corn dough, and local seasonings.

TROPICAL FRUITS
Mango, guava, and pitahaya are used as key ingredients in desserts, salads, salsas, and cocktails at regional resorts and restaurants. The pitahaya cactus fruit, a bright pink-and-yellow dragonfruit that blooms in desert regions, is served on its own, in cocktails, infused into dishes, and even makes its way into jellied candies, jams, and marzipan.

TACOS DE PESCADO
Fish tacos originated in Baja California, so a trip here without eating one or two (or many) is just wrong. Grilled or fried local catches are piled on a corn tortilla and topped with shredded cabbage, cilantro, salsa, lime, and a dribble of a mayo-based sauce.

OAXACAN MOLE
Renowned for the complexity of its flavors, this dark red or brown sauce is typically served over enchiladas, chicken, and tamales. Made with chocolate, nuts, chilies, raisins, and more, it has a smoky, sweet flavor.

Chocolate clams

ALMEJAS CHOCOLATAS
Chocolate clams are neither cooked in nor taste like chocolate; their name derives from their dark brown shells. The meaty clams are a flavor-packed delicacy often roasted and seasoned with rosemary.

ZARZUELA DE MARISCOS
There are numerous versions of this Baja-style seafood stew, but it always has a mix-and-match combination of clams, crab, shrimp, cod, sea bass, red snapper, or mahimahi, along with requisite white wine, garlic, and spices.

CEVICHE
Beautiful presentations of fresh raw fish marinated in lime juice are the perfect way to try Baja's fresh fruits de mer. The poolside favorite is often made with white fish, lime, tomatoes, jalapeños, cilantro, and peppers.

FRIED LOBSTER
Lightly battered fried lobster is a good treat to try alfresco overlooking the sea from which it came. A world-famous version is served in Puerto Nuevo.

What to Buy in Los Cabos

HANDBLOWN GLASS
Artisans at The Glass Factory of Cabo San Lucas (Fábrica de Vidrio Soplado) turn crushed recycled glass into exquisite figures in deep blues, greens, and reds. It's as fun to watch the glass items being crafted as it is to select a colorful piece to take home.

TAMARINDO CANDIES
Made from tamarind fruit and wrapped in a corn husk, these small, sweet-and-sour chewy treats are a good way to bring back the local flavor of Mexico. They are traditionally sold on a stick, to be enjoyed as a lollipop, but there are many bite-size variations. For a little spice, try the jelly version rolled in chili powder.

PAINTED TALAVERA TILES
Colorful Talavera tiles, a craft introduced to Mexico by the Spanish, are usually hand-painted and glazed, and come in striking geometric patterns of ochre, cobalt, and scarlet.

Like many other souvenirs you will find in Los Cabos, they are usually made elsewhere in Mexico, but they are popular gifts and can brighten up a walkway, porch, or kitchen. You can buy them in the shops of Cabo San Lucas and San José del Cabo.

FIRE OPAL
As its name suggests, this bright red-orange stone dazzles like a fiery flame. You can buy it in various forms of jewelry such as rings, necklaces, and pendants, from local vendors at Plaza Artesanos or in the Gallery District of San José del Cabo.

HAMMOCK
What's a beach trip without lazing away in a hammock, cold drink in hand? The woven hammocks you buy in Los Cabos may well hail from the Yucatán, but they are a useful purchase for the beaches you'll encounter—and your favorite quiet spot back home. Find them at Plaza Artesanos, which beckons with stalls featuring handicrafts and curios.

DAMIANA LIQUEUR
Sure, tequila and mezcal can be found in abundance, and Los Cabos' finest restaurants have tastings that may inspire you to take some home, but if you're looking for something truly local, try damiana, a sweet, herbaceous liqueur made here in Baja Sur. The production of the sugar-cane and damiana plant-based liqueur dates back to the time of indigenous inhabitants, who believed it to be an aphrodisiac and relaxation aid. Its bottle is modeled after an Incan Goddess.

FINE ART
Downtown San José's Art District is a must for art lovers. Here, you can stroll through more than a dozen fine-art galleries to find the perfect decorative piece. Pick up a one-of-a-kind painting or sculpture from Galeria Corsica, highlighting Mexican artists, during one of the area's art walks, held each Thursday from November to June.

HUICHOL CRAFTS
The Huichol, or "Peyote People," of Nayarit and Jalisco are known for their ceremonial use of the hallucinogenic drug peyote; their visions, thought to be messages from God, are represented in their colorful, intricately beaded and woven designs on votive bowls, jewelry, bags, and prayer arrows. The price of these pieces can range from $5 to $5,000 depending on quality of the materials and the artist's skill. Spot their distinct rainbow of mesmerizing patterns in shops in Cabo San Lucas and San José del Cabo.

HANDMADE RESORT WEAR
A custom-designed bathing suit or dress from a local boutique is the perfect purchase for soaking up the sun here. A favorite boutique for locally made clothing and accessories is

Eclectic Array, which has locations in the hotel zone of San José del Cabo, Flora Farms, and the marina in Cabo San Lucas. All of their products are made by local Mexican artisans, and their colorful woven camera straps and dog collars are popular gift items. Pepita's Magic of the Moon is another excellent boutique that's stood the test of time with its one-of-a-kind clothing. Plaza del Pescador is another good stop for clothing shops.

GOODIES FROM FLORA FARMS
Artisanal salts, fresh produce and herbs, plus flowers, candies, pots, and candles can be found at Flora Farms Grocery, the store attached to the well-loved Flora Farms. However, shopping is just part of the experience at the working farm, grocery, kitchen, and spa. You can

also get a spa treatment in the open air and dine on fresh produce in a magical garden setting. Flora Farms, along with a host of farm-to-table dining experiences, is located just a short drive from San José del Cabo in the Ánimas Bajas.

ARTISANAL SOAPS
Santo Cabo's pampering, natural line of beauty and apothecary products are a must for wellness enthusiasts, and perhaps the best way to bring the scents of Los Cabos home with you. The local company is best known for their beautiful bar soaps and hand lotions made using regionally grown organic ingredients (think: aloe and cucumber, peppermint and red reef clay, or rosemary and grapefruit). Shops in San José del Cabo and Cabo San Lucas as well as Flora Farms carry the line.

Weddings

Mexico is a growing wedding and honeymoon destination. Many area hotels—from boutiques to internationally known brands—offer honeymoon packages and professional wedding planners. Although Mexican law dictates that an obligatory civil ceremony must accompany the big event, you can get married in a house of worship, on a beach, at a hotel chapel, or on a yacht or sailboat.

Choosing the Perfect Place. Los Cabos is a popular Mexican wedding and honeymoon destination. Many couples choose to marry on the beach, often at sunset because it's cooler and more comfortable for everyone; others opt to marry in an air-conditioned resort ballroom.

Consider booking an all-inclusive, which has plenty of meal options and activities to keep your guests busy before and after the main event.

Beach Wedding Attire. Some brides choose a traditional full wedding gown with veil, but more popular and comfortable—especially for an outdoor wedding—is a simple sheath or a white cotton or linen dress that will breathe in the tropical heat. Some opt for even less formal barefoot attire such as a sundress.

Weddings on the beach are best done barefoot, even when full gowns are worn. Choose strappy sandals for a wedding or reception that's not on the sand. Whatever type of attire you choose, purchase it and get any alterations done before leaving home. Buy a special garment bag and hand-carry your dress on the plane. Don't let this be the one time in your life that your luggage goes missing.

The groom and any groomsmen will want to bring their own wedding attire since there are few places in Los Cabos that rent formal suits.

Time of Year. Planning according to the weather can be critical for a successful Los Cabos wedding. If you're getting married in your bathing suit, you might not mind some heat and humidity, but will your venue—and your future in-laws—hold up under the summer heat? We recommend holding the ceremony between November and February. March through June is usually dry but extremely warm and humid.

By July the heat can be unbearable for an outdoor afternoon wedding, and summer rains, rarely voluminous in Los Cabos, begin to fall here around the same time. Although hurricanes are rarer along the Pacific than the Caribbean, they can occur August through late October and even early November. For an outdoor wedding, establish a detailed backup plan and purchase wedding insurance in case the weather does not comply. Generally insurance will cover the cost of a wedding tent if your outdoor party experiences rain.

Finding a Wedding Planner. Hiring a wedding planner will minimize stress for all but the simplest of ceremonies. A year or more in advance, the planner will, among other things, help choose the venue, find a florist, and arrange for a photographer and musicians.

The most obvious place to find a wedding planner is at a resort hotel that becomes wedding central: providing accommodations for you and your guests, the wedding ceremony venue, and the restaurant or ballroom for the reception. You can also hire an independent wedding coordinator, which you can find easily online by searching "Los Cabos wedding." Be sure to ask for references.

When interviewing a planner, talk about your budget and ask about costs. Are there hourly fees or one fee for the whole event? How available will the consultant and their assistants be? Which vendors are used and why? How long have they been in business? Request a list of the exact services they'll provide, and get a proposal in writing. If you don't feel this is the right person or agency for you, try someone else. Cost permitting, it's helpful to meet the planner in person.

Requirements. A bona fide wedding planner will facilitate completing the required paperwork and negotiating the legal requirements for marrying in Mexico. Blood tests must be done upon your arrival, but not more than 14 days before the ceremony. All documents must be translated by an authorized translator from the destination, and it's important to send these documents by certified mail to your wedding coordinator at least a month ahead of the wedding.

You'll also need to submit an application for a marriage license as well as certified birth certificates (bring the original with you to Los Cabos, and send certified copies ahead of time). If either party is divorced or widowed, official death certificate or divorce decree must be supplied, and you must wait one year to remarry after the end of the previous marriage. (There's no way around this archaic requirement, still on the books, designed to ensure that no lingering pregnancy remains from a former marriage). The two getting married and four witnesses will also need to present passports and tourist cards. Wedding planners can round up witnesses if you don't have enough or any.

Since religious weddings aren't officially recognized in Mexico, a civil ceremony (*matrimonio civil*) is required, thus making your marriage valid in your home country as well. (It's the equivalent of being married in front of a justice of the peace). Cabo San Lucas and San José del Cabo each have one civil judge who performs marriages, a good reason to start planning months in advance. Often for an extra fee, the judge will attend the site of your wedding if you prefer not to go to an office. Civil proceedings take about 10 minutes, and the wording is fixed in Spanish. Most wedding planners will provide an interpreter if you or your guests don't speak the language. For a Catholic ceremony, a priest here will expect evidence that you've attended the church's required pre-wedding sessions back home. If you're planning a Jewish wedding, you'll need to bring your rabbi with you, as Los Cabos has no synagogues. Another option is to be married in your own country and then hold the wedding event in Los Cabos without worrying about all the red tape.

Same-sex civil unions are either allowed or recognized in every state in Mexico; it is legal in both Baja California and Baja California Sur.

Kids and Families

Los Cabos and Baja don't necessarily leap to mind when planning a vacation with the kids. (This isn't Orlando, after all.) It's not that the region is unfriendly to children, but enjoying time with the kids here does take some advance preparation and research.

PLACES TO STAY

Except those that exclude children entirely, many of Los Cabos' beach hotels and all-inclusive resorts cater to families and have children's programs. A few offer little more than kids' pools, but several of the big hotels and their wealth of activities go way beyond that and make fine options for families with kids. Our top picks:

Dreams Los Cabos has an active Explorers Club for children ages 3–12. The climbing wall, splash park, playground, sandcastle contests, video games, and weekly campout adventures are always a crowd pleaser. Older kids will appreciate tennis, Euro-bungee, volleyball, and games.

Grand Velas houses the best spots for kids and teenagers in Los Cabos. Exclusively for children ages 4–12, the Kids' Club teaches little ones how to make piñatas, jewelry, masks, and kites. The Teens' Club, for ages 13–18, has a dance club, juice bar, pool table, Ping-Pong, karaoke, and private gaming pods. These supervised services are open all day, and are free to hotel guests.

Hilton's Cabo Kids' Club is geared toward kids 4–12, with a splash zone, arts and crafts, minigolf, movies, and an outdoor playground. For teens, there are engaging activities like cake decorating, painting, crafts, and even kid-and-teen spa treatments at Eforea Spa. Babysitting service is also available so parents can get some alone time.

Vacation Rentals: Apartments, condos, and villas are an excellent option for families. You can self-cater (a big money saver), spread out, and set up a home away from home. If you decide to go the apartment- or condo-rental route, be sure to ask about the number and size of the swimming pools and whether outdoor spaces and barbecue areas are available.

BEACHES

If you have visions of you and your family frolicking in the surf, revise them a bit. Many Los Cabos–area beaches are notoriously unsafe for swimming, so your day at the beach will be relegated to the sand.

The destination has a handful of beaches where you can swim, the most popular (and crowded) being Playa El Médano in Cabo San Lucas. Although it may be good for swimming, there are some quick drop-offs, not to mention the waters can get congested with party people. Other swimmable beaches include Playa Solmar on the Pacific side of Land's End and Santa Maria Beach off the main highway. Chileno Bay is great for families, but part of the cove is now dominated by Chileno Bay Resort. Estuary Beach at the north end of hotel row in San José del Cabo is relatively calm, as is Playa Hotelera just east of the San José Estuary. Playa Palmilla, near San José del Cabo, offers tranquil water most days, making it a good spot for stand-up paddleboarding or swimming. Playa Buenos Aires in the Corridor is safest between Hilton and Paradisus Resort, where the man-made Tequila Cove serves as a wave breaker. Playa del Amor (Lover's Beach), at Land's End near Cabo San Lucas, is regarded as okay for swimming on the Sea of Cortez side, but not the Pacific side. (You can't swim in any of the Pacific beaches here.)

AFTER DARK

Nightlife here is mostly geared toward grown-ups, but a few kid-friendly dining spots do exist. El Merkado in the Corridor offers an elevated "food court" concept that explores the best of Mexico's gastronomy. Flora Farms, Acre, and Los Tamarindos all have "farm-to-table" dining experiences, meaning kids can explore the grounds while Mom and Dad enjoy live music over a watermelon julep. Most all-inclusives have familiar food that will satisfy the most finicky of eaters, and the U.S. chains are all here, too.

All restaurants in Mexico are nonsmoking (except in outdoor-seating areas). Both San José del Cabo and Cabo San Lucas have modern theaters that show Hollywood movies a few weeks after they premiere back home; note, though, that animated films or G-rated films are often dubbed in Spanish.

BAJA TOP FIVE FOR KIDS

Canyon and Beach Action, Cabo San Lucas: For little adventurers, Baja Outback has turtle-release programs, ziplining, and stand-up paddleboarding. For teens Wild Canyon Adventures dishes up desert action with safari camel rides, dune buggies, and bungee jumping.

Bucaneer Queen, Cabo San Lucas: Kids of all ages can dress up like pirates and go swashbuckling and hunting for treasure on the *Bucaneer Queen*, one of several pirate cruises that operate out of Los Cabos.

La Bufadora, near Ensenada: Literally "the buffalo snort," this natural tidal-wave phenomenon near Ensenada sprays water 100 feet into the air.

Swim with the Dolphins, San José del Cabo: Kids can swim and play with friendly dolphins at the marina in Puerto Los Cabos near San José. A second dolphin center is located at the marina in Cabo San Lucas.

Whale-Watching, Los Cabos, Ensenada, Guerrero Negro, Loreto, Magdalena Bay: You'll find whale-watching venues up and down the peninsula; outfitters here take you out to sea in pangas, small boats that let you get an up-close view of the magnificent beasts. No matter what your age, Baja has no greater thrill.

Wild Wet Fun Water Park, Caduaño: It's worth the one-hour drive inland from Cabo San Lucas to this water park with splash zones and water slides.

LEGALITIES

All children over the age of two require a Mexican Tourist Card (FMT card) to venture beyond the U.S. border region. Kids 16 and under require only a birth certificate or other proof of citizenship to return to the United States by land from Mexico. If you fly home, everyone, regardless of age, must hold a passport to get back into the United States.

Don't forget Mexico's well-known and stringent laws regarding the entry and exit of children under 18. All minors must be accompanied by both parents or legal guardian. In the absence of that, the parent not present must provide a notarized statement granting permission for the child to travel. Divorce, separation, or remarriage complicate these matters, but do not negate the requirement.

If you are traveling as a full family, multiethnic family, or have remarried, adopted, or have different last names, copies of relevant documentation are always beneficial for Mexican immigration officials, just in case there are questions.

Los Cabos Today

INFLATION

By Mexican standards, the Baja Peninsula is prosperous, but things were not always so. It was only some six decades ago that Mexico even deemed part of the region to be economically viable enough for statehood, creating the state of Baja California. This is Mexico, however, and all is relative, even today. Wages here may be higher than those in the rest of the country, but you pause when you realize that about $34 a day is still the national average. The presence of the maquiladora (foreign-run factories in Mexico) economy has brought up the on-paper average level of prosperity to the peninsula.

Urban magnet Tijuana—whose population now stands at 2.1 million—attracts people from all over the country looking for jobs. Agriculture and fishing contribute to Baja's economy, too.

However, like the United States, Mexico also felt the pain of recent inflation. In 2023, food prices increased by 20% in Los Cabos alone. Cabo's location at the tip of Baja adds to distribution costs since supplies are often imported. Despite these challenges, tourism isn't slowing down in a region where hospitality is in high demand, especially with affluent travelers who are looking for luxury experiences, at whatever the cost.

CLIMATE CHANGE

A visitor flying into Los Cabos will readily observe the peninsula's stark, brown terrain—indeed, it feels like you're arriving in the middle of nowhere. You'll realize soon after landing that even though the tip of Baja once also resembled the rest of the dry, inhospitable desert, it has been transformed into an inviting desert oasis.

The landscape, where once only cacti and a few hardy palms resided, is now punctuated by posh hotels, manicured golf courses, and swimming pools. As shown by the thousands of sun-worshipping, partying people seemingly oblivious to the fact that true desert lies, literally across Carretera Transpeninsular (Highway 1) from their beachfront hotel, Los Cabos has beaten back the drylands.

A similar phenomenon exists in the northern sector of the peninsula in the wine region of Valle de Guadalupe, where lack of water has become a concern. Mass growth doesn't come without consequences. Los Cabos has slowly become impacted by climate change in the form of air pollution, water shortages, and lack of infrastructure. Valle de Guadalupe has also suffered from droughts and high temperatures in growing season. In 2022, wine grape production was down by 33%, leaving growers with uncertainty in an era of dramatic climate variations.

THE AFFECTS OF TOURISM

Historically, the peninsula was a land apart, a Wild West where only the intrepid dared to venture to seek their fortunes. But now, Baja's population is over 3.7 million and growing. Some visitors to Los Cabos and Baja experience "Sunshine Syndrome" and want to extend their stay indefinitely. In addition to those who have relocated to make Mexico their home, many foreigners have part-time retirement or vacation homes here. Tourism is a huge business in Baja, with an impressive $1 billion flowing into Los Cabos annually. Despite the pandemic pushing pause on travel, it only gave Los Cabos time to reinvent itself as a high-end traveler's dream. Since 2022, the destination experienced historic growth—1.5 times the rate of Mexico—from travelers who wanted to return to a secure, familiar environment. This growth comes at a cost, however, as Los Cabos is struggling to manage waste generated by this influx of tourists. A recent clean-up campaign resulted in more than 2.3 tons of garbage being collected by local fishermen who cast their nets at sea. The government also pledged to reduce greenhouse gas emissions by 22% by 2030.

CRIME IS RELATIVELY LOW
Considering the amount of people who visit Los Cabos, violence and crime are relatively low. As a whole, Baja California Sur is considered one of the safest states in Mexico, but visit the U.S. State Department website (⊕ *travel.state.gov*) for the most accurate travel warnings. When entering by land, be sure to cross borders (and drive) by daylight and obtain vehicle insurance for the duration of your trip.

SMOKING LAWS
As of 2023, smoking laws have been enforced across Mexico to prohibit smoking in public places. Note that it's also illegal to take vapes or e-cigarettes into Mexico.

TAXIS VS. RIDESHARES
The feud is real, so choose wisely between a taxi or rideshare network like Uber or Lyft. Both companies were still illegal as of 2024 in Los Cabos due to operating permits under Baja's transportation laws. That being said, Uber still operates in Cabo San Lucas and other areas of Baja, but be prepared to wait awhile for your driver to arrive, or even find yourself stranded. Until the government gives the green light, play it safe and rely on registered (albeit costly) taxis to get around town.

WHAT'S NEW
Named after the local postal code in San Jose del Cabo, District 23400 offers a new culinary experience with more than 20 restaurants, bars, and venues. In addition to the popular Thursday Art Walks, this gastronomic hub recently unveiled "Tasty Tuesdays" where local chefs showcase family recipes, street food, and local dishes.

Tapping into the inland drylands of Cabo are outfitters and tour companies going to the heart of rugged Baja with adventures ranging from canyon repelling to mountain biking. Cultural experiences where visitors can learn about communities, traditions, and local history are gaining popularity, and the desert farms on the outskirts of San José are capitalizing on the organic food movement with their farm-to-table restaurants, cooking schools, markets, tours, and other culinary experiences.

To keep pace with air traffic, San José del Cabo International Airport acquired 200 acres to develop an additional landing strip for future expansion. In addition to this growth, officials approved plans for construction on the airport's Terminal 4, scheduled for completion in late 2024.

Luxury hotels are on the rise in Los Cabos, with 540 new rooms added between 2022 and 2024. Hot on the heels of established five-star resorts like Pedregal, Esperanza, Las Ventanas al Paraíso, and One&Only Palmilla are new properties including St. Regis, Four Seasons Resort, Park Hyatt, Soho House Beach Club, and on the East Cape Vidanta and Amanvari.

What to Read and Watch

"JOURNEY TO LAND'S END - CABO SAN LUCAS"
Travel podcast *TripCast360* takes a journey to one of Mexico's most iconic landmarks where the Sea of Cortez meets the Pacific Ocean.

"THE FASCINATING HISTORY OF LOS CABOS"
This episode of the podcast *Unscaled Travel Show* dives into the history of Los Cabos, going from its humble and often violent past, to one of the most visited travel destinations in Mexico.

DUST TO GLORY
This documentary film (2005) gives an inside look at the off-roading motorsport race Baja 1000, which attracts hundreds of riders and thousands of fans each year.

MIDNIGHT RUN FOR YOUR LIFE
Released in 1994, this made-for-television film takes you straight to Mexico when an accused murderer flees to Cabo San Lucas, and a bounty hunter is hired to bring her back with danger hot on his trail.

BLUE MIRACLE
Loosely based on a true story, this 2021 Netflix film tells the story of a cash-strapped orphanage in Los Cabos that found hope from a boat captain (Dennis Quaid) who went all in for a chance to win a lucrative fishing competition.

THE LONG ROAD TO CABO
Take a trip to Cabo with Van Halen's Sammy Hagar & the Waboritas in this documentary that showcases his hot, heavy metal 2002 tour.

LOS CABOS: A HISTORY OF DEVELOPMENT, PEOPLE, PLACES, SEA AND SUN
Authored by Dr. Mark Schrader, this book (2020) offers insight on Cabo's past through to today's developments, and the people who played a pivotal role in its progress.

CALI BAJA CUISINE
Tijuana tacos, Ensenada aguachiles, Baja-style mussels and more are on the menu in this flavor-forward cookbook (2023) by Michael A. Gardiner that sizzles with the vibrant flavors of Baja.

BAJA WATERS: A RICK WATERS NOVEL
When the daughter of a legendary retired footballer vanishes, the intricate web of secrets and rivalries come to the surface in this novel by Eric Chance Stone (2023) where mystique meets danger in Baja.

BAJA LEGENDS: THE HISTORIC CHARACTERS, EVENTS, AND LOCATIONS THAT PUT BAJA CALIFORNIA ON THE MAP
Published in 2002, Author Greg Niemann offers an easy-to-read contemporary history of the people and resorts that helped make Baja what it is today.

Chapter 2

TRAVEL SMART

Updated by
Marlise Kast-Myers

★ CAPITAL:
La Paz (capital of Baja Sur)

♔ POPULATION:
853,026 (Baja Sur)

💬 LANGUAGE:
Spanish

$ CURRENCY:
Mexican Peso (U.S. Dollars accepted)

☎ COUNTRY CODE:
52

⚠ EMERGENCIES:
911

🚗 DRIVING:
On the right

⚡ ELECTRICITY:
120–220 v/60 cycles; plugs have two or three rectangular prongs

🕐 TIME:
2 hours behind New York

🌐 WEB RESOURCES:
www.visitloscabos.travel;
www.gringogazette.com;
www.discoverbaja.com;
www.visitbajasur.travel;
www.golapaz.com

✈ AIRPORT:
SJD

○ Ciudad Constitución

BAJA
CALIFORNIA
SUR

La Paz ○

San Juan
○ de los Planes

○ Punta Pescadero
○ Los Barriles

Todos Santos ○   EAST
CAPE ○ Cabo Pulmo

THE
CORRIDOR
○ \ ○ San José del Cabo
Cabo San Lucas

Know Before You Go

Is Baja kid-friendly? Can you drink the water? Do you need special documents to enter the country? You may have a few questions before your trip to Mexico. We've got answers and a few insider tips to help you make the most of your visit, so you can rest easy in paradise.

GET THE LAY OF THE LAND

Located at the southern tip of the Baja peninsula (Baja California Sur), Los Cabos is comprised of two towns— Cabo San Lucas and San José del Cabo—as well as their connecting "Corridor." Each of these three areas has its own vibe: Cabo San Lucas is a popular nightlife haven; San José del Cabo is quiet and artistic; and the Corridor is home to a string of luxurious resorts. Many visitors make day trips to nearby destinations, including Todos Santos, La Paz, and East Cape. Note that Baja California at the northern end of the peninsula is not within driving distance of Los Cabos; you will need to fly or take a multiday car trip to reach its beach towns, and its world-class wine region in Valle de Guadalupe 30 minutes inland. Both are close enough to the U.S. border for a weekend road trip.

SOME BEACHES AREN'T SAFE FOR SWIMMING

While there are plenty of spots to dip your toes along the coast, most resorts are on stretches of beach where swimming is dangerous or forbidden due to strong currents. The Pacific side is notorious for rogue waves and intense undertows. Unswimmable beaches include Divorce, Solmar, Pedregal, Monuments, Hotel, El Tule, and Estuary Beach. But Los Cabos proper has 22 swimmable beaches, including Cabo San Lucas's Lover's Beach (the most photographed beach, closest to the iconic "El Arco" arch) and Playa Médano (the party beach). In the Corridor, the most popular surfing beaches are Costa Azul and Zippers. In this area, you'll also find the less-congested swimming beaches of Playa Palmilla, Las Viudas, Bahía Santa María, and Bahía Chileno. When in doubt, look for green flags that indicate waters are safe for swimming. A red flag will indicate swimming conditions are unsafe.

TIPPING IS EXPECTED

Tipping is appreciated and expected in Los Cabos. If the service was good, leave 15% to 20% of the bill. Double-check to make sure this *servicio* amount was not already added to your bill. With tours and private guides, tip accordingly since some depend on tips as their main source of income. When you arrive, it's a good idea to have smaller bills to pay for tips.

A RENTAL CAR IS HANDY

Rental cars, taxis, and public transportation are all options in Los Cabos, but a rental car will offer flexibility to visit surrounding sites and explore outside of town. Rental agencies can be found at SJD airport and even at some larger hotels. If you plan on spending a great deal of time at your resort with few outside excursions, you might not need a car. Many tour operators include transportation in their rates, and taxis, while expensive, offer impeccable service and are available 24 hours a day from all hotel lobbies.

YOU MUST GET CAR INSURANCE FOR RENTALS

Regardless of the coverage you have from your credit card or travel insurance, you must (by law) have additional Mexican auto insurance to rent a car. This mandatory cost is as much as $40 per day, which is often more than the daily rental fee if you happen to find a good deal online. When renting a car, make sure that your insurance coverage includes an attorney and claims adjusters who will come to the scene of an accident.

KNOWING SOME SPANISH IS HELPFUL

If you stay within the main tourist areas, nearly everyone will speak English, and if they don't, someone nearby certainly will. In remote towns and areas less visited by travelers, you'll have to speak "Spanglish" or rely on Siri to give you the translation. Speaking the local language is always helpful and appreciated.

IT'S SAFER NOT TO DRINK THE WATER

Tap water in Mexico is not potable and comes from the surrounding mountains. It's filtered through natural sand beds and then desalinated and purified by major hotels and restaurants. To err on the side of caution, you may want to ask for your beverage *sin hielo* (without ice), as a contaminated piece could ruin a vacation; or opt for bottled water, which is readily available.

HOLD ON TO YOUR PASSPORT

You must have a valid passport to enter Mexico and to reenter the United States. The Forma Migratoria Multiple (FMM), commonly known as the Tourist Card, is no longer required for travelers arriving or departing from the Los Cabos International Airport (SJD).

ALL-INCLUSIVE RESORTS HAVE PROS AND CONS

All-inclusives are like all-you-can-eat buffets—and that has its benefits. You fork over one lump payment and have at it, from food and drink to an expansive pool complex and often water sports and excursions, too. You might consider this as one way for first-time visitors (especially families) to experience Los Cabos and not to break the bank. But it also means you're less likely to venture off-property to try local food. Note that while some all-inclusives offer endless complimentary amenities, others have a list of exclusions (in fine print) that you'll be billed for in the end.

THERE'S PLENTY OF KID-FRIENDLY ENTERTAINMENT

From stellar kids' clubs in Cabo San Lucas to epic surf breaks near Rosarito, the entire Baja peninsula has something to appease every age group. Barring the wine region in Valle de Guadalupe, many properties are kid-friendly and go out of their way to entertain children. In La Paz, kids can swim with whale sharks and a seal colony. In Cabo there are adrenaline-pumping water activities like Jet Skiing, banana boat rides, snorkeling, surfing, kayaking, and whale-watching (December–April). Smaller children may prefer a pirate boat tour, submarine tour, or interactive program at a Kids' Club. Cabo's desert adventures range from camel rides to canyon ziplining. To blend nature and education, visit between August and October when children can see rescued turtle hatchlings.

WHEN TO GO, AND NOT GO

The winter holiday season is busy, and people often book months in advance. Spring break is another busy time. Late May through September is when it's hottest and least crowded.

SENTRI SAVES THE DAY

Cut your border wait time—and frustration—in half with the Secure Electronic Network for Travelers Rapid Inspection (SENTRI) pass that expedites clearance when entering the United States from Mexico by land or air. The five-year membership includes Global Entry perks and costs around $125. To apply, create a TTP account (⊕ *ttp.dhs.gov*)and complete the online application. Upon conditional approval, you can schedule an interview at a SENTRI Enrollment Center.

BUTTS OUT

Leave those cigarettes at home, including all vaping devices, since customs will confiscate, and possibly even fine and arrest you for doing otherwise. Drug possession and use, including medical marijuana, is illegal in Mexico and may result in jail time. In 2023, Mexico imposed one of the world's strictest antismoking laws, banning smoking in public places including outdoor locations. If you're caught lighting up, expect to pay up to $550 in fines.

Getting Here and Around

Compared to other parts of Mexico, the roads in Los Cabos are nicely paved, but you should still watch out for speed traps and large *topes* (speed bumps). In Valle de Guadalupe, stop signs are often hidden and oddly placed to the far right of the street corner, so be extra careful at four-way intersections. The cheapest way to get around is by bus, but you'll be locked into a schedule and will have to walk or organize additional transportation from the bus stop.

Air

You can fly nonstop to Los Cabos from Atlanta, Austin, Charlotte, Chicago, Culiacán, Dallas/Fort Worth, Denver, Guadalajara, Houston, Los Angeles, Mexico City, Minneapolis, Monterrey, New York, Phoenix, Portland, Sacramento, Salt Lake City, San Diego, San Francisco, San Jose, Seattle, and Tijuana. From most other destinations, you will have to make a connecting flight, either in the United States or in Mexico City. Via nonstop service, Los Cabos is about 2 hours from San Diego, about 2¼ hours from Houston, 3 hours from Dallas/Fort Worth, 2½ hours from Los Angeles, and 2½ hours from Phoenix. Flying time from New York to Los Cabos is a little more than 6 hours if you're flying nonstop. Los Cabos is about a 2½-hour flight from Mexico City.

AIRPORTS

Aeropuerto Internacional de San José del Cabo (SJD) is 1 km (½ mile) west of the Carretera Transpeninsular (Highway 1), 13 km (8 miles) north of San José del Cabo, and 48 km (30 miles) northeast of Cabo San Lucas. The airport has restaurants, duty-free shops, and car-rental agencies. Los Cabos flights increase in winter with seasonal flights from U.S. airlines, and, despite growing numbers of visitors to the area, the airport manages to keep up nicely with the crowds.

Aeropuerto General Manuel Márquez de León serves La Paz. It's 11 km (7 miles) northwest of the Baja California Sur capital, which itself is 188 km (117 miles) northwest of Los Cabos.

FLIGHTS

Aeroméxico, an airline partner with Delta, has flights to La Paz from Los Angeles, San Diego, Tijuana, and Mexico City.

Alaska Airlines flies nonstop to Los Cabos from Los Angeles, San Diego, San Jose, Seattle, Portland, and San Francisco. American Airlines flies to Los Cabos from Albany, Austin, Boston, Charlotte, Dallas–Fort Worth, Chicago, Los Angeles, Las Vegas, Miami, New York (JFK), Philadelphia, Phoenix, Sacramento, and Spokane. British Airways and other European carriers fly to Mexico City where connections can be made for the 2½-hour flight to Los Cabos.

United Airlines has nonstop service from Denver, Houston, Los Angeles, and New York. Delta flies to Los Cabos from Atlanta, Detroit, Los Angeles, Minneapolis, New York, Salt Lake, and Seattle. Southwest offers direct flights on weekends from San Diego to Los Cabos.

GROUND TRANSPORTATION

If you have purchased a vacation package from an airline or travel agency, transfers are usually included. Otherwise, only the most exclusive hotels in Los Cabos offer transfers. Fares from the airport to hotels in Los Cabos are expensive. The least expensive transport is by city bus Ruta del Desierto ($5) or by shuttle buses that stop at various hotels along the route;

fares run $20 to $30 per person. Private taxi fares run from $70 to $100. Some hotels can arrange a pickup, which is much faster and costs about the same as a shuttle. Ask about hotel transfers, especially if you're staying in the East Cape, La Paz, or Todos Santos and not renting a car—cab fares to these areas are astronomical.

Sales representatives from various time-share properties compete vociferously for clients; often you won't realize you've been suckered into a time-share presentation until you get in the van. To avoid this situation, go to the official taxi booths inside the baggage claim or just outside the final customs clearance area and pay for a ticket for a regular shuttle bus. Private taxis, often U.S. vans, are expensive and not metered, so always ask the fare before getting in. Rates change frequently, but it costs about $70 to get to San José del Cabo, $85 to a hotel along the Corridor, and $110 to Cabo San Lucas. After the fourth passenger, it's about an additional $20 per person. Usually only vans accept more than four passengers. At the end of your trip, don't wait until the last minute to book return transport. Make arrangements a few days in advance for shuttle service, and then reconfirm the morning of your departure. Or at least a day in advance, sign up at your hotel's front desk to share a cab with other travelers, reconfirming the morning of your departure.

 Bus

In Los Cabos the main Terminal Central Cabo San Lucas Águila (Los Cabos Bus Terminal) is about a 10-minute drive west of Cabo San Lucas. There are also terminals in San José del Cabo and La Paz. Express buses, including Águila and ABC, have air-conditioning and restrooms and travel frequently from the terminal to Todos Santos (one hour) and La Paz (two hours). One-way fare from Cabo San Lucas or San José del Cabo to Todos Santos is about $13 (payable in pesos or dollars). From either terminal to La Paz will cost around $20. From the Corridor expect to pay about $25 for a taxi to the bus station.

The city's purple-and-yellow bus, Ruta del Desierto, has nine stops along the highway between the airport in San José del Cabo and Terminal Águila in Cabo San Lucas. Although affordable ($5), the trip from the airport to Cabo San Lucas takes over an hour and only departs from Terminal 1 (international flights arrive in Terminal 2). Plus, drop-off points are on Carretera Transpeninsular, meaning you'll still have to get from the highway to your hotel. If you have time and a sense of adventure, this is your cheapest way into San Jose Del Cabo Downtown, the Tourist Corridor, and Cabo San Lucas.

In La Paz the main Terminal de Autobus is in front of the *malecón*, the seaside promenade.

 Car

Rental cars come in handy when exploring Baja. Countless paved and dirt roads branch off Highway 1 beckoning adventurers toward the mountains, ocean, and sea. Baja Sur's highways and city streets are under constant improvement, and Highway 1 is usually in good condition except during heavy rains. The toll road between Tijuana and Ensenada is your best bet when in the northern region, with each toll costing about $2. Either

Getting Here and Around

U.S. dollars or Mexican pesos are accepted, however, change will be returned in pesos. Four-wheel drive comes in handy for hardcore backcountry explorations, but isn't necessary most of the time. Just be aware that some car-rental companies void their insurance policies if you run into trouble off paved roads. If you are even slightly inclined to impromptu adventures, it's best to find out what your company's policy is before you leave the pavement.

GASOLINE

Pemex (the government petroleum monopoly) franchises all gas stations in Mexico. Stations are to be found in both towns as well as on the outskirts of San José del Cabo and Cabo San Lucas and in the Corridor, and there are also several along Carretera Transpeninsular (Highway 1). Gas is measured in liters. Prices run higher than in the United States. Premium unleaded gas (*magna premio*) and regular unleaded gas (*magna sin*) are available nationwide, but it's still a good idea to fill up whenever you can. Fuel quality is generally lower than that in the United States and Europe. Vehicles with fuel-injected engines are likely to have problems after driving extended distances.

Gas-station attendants pump the gas for you and may also wash your windshield and check your oil and tire air pressure. A tip of MX$10 or MX$20 (about 50¢ or $1) is customary depending on the number of services rendered beyond pumping gas.

Always make sure the gas pump is displayed at zero on the liters before the attendant pumps your gas. Otherwise, this scam could cost you extra money, which ends up in the pocket of the business.

If you have an electric car, there are over 50 Tesla charging stations on the Baja peninsula, most of which are Los Cabos. You'll also find several charging stations in Tijuana, Ensenada, and at vineyards in Valle de Guadalupe.

RENTAL CARS

When you reserve a car, ask about cancellation penalties, taxes, drop-off charges (if you're planning to pick up the car in one city and leave it in another), and surcharges (for being under or over a certain age, for additional drivers, or for driving across state or country borders or beyond a specific distance from your point of rental). All these things can add substantially to your costs. If you need extras such as a car seat or a GPS, request this at time of booking.

Rates are sometimes—but not always—better if you book in advance or reserve through a rental agency's website. There are other reasons to book ahead though: for popular destinations, during busy times of the year, or to ensure that you get certain types of cars (vans, SUVs, sports cars). We've also found that car-rental prices are much better when reservations are made ahead of travel, from the United States. Prices can be as much as 50% more when renting a car upon arrival in Los Cabos. Shockingly low rates through third-party sites usually result in hidden fees when you actually pay for the car on-site. Los Cabos–based Cactus Car includes insurance, taxes, and unlimited mileage in the quoted rate and have a solid fleet of compact cars, SUVs, and vans. They have some of the best prices in the area and include 30% discounts on local attractions when booking through their website.

■ TIP→ **Make sure that a confirmed reservation guarantees you a car. Agencies sometimes overbook, particularly for busy weekends and holiday periods.**

Taxi fares are especially steep in Los Cabos, and a rental car can come in handy if you'd like to dine at the Corridor hotels, travel frequently between the two towns, stay at a hotel along the Cabo Corridor, spend more than a few days in Los Cabos, or plan to see some of the sights outside Los Cabos proper, such as La Paz, Todos Santos, or even farther afield. If you don't want to rent a car, your hotel concierge or tour operator can arrange for a car with a driver or private transfer service.

Convertibles and jeeps are popular rentals, but beware of sunburn and wind-burn, and remember there's nowhere to stash your belongings out of sight. Most rental fleets only have automatics vs manual transmission. If you rent from a major U.S.-based company, you can find a compact car for about $60 per day ($420 per week), including unlimited mileage, and 16% tax; however, having the pro-tection of complete coverage insurance will add another $25 per day, depending on the company, so you should figure the cost of insurance into your budget. You will pay considerably more (probably dou-ble) for a larger or higher-end car. Most vendors negotiate considerably if tourism is slow; ask about special rates if you're renting by the week.

To increase the likelihood of getting the car you want and to get considerably bet-ter car-rental prices, make arrangements before you leave for your trip. You can sometimes find cheaper rates online. No matter how you book, rates are generally much lower when you reserve a car in advance outside Mexico.

In Mexico your own driver's license is acceptable. In most cases the minimum rental age is 21, although some compa-nies may tack on a surcharge for drivers under 25. A valid driver's license, major credit card, and Mexican car insurance are required.

CAR-RENTAL INSURANCE

In Mexico, the law states that drivers must carry mandatory Third Party Liability, an expense that is not covered by U.S. insurance policies or by credit card companies. To be safe, agree to at least the minimum rental insurance. It's best to be completely covered when driving in Mexico. Also, if you're driving across the border from the United States, you're required to bring appropriate identifica-tion and proof of Mexico auto insurance. If your car is financed, you'll also need a letter of permission from your lender.

Even if you have auto insurance back home, you must buy the collision- or loss-damage waiver (CDW or LDW) from the car-rental company, which eliminates your liability for damage to the car. Some credit cards offer CDW coverage, but it's **secondary rental car insurance**, mean-ing you must first file a claim with your personal insurance company. But no credit-card insurance is valid unless you use that card for all transactions, from reserving to paying the final bill.

Rather than fear what might happen, always purchase a Mexican liabili-ty insurance package so you know you're covered.

Getting Here and Around

RIDE-SHARING

Ride shares such as Uber and Lyft are not readily available in Los Cabos. Although they operate around town, they are not permitted to pick up passengers due to operating permits under Baja's transportation laws. If you end up using the app for a ride, be prepared to wait awhile, or even find yourself stranded due to lack of vehicles in your area.

ROAD CONDITIONS

Mexico Highway 1, also known as the Carretera Transpeninsular, runs the entire 1,700 km (1,054 miles) from Tijuana to Cabo San Lucas. Do not drive the highway at high speeds or at night—it is not lighted and is very narrow much of the way. For a faster option, the toll road begins just after the airport with exit points in San José del Cabo ($2.50) and Cabo San Lucas ($5.50). From there you can jump on Highway 19 to Todos Santos.

Four-lane Highway 19 runs between Cabo San Lucas and Todos Santos, joining Highway 1 below La Paz. The four-lane road between San José del Cabo and Cabo San Lucas is usually in good condition. Roadwork along the highway is common and may cause delays or require detours.

In rural areas roads tend to be iffy and in unpredictable conditions. Use caution, especially during the rainy season, when rock slides and potholes are a problem, and be alert for animals—cattle, goats, horses, coyotes, and dogs in particular—even on highways. If you have a long distance to cover, start early, fill up on gas, and remember to keep your tank full, as gas stations are not as abundant here as they are in the United States or Europe. Allow extra time for unforeseen obstacles.

Signage is not always adequate in Mexico, and the best advice is to travel with a companion and a good map. Take your time. Always lock your car, and never leave valuables in plain sight (the trunk will suffice for daytime outings, but be smart about stashing expensive items in there in full view of curious onlookers).

Your smart phone's map should suffice to get you around, but it's a good idea to stock up on every map your rental-car company has for back up. Gas stations generally do not carry maps.

ROADSIDE EMERGENCIES

The Mexican Tourism Ministry operates a fleet of more than 350 pickup trucks, known as the Angeles Verdes, or Green Angels. Bilingual drivers provide mechanical help, first aid, radio-telephone communication, basic supplies and small parts, towing, tourist information, and protection. Services are free; spare parts, fuel, and lubricants are provided at cost. Tips are always appreciated ($20–$30 for big jobs, $10–$15 for minor repairs). The Green Angels patrol sections of the major highways daily 8–6 (later on holiday weekends). If you break down, call Green Angels at 078. If you witness an accident, do not stop to help—it could be a ploy to rob you or could get you interminably involved with the police. Instead, notify the nearest official.

SAFETY ON THE ROAD

The mythical *banditos* are not a big concern in Baja. Still, **do your best to avoid driving at night,** especially in rural areas. Cows and burros grazing alongside the road can pose as real a danger as the ones actually in the road—you never know when they'll decide to wander into traffic.

Though it isn't common in Los Cabos, police may pull you over for supposedly breaking the law, or for being a good prospect for a scam. If it happens to you, remember to be polite. Tell the officer that you would like to talk to the police captain when you get to the station. The officer will usually let you go. If you're stopped for speeding, the officer should hold your license until you pay the fine at the local police station, but he will always prefer taking a *mordida* (small bribe) to wasting his time at the police station. Corruption is a fact of life in Mexico, and the $20–$40 it costs to get your license back is supplementary income for the officer who pulled you over with no intention of taking you to police headquarters.

 # Taxi

Taxis are plentiful throughout Baja Sur, even in the smallest towns. Government-certified taxis have a license with a photo of the driver and a taxi number prominently displayed. Fares are exorbitant in Los Cabos, and the taxi union is very powerful. Some visitors have taken to boycotting taxis completely, using rental cars and buses instead, the latter of which can be the most time-consuming. The fare between Cabo San Lucas and San José del Cabo runs about $80–$120 at night. Cabs from Corridor hotels to either town run at least $50 each way. Expect to pay at least $75 from the airport to hotels in San José, and closer to $120 to Cabo.

In La Paz taxis are readily available and inexpensive. A ride within town costs under $10; a trip to Pichilingue costs between $15 and $20. Illegal taxis aren't a problem in this region.

Essentials

🏃 Activities

Los Cabos has something for everyone in a relatively small area. Whether you want a lively beach or a secluded cove, high-speed Jet Ski rides or leisurely fishing trips, deep-sea scuba expeditions or casual snorkeling, the waters off Cabo and the surrounding area offer endless possibilities.

Long stretches of coastline along the Sea of Cortez and the Pacific Ocean make Los Cabos a beautiful spot for a beach vacation. Be careful about where you take a dip, though—many of the beaches border sea waters that are too dangerous for swimming due to strong undercurrents. Nearly 360 warm and sunny days per year make Los Cabos a natural wonderland, where outdoor activities—both land- and water-based—can be enjoyed year-round.

Jet-Skiing and sailing are found almost exclusively at Cabo San Lucas's Playa El Médano, where you can also go kayaking. At least eight good scuba-diving sites are near Playa del Amor. The East Cape, which includes the town of Cabo Pulmo, is a great area for kayaking, fishing, diving, and snorkeling. In fact, Cabo Pulmo has the only coral reef ecosystem in the Gulf of California, making it a protected National Marine Park recognized as a World Heritage Site by UNESCO. There are numerous spots to dive—even just snorkeling right off the beach is an experience. Both the Sea of Cortez and the Pacific provide great waves for year-round surfing whether you're a longboarder or a hotshot on a short board. Still, in the spot known as the "Marlin Capital of the World," sportfishing remains one of the most famous and popular water sports.

If you'd like to mix up your Los Cabos experience with some land-based adventures, the area's desert terrain lends itself to all sorts of possibilities, whether you're a thrill seeker or a laid-back bird-watcher. You can explore cactus fields, sand dunes, waterfalls, and mountain forests on foot or horseback. Ziplining, camel rides, dune buggy tours, and electric bikes are all the rage around Arroyo Azul. Back in town you can play beach volleyball on Playa El Médano, tennis at one of the hotels, or golf at one of the many courses available. If you are fortunate enough to be in Los Cabos during the whale migration (December through April)—when the weather is perfect—a whale-watching trip with one of the many tour-boat operators is a must.

⚓ Beaches

Along the rocky cliffs of the Pacific Ocean and the Sea of Cortez lie many bays, coves, and roughly 80 km (about 50 miles) of sandy beach. The waters range from translucent green to deep navy, and even a stunning turquoise on some days of the year.

The destination has 22 swimmable beaches but most people come to Médano's active 3-km (2-mile) stretch for the crowds, since there's no better place to people-watch. Gorgeous Playa del Amor (Lover's Beach) near the famous El Arco (the Arch) is five minutes across the bay by water taxi ($15–$20). Do not pay a round-trip fare since the likelihood of your boat returning is slim. There are plenty of boats that will take you back to the mainland. It's a great spot for swimming, though the waters can be somewhat busy with all the *panga* (skiff) traffic. Just southwest of San José in the Corridor, the most popular surfing beach is Costa Azul. For less congested beaches, stay along this stretch between San Jose and Cabo San Lucas where you'll find Playa

Palmilla, Las Viudas, Bahía Santa María, and Bahía Chileno.

No other beaches are within walking distance of either Cabo San Lucas or San José del Cabo; some can be accessed by boat, but most require a car ride (unless you're staying at a Corridor hotel nearby). Since beach service and amenities are limited to hotel guests, it is imperative that you lug extra water, especially if you are adventuring during the searing summer months.

SUN AND SAFETY
If swimming in the ocean or sea is at the top of your vacation checklist, opt for a property on a protected cove, where swimming is permitted. Most resorts in the region are on stretches of beach where swimming is dangerous or forbidden due to strong currents. Look for the beach warning flags posted outside resorts: red means conditions are dangerous, yellow signals to use caution, and green signifies conditions are safe. Barely visible rocks and strong undertows make many of the beaches unsuitable for swimming. Use precaution as tides change from serenely calm or dangerously turbulent, depending on the day or even the hour. The Pacific side is notorious for rogue waves and intense undertows. Also, the sun here is fierce: don't underestimate the need for waterproof sunscreen and a wide-brimmed hat.

BEACH ETIQUETTE
As on most beaches in Mexico, nudity is not permitted on Los Cabos beaches. If you head to a beachside bar, it's appropriate to put on a cover-up, although you'd be hard-pressed to find a strict dress code at any of these places unless you're at one of the more posh resorts. As tempting as it is to pick up seashells from the beach, be advised that U.S. Customs commonly seizes these items

upon reentry to the United States. A few beaches have vendors offering umbrella rentals, but if you're really keen on having one for shelter, it's best to take your own. In Mexico, smoking is prohibited in public places including beaches and parks.

BEACH FACILITIES
Despite the lure, many of the beaches in Los Cabos are unswimmable including Divorce, Solmar, Pedregal, Monuments, Hotel, El Tule, and Estuary Beach.

There is now an established lifeguard program at the popular beaches of Viudas, Chileno, and Santa María. Staffed with even more support is the crowded strand of Medano Beach, that has four lifeguards on duty. Some hotels have their own lifeguards as well. During spring break and peak season, Jet Skis are prohibited to help avoid accidents.

Hotels will often post a red flag on the beach to alert swimmers to strong currents and undertows, but you won't see such warnings on the stretches of public beach along the coasts.

Many public beaches have toilets, but you'll still be hard-pressed to find a shower. The picnic tables, grills or fire pits, playgrounds, and other amenities common at U.S. beaches simply aren't part of the scene in Los Cabos. If you want or need anything for your day at an isolated beach, it's best to pack it yourself. If any of the following facilities are present at a beach, we'll list them: food and drink, lifeguards, parking (fee or free), showers, toilets, and water sports.

Mexican beaches are free and open to the public, though some of the resort developments along the Corridor are doing their best to keep their beaches private for guests. Resort boundaries are usually very well marked; any beach after that is free to all.

If you like:	In Cabo San Lucas	Along the Corridor	In San José del Cabo or beyond
Crystal-clear water	El Médano, Playa del Amor	Bahía Santa María	San José del Cabo's main beach (aka Playa del Sol)
Snorkeling/swimming	Lover's Beach (near the Sand Falls area)	Bahía Santa María, Bahía Chileno	For snorkeling, keep going to the East Cape and Cabo Pulmo area.
Surfing	Monuments Beach (at eastern end of El Médano Beach)	Costa Azul stretch, Acapulquito Beach (at the Cabo Surf Hotel)	Shipwreck, 14½ km (9 miles) northeast of San José; Nine Palms, just beyond
Beachside or ocean-view bars	The Office, Mango Deck, Billygan's Beach Club	Zipper's at Costa Azul, or Acapulquito Beach at 7 Seas at Cabo Surf Hotel	Buzzard's Bar & Grill (east of La Playita) or El Ganzo Beach Club
Undiscovered beaches	El Faro Viejo Beach is difficult to access, with dangerous waves, but is a gem for sunbathing.	A drive along the highway will reveal many *acceso a playa* signs—be wary of waves.	Los Frailes and Cabo Pulmo at Playa Los Arbolitos is distant—a full day's adventure—but pristine for water activities and well worth the time.

Dining

Prepare yourself for a gourmand's delight. The competition, creativity, selection, and, yes, even the prices are utterly beyond comprehension. From elegant dining rooms to casual seafood cafés to simple *taquerías,* Los Cabos serves up anything from standard to thrilling fare.

Seafood is the true highlight here. Fresh catches that land on the menus include dorado (mahimahi), *lenguado* (halibut), *cabrilla* (sea bass), *jurel* (yellowtail), wahoo, and marlin. Local lobster, shrimp, and octopus are particularly good. Fish grilled over a mesquite wood fire is perhaps the most indigenous and tasty seafood dish, while the most popular may be the tacos *de pescado* (fish tacos): traditionally a deep-fried fillet wrapped in a handmade corn tortilla, served with shredded cabbage, cilantro, and salsas. Beef and pork—commonly served marinated and grilled—are also delicious. Many restaurants import their steak,

lamb, duck, and quail from the state of Sonora, Mexico's prime pastureland, and also from the United States, though many of the high-end spots are only using local ingredients.

In San José international chefs prepare excellent Continental, French, Asian, and Mexican dishes in lovely, intimate restaurants. Following in the footsteps of Northern Baja's Valle de Guadalupe, several restaurants on the outskirts of San José del Cabo are offering farm-to-table cuisine, as well as cooking courses and tours. This organic movement has spread from the farmers' market in San José del Cabo to the luxury resorts along the coast that rely on the farms for their daily menu. The Corridor is the place to go for exceptional (and expensive) hotel restaurants, while intense competition for business in Los Cabos means many restaurants go through periodic remodels and reinvention, the Corridor restaurants included.

MEALS AND MEALTIMES

Although Mexicans often prefer dining late into the evening, be warned that if you arrive at restaurants in Los Cabos after 10 pm, you're taking your chances. Most places are open year-round, sometimes closing for a month in the middle of the hot Baja summer, and many Los Cabos restaurants close one night a week, typically Sunday or Monday.

RESERVATIONS AND DRESS

Reservations are mentioned when essential, but are a good idea during high season (mid-November to May). Restaurant websites are common, and many let you make online reservations.

Dress is often casual. Only in the most formal restaurants are collared shirts (short sleeve is fine), pants, and close-toed shoes required for men; women can always wear dress sandals with elegant evening wear. Shirts and shoes (or sandals) should be worn anytime you're away from the beach.

SMOKING AND DRINKING

Mexican law prohibits smoking in all public places including beaches, parks, hotels, and restaurants. The drinking age here is 18. Establishments do ask for IDs.

What It Costs in U.S. Dollars			
$	$$	$$$	$$$$
AT DINNER			
under $15	$15–$25	$26–$50	over $50

⚠ Emergencies

Mexico's emergency number for police and the fire department is 911. The number can be used throughout the state, and there are English-speaking operators.

Another option is air medical services—find a provider through the Association of Air Medical Services (AAMS); several of the U.S.-headquartered operations have bases around Mexico so they can reach you more quickly.

⊕ Health and Safety

In Mexico the biggest health risk is *turista* (traveler's diarrhea) caused by consuming contaminated fruit, vegetables, or water. To minimize risks, avoid questionable-looking street stands and bad-smelling food even in the toniest establishments; and if you're not sure of a restaurant's standards, pass up ceviche (raw fish cured in lemon juice). The Mexican Department of Health warns that marinating in lemon juice does not constitute the "cooking" that would make the shellfish safe to eat. Also avoid raw vegetables that haven't been, or can't be, peeled (e.g., lettuce and tomatoes).

In general Los Cabos does not pose as great a health risk as other parts of Mexico. Nevertheless, watch what you eat, and drink only bottled water. Most hotels have water-purification systems, and, regardless, tap water in Cabo meets regular standards for purity and cleanliness, however, pipes may be old. To avoid any risk, use bottled water.

Stay away from uncooked food and unpasteurized milk and milk products. Mexicans excel at grilling meats and seafood, but be smart about where you eat—ask locals to recommend their favorite restaurants or taco stands, and if you have the slightest hesitation about cleanliness or freshness, skip it. Fruit and *licuados* (smoothies) stands are wonderful for refreshing treats, but again, ask around, be fanatical about freshness, and watch to see how the vendor handles

Essentials

the food. Mexico is a food lover's adventure land, and many travelers wouldn't dream of passing up the chance to try something new and delicious.

Mild cases of turista may respond to Imodium (known generically as loperamide), Lomotil, or Pepto-Bismol, all of which you can buy over the counter. Keep in mind that these drugs can complicate more serious illnesses. You'll need to replace fluids, so drink plenty of purified water.

Chamomile tea (*té de manzanilla*) and peppermint tea (*té de menta/hierbabuena*) can be good for calming upset stomachs, and they're readily available in restaurants throughout Mexico.

It's smart to travel with a few packets of drink mix such as EmergenC when you travel to Mexico. You can also make a salt-sugar solution (½ teaspoon salt and 4 tablespoons sugar per quart of water) to rehydrate. Drinking baking soda dissolved in water can neutralize the effects of an acidic meal and help with heavy indigestion or an upset stomach. It might also help prevent a painful hangover if taken after excessive drinking.

If your fever and diarrhea last longer than a day or two, see a doctor—you may have picked up a parasite or disease that requires prescription medication.

⚠ **Divers' Alert: Do not fly within 24 hours of scuba diving.**

IMMUNIZATIONS

Although no immunizations are currently required for travel to Mexico, it's a good idea to keep up to date with routine vaccinations and boosters.

SAFETY

Considering the amount of people who visit Los Cabos, violence and crime are low. Stay up to date with travel warnings on the U.S. State Department website (⊕ *www.travel.state.gov*). While travelers are generally safe, standard precautions always apply: don't drive at night; distribute your cash, credit cards, and IDs between a deep front pocket and an inside jacket pocket, and don't carry excessive amounts of cash. Leave your passport, along with other valuables, in your in-room safe—and be sure to make copies of your passport and credit cards to leave with someone back home.

🛏 Lodging

Expect high-quality accommodations wherever you stay in Los Cabos—whether at a huge resort or a small bed-and-breakfast. Much of the area's beaches are now backed by major properties, all vying to create the most desirable stretch on the sand. For the privilege of staying in these hot properties, you'll pay top dollar—and more for oceanfront rooms with incredible views.

Sprawling Mediterranean-style resorts of generally 200 to 400 rooms dominate the coastline of Los Cabos, especially on the 29-km-long (18-mile-long) Corridor, but also on the beaches in Cabo San Lucas and San José (the town of San José is not on the coast, but inland just a bit). Currently Los Cabos has more 3 million annual visitors and 85 hotels including luxurious properties from St. Regis, Montage, and Four Seasons.

Los Cabos resorts are known for their lavish pools and lush grounds in addition to their beachfront access, although the majority of beaches on the densely developed coastline, with the notable exception of Playa Médano in Cabo San Lucas, can have an oddly deserted appearance because of the dangerous currents in the water and the predominance of luxurious pools.

If you're inclined to go beyond the beach-and-party vibe of Cabo San Lucas, it's well worth spending time in Todos Santos and San José del Cabo (⇨ *See Los Cabos Side Trips chapter*). Both towns offer exceptional independent hotels and inns, as well as burgeoning art scenes, great restaurants, and ambiance you won't find elsewhere.

ALL-INCLUSIVES
Many of the resorts along the Corridor offer all-inclusive plans that cover everything from the food and drink to an expansive pool complex and often water sports and excursions, too. Choosing that option is good if you want to check into your hotel and stay put for the duration of your stay, but it also means you'll have little reason to venture out and taste some of the diverse and remarkable food available in this region. Guests looking to get a feel for the local culture may find the generic, chain-hotel atmosphere frustrating. On the other hand, first-time visitors might consider this a viable option to whet the appetite without draining the annual vacation fund.

CABOS WITH KIDS
If you're heading down to Los Cabos with the little ones in tow, you're in luck, because many properties are kid-friendly. Unless they are adults-only properties, most of them welcome children with Kids' Clubs. Many of the independent hotels listed don't restrict children, but their size and arrangement suggest more adult-oriented accommodations. We've mentioned these factors in our reviews.

CABO CONDOS
If you're planning to stay a week or more, staying at a private property through a rental or Airbnb can be more economical and convenient than a hotel. Los Cabos has countless rental properties, ranging from modest homes to ultraluxurious villas in such exclusive areas as Palmilla near San José del Cabo and the hill-clinging Pedregal neighborhood above Cabo San Lucas and its marina. Many private owners rent out their condos, either through the development's rental pool or property management companies. The price is the same for both, but with the latter you might get a better selection. Some hotels have "residences" with two- or three-bedroom villas equipped with kitchens, laundry facilities, a housekeeping service, and access to hotel amenities.

A minimum stay of one week is typically required, though rules can vary by property. Check reviews and start the booking process at least four months in advance, especially for high-season rentals.

PRICES
Bargains here are few; rooms generally start at $250 a night and can climb into the thousands. For groups of six or more planning an extended stay, condos or villas can be a convenient and economical option, though you should always book early.

Hotel rates in Baja California Sur are subject to a 16% sales tax. Service charges (at least 15%) and meals generally aren't included in hotel rates, except at some all-inclusive resorts. Several of the high-end properties include a daily service charge in your bill; be sure you know the policy before tipping (though additional tips are always welcome). We always list the available facilities, but we don't specify extra costs; so always ask about what's included.

Essentials

What It Costs in U.S. Dollars			
$	$$	$$$	$$$$
HOTELS			
under $250	$250–$350	$351–$500	over $500

RESERVATIONS

With its growing popularity, Los Cabos has a high season that seems to keep gaining months. It's been said that high season is now mid-November through May, though the crowds are a bit more manageable in October and after mid-April. Summers can be scorchers in this desert landscape, reaching temperatures in the 90s and above. No matter what time of year you visit, rain is pretty unlikely. Los Cabos gets most of its rain between July and October—about 15 days—so book accordingly. Book your trip early, as many as four months in advance for top holidays such as Thanksgiving, the December celebrations, and New Year's and at least three months in advance for other high-season stays. Note that during any holidays, a seven-night minimum stay is required at most high-end resorts.

WEDDINGS

If you decide to get married in Los Cabos, you'll be able to enjoy nuptials with friends and family in a gorgeous setting, and there'll be no worries about heading out for the honeymoon the morning after—you're already there. Los Cabos has a bevy of choices, and prices, for dream destination weddings. If money is no object, look into the big-name properties such as One&Only Palmilla, Las Ventanas al Paraíso, Esperanza, Grand Velas, and the Marquis Los Cabos, where celebs often say "I do." Palmilla and Grand Velas even have official directors of celebrations to assist.

At Las Ventanas the romance director has an entire program dedicated to dream weddings, offering everything from a fireworks display to a ring bearer on horseback. But the true champion of weddings has got to be the Dreams Los Cabos property, where as many as five couples get hitched each week.

⇨ *For more information on planning a wedding, civil ceremony, or civil union in Los Cabos, see Weddings in the Experience chapter.*

 Money

Mexico has a reputation for being inexpensive, but Los Cabos is one of the most expensive places to visit in the country. Prices rise from 10% to 18% annually and are comparable to those in Southern California.

Prices in this book are quoted most often in U.S. dollars, which are readily accepted in Los Cabos (although you should always have pesos on you if you venture anywhere beyond the walls of a resort).

ATMS AND BANKS

ATMs (*cajas automáticas*) are commonplace in Los Cabos and La Paz. Be sure to inform your bank of upcoming travel so that your card is not declined. If you're going to a less-developed area, though, go equipped with cash. Cirrus and Plus cards are the most commonly accepted. The ATMs at Citibanamex tend to be the most reliable. BBVA México, Santander, and HSBC are other banks with many ATM locations.

Many Mexican ATMs cannot accept PINs with more than four digits. If yours is longer, change your PIN to four digits before you leave home. If you've entered your PIN correctly yet your transaction still can't be completed, chances are that the computer lines are busy, the machine has run out of money, or it's being serviced. Don't give up. Expect to pay a $5 withdrawal fee with each ATM transaction.

CREDIT CARDS

When shopping you can often get better prices if you pay with cash, particularly in small shops. But you'll receive wholesale exchange rates when you make purchases with credit cards. These exchange rates are usually better than those that banks give you for changing money. The decision to pay cash or to use a credit card depends on whether the establishment finds bargaining acceptable, and whether you want the safety net of your card's purchase protection. To avoid fraud or errors, it's wise to make sure that pesos are clearly marked on all credit-card receipts. Keep in mind that foreign transaction fees tack on an additional 3% for every purchase made abroad. If you travel often, consider getting a credit card with no foreign transaction fees and flexible travel rewards.

CURRENCY AND EXCHANGE

The currency in Los Cabos is the Mexican peso (MXP), though prices are often given in U.S. dollars. Mexican currency comes in denominations of 20-, 50-, 100-, 200-, and 500-peso bills. Coins come in denominations of 1, 2, 5, 10, and 20 pesos and 20 and 50 centavos (20-centavo coins are only rarely seen). Many of the coins are very similar, so check carefully; bills, however, are different colors and easily distinguished.

At this writing US$1 was equivalent to approximately MXP 16.94.

Nightlife

Crowds roam the main strip of Cabo San Lucas every night from happy hour through last call, staggering home just before dawn. It's not hard to see why this is *the* nightlife capital of southern Baja.

It's not all about the parties though; enjoying a fine dinner is a time-honored way to spend a Los Cabos evening. During the slow, sweltering months of August and September, some establishments curtail their offerings or close for a few weeks altogether. Don't fret though: you'll find nightlife here no matter what season you visit.

WHAT'S WHERE

Cabo San Lucas: Cabo is internationally famous (or infamous) for being a raucous party town. If Vegas hadn't already co-opted the "what happens here, stays here" mentality, Cabo San Lucas might have snatched it up. You can experience spring break here, even if you went to college 30 years ago. Quiet Cabo nightlife does exist; you just need to look a bit harder.

The Corridor: This sprawling strip between the two cities is the province of big resorts and their in-house cocktail bars. Expect upscale venues (and patrons). A few nightspots not affiliated with any hotel do exist here and are quite popular.

San José del Cabo: Proprietors here say that you "graduate" to San José del Cabo after you go through your party phase in Cabo San Lucas. For a cozy, romantic, and often cultural evening, nothing beats the quieter and more intimate San José nightlife, where it's all about a good drink and conversation.

Where Should I Stay?

	NEIGHBORHOOD VIBE	PROS	CONS
Cabo San Lucas	With lively beaches and a party atmosphere, Cabo continues its meteoric climb into the five-star stratosphere.	Close to the action; nearly every hotel in Cabo has undergone some kind of renovation recently; near swimmable Playa El Médano.	Not for those who want a quiet vacation or a truly authentic lodging experience.
The Corridor	The stretch that connects San José with Cabo San Lucas is booming with luxurious megaresorts made for visitors.	You'll have your choice of golf courses, private villas, and upscale resorts. Many hotels have all-inclusive options.	Most beaches on the Corridor are not swimmable; no reason to venture out; lacks local culture of other neighborhoods.
San José del Cabo	The most charming of the Los Cabos region, the area retains its Mexican colonial roots and offers boutique hotels and bed-and-breakfasts.	Closest to the international airport; some areas are very walkable; a nod to history and art; farthest from the crowds that gravitate toward downtown Cabo San Lucas's fiesta atmosphere.	Some areas are remote from town centers; not as lively as Cabo San Lucas if you're looking for a party.
Todos Santos	Forty-five miles north of Cabo San Lucas, this charming Pueblo Mágico (magical town) has shifted from day-trip town to a destination in its own right.	Local flavor, boutique B&Bs, and great shopping abound in Todos Santos. But the area isn't short on luxury either, thanks to its new Paradero Todos Santos eco-hotel.	It's far enough from Cabo San Lucas that you'll need a car to reach its lively bars and restaurants, although the neighborhood has some great options itself.
East Cape	The "other" side of Los Cabos most visitors don't see, this off-the-beaten path area is for adventurers and trendsetters who prioritize natural beauty and quiet over nightlife.	Few crowds flock here, and you're close to the stunning Cabo Pulmo National Park. You can still find luxury at the Four Seasons Resort Costa Palmas.	The East Cape is far from the more developed neighborhoods of Los Cabos and there isn't much nightlife. The roads are often rough and unpaved.

WHAT IT COSTS

Baja's very own Tecate beer can be pricier here than at home. Many places compete for the best happy-hour deals, often about $5 for a *cerveza*. Margaritas cost around $10. A glass of wine in an upscale venue should run $15 and up. The rowdy beach bars in Cabo San Lucas have waitstaff blowing whistles while handing out test tubes of vodka. Don't be fooled—there's a charge and tip behind each offer, so expect to pay around $8 for each. Many places add a 16%–20% tip to your tab. (Look for the word *servicio* on your bill.) A big musical event means a nominal cover charge of a few dollars; those are rare.

WHAT'S GOING ON

You'll find copies of Los Cabos publications in hotels, restaurants, and bars all over the city. The most helpful is *Visit Los Cabos* (⊕ *www.visitloscabos.travel*). The free English-language newspapers *Gringo Gazette* (⊕ *www.gringogazette. com*) and *Destino: Los Cabos* (⊕ *www. destinomagazine.com*) offer timely and cultural articles on the ever-changing scene. (We especially like the *Gringo Gazette* for its fun-loving, humorous look at expatriate life in Los Cabos.) These publications are available free at many hotels and stores or at racks on the sidewalk.

DRINKING AGE

Mexico's nationwide drinking age is 18. Bars here check IDs at the door if they have any doubts about your age. Consumption of alcohol or the possession of an open beverage container is not permitted on public sidewalks, streets, or beaches (outside of licensed establishments), or in motor vehicles, whether moving or stationary.

Smoking is prohibited anywhere in public and is restricted to private residences. Customs will confiscate vaping devices including electronic cigarettes.

Drug possession and use, including medical marijuana, is illegal in Mexico.

SAFETY

Nighttime is reasonably safe and secure here. Ask the bar or restaurant to call a taxi for you if you're going far. Taxis aren't cheap, but you shouldn't put a price on getting home safely. All the standard precautions apply: stick to well-lighted areas where people congregate. Wandering dark, deserted streets or lonely stretches of beaches is never wise, nor is staggering home in a state of inebriation.

 Passport and Visa

A valid passport is required to enter Mexico. As of 2024, the paper FMM Tourist Card is no longer necessary, as Mexican immigration implemented a digital process called FMMD. This new process is in place at all 66 international airports in Mexico, which allows border authorities to determine a traveler's authorized length of stay and either place a passport date stamp or direct the traveler through a self-service electronic gate that will generate a printed receipt with QR code.

This allows entry into Mexico for up to 180 days. If entering by land, Baja California, Baja California Sur, and Sonora have a "hassle-free" zone that allows cars traveling without an entry permit or car registration within the zone. Traveling beyond that zone requires a temporary vehicle import permit to bring a U.S.-registered vehicle into Mexico. These permits are processed through Banjercito and require a deposit that will be refunded once the vehicle leaves Mexico.

■ TIP→ **Mexico has some of the strictest policies about children entering the country. Minors traveling with one parent need notarized permission from the absent parent.**

If you're a single parent traveling with children up to age 18, you must have a notarized letter from the other parent stating that the child has their permission to leave their home country. The child must be carrying the original letter—not a facsimile or scanned copy—as well as proof of the parent-child relationship (usually a birth certificate or court document), and an original custody decree, if applicable. If the other parent is deceased or the child has only one legal parent, a notarized statement saying so must be obtained as proof.

Essentials

Shipping

DHL has express service for letters and packages from Los Cabos to the United States and Canada; most deliveries take three to four days (overnight service is not available). To the United States, letters take three days and boxes and packages take four days. Cabo San Lucas, San José del Cabo, and La Paz have a DHL drop-off location. ■TIP→ **Many stores and galleries offer shipping services for large or unwieldy items.**

Shopping

Los Cabos may not have many home-grown wares, but the stores are filled with beautiful and unusual items from all over mainland Mexico. You can find hand-painted blue Talavera tiles from Puebla; blue-and-yellow pottery from Guanajuato; black pottery from San Bartolo Coyotepec (near Oaxaca); hammocks from the Yucatán; embroidered clothing from Oaxaca, Chiapas, and the Yucatán; silver jewelry from Taxco; fire opals from Queretaro; and the fine beaded crafts of the Huichol tribe from Nayarit and Jalisco.

If you're on the hunt for custom or locally made goods, Fábrica de Vidrio Soplado (Blown-Glass Factory) in Los Cabos produces beautiful glassware. Dozens of shops will custom-design gold and silver jewelry for you, fashioning pieces in one to two days. Liquor shops sell a locally produced herbal-based liqueur called *damiana,* which is touted as an aphrodisiac. A few shops will even create custom-designed bathing suits for you in a day or so. National and international artists have opened galleries across the region as part of its burgeoning arts scene in Los Cabos, with many in San José del Cabo's historic center, and even more dotted throughout Todos Santos's downtown.

While you can still find T-shirts, belt buckles, and trinkets, Cabo's shopping scene is up to par with high standards of other Mexican resorts. Its streets are lined with designer boutiques, open-air bazaars, artisan markets, souvenir shops and luxury malls. Near Marina Cabo San Lucas, you'll find Puerto Paraiso Mall and Luxury Avenue selling high-end brands from brands Yves Saint Laurent to Dior.

HOURS OF OPERATION

Many stores are open as early as 9 am and often stay open until 9 or 10 pm. A few close for siesta at 1 pm or 2 pm, then reopen at 4 pm. About half of Los Cabos' shops close on Sunday; those that do open usually close up by 2 or 3 in the afternoon.

It's not uncommon to find some shops and galleries closed in San José del Cabo or Todos Santos during the hot season (roughly June to September), though very few shops close in Cabo San Lucas. We've noted this whenever possible. In any case, low-season hours are usually reduced, so call ahead during that time of year.

A NOTE OF CAUTION

One of the benefits of traveling in Los Cabos is the low crime rate, thanks in part to the large population of expats and year-round tourists, and the *tranquilo* nature of locals. That being said, it's always wise to pay attention to what's going on when money is changing hands. Some tips: watch that your credit card goes through the machine only once, so that no duplicates of your slip are made. If there's an error and a new slip needs to be drawn up, make sure the original is destroyed. Don't let your card leave a store without you. One scam is to ask you to wait while the clerk runs next door ostensibly to use another business's phone or to verify your number—but really to make extra copies. Again, this area is refreshingly safe and incident-free compared to many areas on the mainland, but it's always wise to be aware.

BEST LOCAL GIFTS AND SOUVENIRS

Cabo San Lucas is a great shopping town. Works of art by local artists make great treasures to take back home—and galleries will usually ship the items for you. T-shirts, resort wear, and clothing from hip Mexican designers will all compete for space in your suitcase.

If you're looking for something truly authentic and *hecho en Cabo* (made in Cabo), check out the blown glass at the intriguing **Fábrica de Vidrio Soplado.** Other fun souvenirs include the new labels of tequila offered from such outlets as Cabo Wabo, Hotel California in Todos Santos, and the Cabo Surf Hotel.

WHAT YOU CAN'T BRING HOME

Don't buy items made from tortoiseshell or any sea turtle products: it's illegal (Mexico's turtle species are endangered or threatened, and these items aren't allowed into the United States, Canada, or the United Kingdom). Cowboy boots, hats, and sandals made from the leather of endangered species such as crocodiles may also be taken from you at customs, as will birds, or stuffed iguanas or parrots. It isn't uncommon for U.S. Customs agents to seize seashells, so leave shells and sea creatures where you found them.

Both the U.S. and Mexican governments also have strict laws and guidelines about the import/export of antiquities. Check with customs beforehand if you plan to buy anything unusual or particularly valuable.

Do not bring back any agricultural items or animal products. American visitors can bring back cigars, even if they originated in Cuba but were purchased in Mexico.

For the latest official guidelines on what you can and cannot bring back from your trip, check with U.S. Customs and Border Protection.

TIPS AND TRICKS

Better deals are often given to cash customers—even though credit cards are nearly always accepted—because stores must pay a commission to the credit-card companies. If you are paying in cash, it is perfectly reasonable to ask for a 5%–10% discount—though you shouldn't assume you'll be given one.

U.S. dollars are widely accepted in Los Cabos, although most shops pay a lower exchange rate than a bank (or ATM) or *casa de cambio* (money exchange).

Bargaining is common in markets and by beach vendors, who may ask as much as two or three times their bottom line. Occasionally an itinerant vendor will ask for the real value of the item, putting the energetic haggler into the awkward position of offering far too little. One vendor says he asks *norteamericanos* "for twice the asking price, since they always want to haggle." The trick is to know an item's true worth by comparison shopping. It's not necessary to bargain for already inexpensive trinkets like key chains or quartz-and-bead necklaces or bracelets.

Taxes

Mexico charges a departure and airport tax of about $65 that is almost universally included in the price of your ticket, but check to be certain.

A 4% lodging tax on accommodations is charged in Los Cabos, with proceeds used for tourism promotion.

All of Mexico has a federal tax, or Value-Added Tax of 16%, called I.V.A. (*impuesto de valor agregado*), which is

Essentials

occasionally (and illegally) waived for cash purchases. Other taxes and charges apply for phone calls made from your hotel room.

Time

Baja California Sur is on Mountain Standard Time, Baja California is on Pacific Standard Time. And the unofficial standard for behavior is "Mexican time"—meaning stop rushing, enjoy yourself, and practice being *tranquilo.*

Tipping

In 2024, Baja's minimum wage increased by 20%, raising it to about $22 per day ($14 in the rest of Mexico). Nevertheless, there are Mexicans who think in dollars and know, for example, that in the United States porters are tipped about $5 a bag; many of them expect the peso equivalent. Following are some guidelines. Naturally, larger tips are always welcome.

For porters and bellboys at airports and hotels, $5 per bag should be sufficient. Leave at least $10 per night for maids at all hotels. The norm for waiters is 15% to 20% of the bill, depending on service (make sure a 15% service charge hasn't already been added to the bill, although this practice is more common in resorts). Tipping taxi drivers is necessary only if the driver helps with your bags; $1 to $2 should be enough, depending on the extent of the assistance. Tip tour guides and drivers at least 10% of the tour fee, minimum. Gas-station attendants receive 50¢ to $2, more if they check the oil, tires, etc. Parking attendants—including those at restaurants with valet parking—should be tipped $3 to $5.

Visitor Information

Avoid tour stands on the streets; they are usually associated with time-share operations. The free English-language *Gringo Gazette* newspaper, *Visit Los Cabos* ⊕ *www.visitloscabos.travel*), and *Destino: Los Cabos* (⊕ *www.destinomagazine.com*) are the most helpful. Discover Baja (⊕ *www.discoverbaja.com*), a membership club for Baja discounts, has links and info at its website.

The Baja California Sur State Tourist Office is in La Paz about a 10-minute drive north of the *malecón*, the seaside promenade. It serves as both the state and city tourism office. There's also an information stand on the malecón across from Los Arcos hotel. The booth is a more convenient spot, and it can give you info on La Paz, Scammon's Lagoon, Santa Rosalia, and other smaller towns. Both offices and the booth are open weekdays 9–5.

When to Go

Los Cabos enjoys a nearly endless summer, with pleasant warm temperatures and sunshine year-round. June is the hottest and most humid month, with temperatures averaging 80°F and reaching into the 90s F. It never really gets cold in Los Cabos, but January is the coolest month with an average temperature of 70°F. The water can be chilly during this time but is generally still pleasant enough for water sports. The rainy season spans July to October (peak month September).

HIGH SEASON

Although Los Cabos hotels are often busiest starting in mid-October for the sportfishing season, the high season doesn't technically begin until mid-December, running through the end of Easter week. It's during this busy period that you'll pay the highest hotel and golf rates. Spring break, which can stagger over several weeks in March and April, is also a particularly crowded and raucous time. Downtown Cabo gets very busy, especially on weekends, throughout the year. Whale-watching season (December–April) coincides with high season, but whale-watchers tend to stay in La Paz, not Los Cabos (though there are plenty of tours in Los Cabos, too).

LOW SEASON
July through October is the so-called short "rainy" season, but most summer tropical storms pass through quickly. This season is prime time for marlin fishing, which is when big-money fishing tournaments take place in Cabo San Lucas. It's also a great time to score deals on hotels that are experiencing low occupancy. Surfing is best in the summer months, and sea turtles lay their eggs at this time, when visitors can watch them scurry to the sea.

VALUE SEASON
For the best of both worlds—not too expensive, not too crowded—plan your trip during shoulder season in the spring and fall months. November and May are both excellent times to visit, because they still have pleasant weather and just miss the crowds of high season (November precedes the influx of winter snowbirds and May follows the spring break rush in March and April). November through May is also the time for Art Walks in San José (every Thursday from 5 to 9 pm).

HURRICANE SEASON
The Pacific hurricane season mirrors that of the Atlantic and Caribbean, so there is always a slight chance of a hurricane May 15 through November 30 with the peak month being September. Hurricanes rarely hit Los Cabos head-on thanks to the natural protection it receives from the bay and surrounding mountains, but the effects can reverberate when a large hurricane hits Mexico's Pacific coast. For peace of mind, track Eastern Pacific hurricanes before your trip at ⊕ www.nhc.noaa.gov and be sure to heed any and all warnings for evacuation if a storm does come.

Contacts

Air

AIRPORTS Aeropuerto Internacional Los Cabos. (*Los Cabos International Airport*). ✉ *Carretera Transpeninsular, Km 43.5* ☎ *624/146–5111* ⊕ *www.loscabosairport. com.* **Manuel Márquez de León International Airport.** (*La Paz International Airport*). ✉ *Carretera Transpeninsular, Km 13* ☎ *612/124–6307.*

AIRLINE CONTACTS Aeroméxico. ☎ *800/237–6639 in U.S., 624/146–5097 in Los Cabos, 612/124–6366 in La Paz* ⊕ *www. aeromexico.com.* **Alaska Airlines.** ☎ *800/252–7522* ⊕ *www.alaskaair. com.* **American Airlines.** ☎ *800/433–7300* ⊕ *www. aa.com.* **British Airways.** ☎ *800/247–9297 in U.S.* ⊕ *www.britishairways. com.* **Delta Airlines.** ☎ *800/221–1212, 624/146–5005 in Los Cabos* ⊕ *www. delta.com.* **Southwest.** ☎ *800/435–9792* ⊕ *www. southwest.com.* **United Airlines.** ☎ *800/241–6522, 01800/900–5000 toll-free in Mexico* ⊕ *www.united. com.*

Bus

BUS ABC. ☎ *664/104–7400* ⊕ *www.abc.com.mx.* **Ruta del Desierto.** ☎ *624/146–5320.* **Terminal Central Cabo San Lucas Águila.** (*Transportes Águila*). ✉ *Av. Hidalgo, Block Ejidal* ☎ *01800/026–8931 toll-free in Mexico* ⊕ *www. autobusesaguila.com.* **Terminal Central La Paz Águila.** ✉ *Alvaro Obregon 125, entre 5 de Mayo e Independencia* ☎ *01800/026–8931 toll-free in Mexico* ⊕ *www.autobusesaguila. com.* **Terminal Central San José del Cabo Águila.** ✉ *Calle Valerio González 1, Colonia Primero de Mayo* ☎ *01800/026–8931* ⊕ *www.autobusesaguila. com.*

Car

ROADSIDE EMERGENCIES Federal Highway Patrol. ☎ *624/125–3584.* **Green Angels, La Paz.** ☎ *01800/987–8224 toll-free in Mexico, 078 from any Baja phone.*

RENTAL CARS Alamo. ✉ *Carretera Transpeninsular, Km 43.5, at Los Cabos Intl. Airport* ☎ *624/146–1900* ⊕ *www.alamo.com.* **Cactus Car.** ✉ *Carretera*

Transpeninsular, Km 45, at Aeropuerto Internacional de Los Cabos ☎ *624/146–1839* ⊕ *www.cactuscar. com.*

Lodging

CONDOS AND VILLAS Cabo Homes and Condos. ☎ *866/321–CABO(2226) in U.S.* ⊕ *www.caboboundvacations.com.* **Cabo Villas.** ☎ *855/745–2226 in U.S. and Canada* ⊕ *www. cabovillas.com.*

Safety

EMBASSY Consular Agent in Cabo San Lucas. ✉ *Carretera Transpeninsular, Km 27.5, Shoppes at Palmilla* ☎ *624/143–3566.* **Mexican Embassy.** ☎ *202/728–1600* ⊕ *www.mx.usembassy. gov.*

EMERGENCIES AAMS. (*Association of Air Medical Services*). ☎ *703/836–8732* ⊕ *www. aams.org.* **Highway Patrol.** ☎ *624/143–0135 in Los Cabos, 612/122–0429 in La Paz.* **Police.** ☎ *624/142–0361 in San José del Cabo, 624/143–3977 in Cabo San Lucas, 612/122–0477 in La Paz.*

HOSPITALS American Medical Center. (*AMC*). ✉ *Col. El Medano, Paseo de la Marina #4116* ☎ *624/143–4911* ⊕ *www.amchospitals.com*. **Centro de Especialidades Médicas.** ✉ *Calle Delfines 110, La Paz* ☎ *612/124–0400* ⊕ *www.centraldeespecialidadesmedicas.com*. **Farmacia Baja California.** ✉ *Transpeninsular Hwy. 403* ⊕ *Ensenada* ☎ *616/166–6320*.

📦 Shipping
MAJOR SERVICES DHL Worldwide Express. ✉ *Blvd. Lazaro Cardenas, Corner of Ignacio Zaragoza s/n, Marina San Lucas* ☎ *52/55–5345–7000* ⊕ *www.dhl.com*. **DHL Worldwide Express.** ✉ *Prolongacion Leona Vicario Sn Lote 1, corner of Revolución 1810, Cabo San Lucas* ⊕ *Zona Industrial Firet* ☎ *624/5345–7000* ⊕ *www.dhl.com*. **Mailbox Store.** ✉ *Carretera Transpeninsular, San José del Cabo* ☎ *624/142–6075* ⊕ *www.mbstorecabo.com*.

POST OFFICES Cabo San Lucas Oficina de Correo. ✉ *El Medano Ejidal, Lázaro Cárdenas 22, Centro* ☎ *800/701–7000*. **San José del Cabo Oficina de Correo.** ✉ *Mijares and Margarita Maya de Juárez, San José del Cabo* ☎ *800/701–7000*.

📍 Visitor Information
CONTACTS Baja California Sur State Tourist Office. ✉ *Mariano Abasolo s/n* ☎ *612/124–2155, 612/124–1988* ⊕ *www.visitbajasur.travel*. **Discover Baja.** ✉ *8322 Clairemont Mesa Blvd., Suite 101–102* ☎ *800/727–2252 in San Diego* ⊕ *www.discoverbaja.com*. **Gringo Gazette.** ☎ *562/714–6735 in U.S., 624/121–1214 in Baja Sur* ⊕ *www.gringogazette.com*. **Los Cabos Tourism Board.** ✉ *Plaza Providencia, Hwy. 1, Km 43, next to Costco, No. 209* ☎ *624/143–5531 in Mexico* ⊕ *www.visitloscabos.travel*.

Great Itineraries

Los Cabos Daily Itineraries

Each of these fills one day in Los Cabos. Together they span the area's most quintessential experiences, from boating to El Arco and visiting the blown-glass factory, to grabbing a beer at a local brewpub and discovering Cabo's Golden Zone.

LEARN THE LAY OF THE LAND

On Day 1 take it easy, enjoy your hotel, take a swim in the pool, and get to know the beach in your general area. If staying in Cabo, meander around town, mentally noting the many restaurants and shops on the way that you might wish to sample later. Walking the length of the marina boardwalk will introduce you to Cabo's Golden Zone shopping area and a few waterfront bars: from the boardwalk's western end beginning near the **Marina Fiesta Hotel**, you'll pass through the marina's Luxury Avenue mall toward the infamous **Nowhere ¿Bar?**). The marina walk ends at the **Tesoro Los Cabos Hotel.** Here you can catch a boat for sunset cruises, whale-watching, and sportfishing.

TRAVERSING THE CORRIDOR

To see the Corridor and make it over to San José del Cabo from Cabo San Lucas, it's most convenient and least expensive if you rent a car for a few days. (Taxis are expensive, and buses limit you to their schedule and stops.) Shop around for rentals and you'll be amazed at the range. Take your time driving along the Corridor, both to enjoy the sights of the coast, and to become accustomed to the unique traits of this quirky highway. On- and off-ramps are challenging, as you'll see. About mid-Corridor you pass **Bahía Santa María** and **Chileno Bay,** fun for stops to sun, swim, and snorkel. Bring your own equipment and refreshments.

As you near San José del Cabo, you can't miss the **Koral Center** or **Tiendas de Palmilla** (Palmilla Shopping Center) across from the **One&Only Palmilla Resort.** Koral Center has El Merkado, with food stalls inspired by the marketplaces of Europe. "Tiendas" comprises upscale shops and some excellent restaurants, including Nicksan. Walmart, Costco, and Sam's Club are also along Highway 1 for your more basic shopping needs. Heading farther east, you'll see a turnout and large parking lot—a great panoramic overlook of the Sea of Cortez. It's a lovely spot to watch the surf at **Playa Acapulquito** to your right, in front of the **Cabo Surf Hotel.**

LOS CABOS BEACHES

All hotels provide beach towels, chairs, and umbrellas. To get to the most pristine beaches along the Sea of Cortez, head east out of San José del Cabo by car. At the corner of Boulevard Mijares and Calle Benito Juárez in San José, turn east at the sign marked "pueblo la playa." The paved street becomes a dirt road that leads to the small fishing villages of **La Playa** (The Beach) and **La Playita** (The Little Beach), about 1½ km (1 mile) from San José. As the gateway between San José del Cabo and the East Cape coastline, this area known as Puerto Los Cabos is marked by a series of roundabouts that branch to the marina, organic farms (Flora Farms, Acre, and Los Tamarindos), and luxury resorts like Secrets and JW Marriott.

From La Playita, drive 60 km (37 miles) up the coast to the ecological reserve **Cabo Pulmo,** home of Baja Sur's largest coral reef. Water depths range from 15 to 130 feet, and colorful marine animals live among the reef and shipwrecks. When hunger calls, stroll up the beach from Cabo Pulmo to **Tito's** for a fish taco and an ice-cold cerveza. Try to get back to La Playa by late afternoon to avoid driving

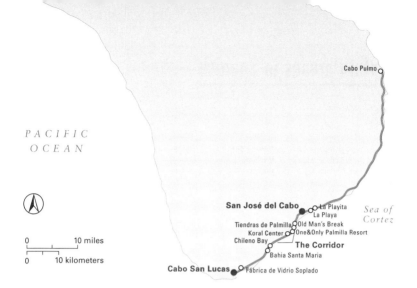

PACIFIC OCEAN

Cabo Pulmo

San José del Cabo

La Playita
La Playa

Sea of Cortez

Tiendras de Palmilla — Old Man's Break
Koral Center — One&Only Palmilla Resort
Chileno Bay

The Corridor

Bahia Santa Maria

Cabo San Lucas — Fábrica de Vidrio Soplado

0   10 miles
0   10 kilometers

the East Cape's dirt road at night. Stop for fresh seafood and a frozen margarita at **Buzzard's Bar and Grill** near the beach just north of La Playa. San José is 10 minutes away.

ARTSY LOS CABOS
Set out from Cabo San Lucas for the **Fábrica de Vidrio Soplado** (Blown-Glass Factory)—a bit hard to find if you're driving yourself. First head toward San José on Avenida Lázaro Cárdenas, which becomes Highway 1. Turn left at the stoplight and signs for the bypass to Todos Santos, then look for signs to the factory. It's in an industrial area two blocks northwest of Highway 1. At the factory you can watch the talented artisans use a process little changed since it was first developed some 4,000 years ago.

From the factory, head east for the 20-minute drive to San José del Cabo. Park at the south end of Boulevard Mijares near the Tropicana Inn, since parking is limited from here on in. Grab some lunch at **Baja Brewing Company**, located on Avenida Morelos. The pub has a tasty San José Especial cerveza, and offers international fare to go along with it. Then stroll through the central plaza, or *zócalo*, directly in front of the **Mision de San José del Cabo Anuiti** (mission church)

and peruse the several art galleries north and west of the church.

For dinner, try **Don Sanchez's** in San José proper, where Canadian-born chef Tadd Chapman is elevating the presentation of local ingredients and Mexican wines.

Alternatively, from the glass factory, head north on Highway 19 for the one-hour drive to the laid-back town of Todos Santos. Spend the afternoon visiting in-town galleries near the **Misión de Nuestra Señora de Pilar** (Mission of Our Lady of Pilar) church.

ORGANIC, GREEN, AND GOOD
Start off your morning with green juice and homemade granola at **Lolita Café** in the heart of San José del Cabo. For lunch, join a cooking class at **Los Tamarindos** organic farm, which includes a property tour and four-course meal. If you're in the area on Saturday, be sure to visit **Mercado Orgánico**, the farmers' market that takes place in San José on Wednesday and Saturday from 7 am to 1 pm. End the day with a sunset surf session at **Costa Azul Surf Shop** or participate in **Baja Outback's** evening turtle release program (August to November only). Finish with a healthy dinner at **7 Seas Seafood Grille** restaurant, known for their local products and sustainable seafood.

Helpful Phrases in Spanish

BASICS

Hello	Hola	**oh**-lah
Yes/no	Sí/no	see/no
Please	Por favor	pore fah-**vore**
May I?	¿Puedo?	**Pweh**-doh
Thank you	Gracias	**Grah**-see-as
You're welcome	De nada	day **nah**-dah
I'm sorry	Lo siento	lo see-**en**-toh
Good morning!	¡Buenos días!	**bway**-nohs **dee**-ahs
Good evening!	¡Buenas tardes! (after 2pm)	**bway**-nahs-**tar**-dess
	¡Buenas noches! (after 8pm)	**bway**-nahs **no**-chess
Good-bye!	¡Adiós!/¡Hasta luego!	ah-dee-**ohss/ah**-stah **lwe**-go
Mr./Mrs.	Señor/Señora	sen-**yor**/sen-**yohr**-ah
Miss	Señorita	sen-yo-**ree**-tah
Pleased to meet you	Mucho gusto	**moo**-cho **goose**-toh
How are you?	¿Cómo estás?	**koh**-moh ehs-**tahs**

NUMBERS

one	un, uno	oon, **oo**-no
two	dos	dos
three	tres	tress
four	cuatro	**kwah**-tro
five	cinco	**sink**-oh
six	seis	saice
seven	siete	see-**et**-eh
eight	ocho	**o**-cho
nine	nueve	new-**eh**-vey
ten	diez	dee-**es**
eleven	once	**ohn**-seh
twelve	doce	**doh**-seh
thirteen	trece	**treh**-seh
fourteen	catorce	ka-**tohr**-seh
fifteen	quince	**keen**-seh
sixteen	dieciséis	dee-es-ee-**saice**
seventeen	diecisiete	dee-es-ee-see-**et**-eh
eighteen	dieciocho	dee-es-ee-**o**-cho
nineteen	diecinueve	dee-es-ee-new-**ev**-eh
twenty	veinte	**vain**-teh
twenty-one	veintiuno	**vain**-te-oo-noh
thirty	treinta	**train**-tah
forty	cuarenta	kwah-**ren**-tah
fifty	cincuenta	seen-**kwen**-tah
sixty	sesenta	sess-**en**-tah
seventy	setenta	set-**en**-tah
eighty	ochenta	oh-**chen**-tah
ninety	noventa	no-**ven**-tah
one hundred	cien	see-**en**
one thousand	mil	meel
one million	un millón	oon meel-**yohn**

COLORS

black	negro	**neh**-groh
blue	azul	ah-**sool**
brown	café	kah-**fehg**
green	verde	**ver**-deh
orange	naranja	na-**rahn**-hah
red	rojo	**roh**-hoh
white	blanco	**blahn**-koh
yellow	amarillo	ah-mah-**ree**-yoh

DAYS OF THE WEEK

Sunday	domingo	doe-**meen**-goh
Monday	lunes	**loo**-ness
Tuesday	martes	**mahr**-tess
Wednesday	miércoles	me-**air**-koh-less
Thursday	jueves	hoo-**ev**-ess
Friday	viernes	vee-**air**-ness
Saturday	sábado	**sah**-bah-doh

MONTHS

January	enero	eh-**neh**-roh
February	febrero	feh-**breh**-roh
March	marzo	**mahr**-soh
April	abril	ah-**breel**
May	mayo	**my**-oh
June	junio	**hoo**-nee-oh
July	julio	**hoo**-lee-yoh
August	agosto	ah-**ghost**-toh
September	septiembre	sep-tee-**em**-breh
October	octubre	oak-**too**-breh
November	noviembre	no-vee-**em**-breh
December	diciembre	dee-see-**em**-breh

USEFUL WORDS AND PHRASES

Do you speak English?	¿Habla Inglés?	**ah**-blah in-**glehs**
I don't speak Spanish.	No hablo español	no **ah**-bloh es-pahn-**yol**
I don't understand.	No entiendo	no en-tee-en-doh
I understand.	Entiendo	en-tee-**en**-doh
I don't know.	No sé	no **seh**
I'm American.	Soy americano (americana)	soy ah-meh-ree-**kah**-no (ah-meh-ree-**kah**-nah)
What's your name?	¿Cómo se llama?	koh-mo seh **yah**-mah
My name is . . .	Me llamo . . .	may **yah**-moh
What time is it?	¿Qué hora es?	keh **o**-rah es
How?	¿Cómo?	**koh**-mo
When?	¿Cuándo?	**kwahn**-doh
Yesterday	Ayer	ah-**yehr**
Today	hoy	oy
Tomorrow	mañana	mahn-**yah**-nah
Tonight	Esta noche	**es**-tah **no**-cheh
What?	¿Qué?	keh

What is it?	¿Qué es esto?	keh es **es**-toh
Why?	¿Por qué?	pore **keh**
Who?	¿Quién?	kee-**yen**
Where is . . .	¿Dónde está . . .	**dohn**-deh es-**tah**
. . . the bus station?	la central de autobuses?	lah sehn-**trahl** deh ow-toh-**boo**-sehs
. . . the subway station?	estación de metro	la es-ta-see-**on** del **meh**-tro
. . . the bus stop?	la parada del autobus?	la pah-**rah**-dah del ow-toh-**boos**
. . . the terminal? (airport)	el aeropuerto	el air-oh-**pwar**-toh
. . . the post office?	la oficina de correos?	la oh-fee-**see**- nah deh koh-**rreh**-os
. . . the bank?	el banco?	el **bahn**-koh
. . . the hotel?	el hotel?	el oh-**tel**
. . . the museum?	el museo?	el moo-**seh**-oh
. . . the hospital?	el hospital?	el ohss-pee-**tal**
. . . the elevator?	el elevador?	ehl eh-leh-bah-**dohr**
Where are the restrooms?	el baño?	el **bahn**-yoh
Here/there	Aquí/allí	ah-**key**/ah-**yee**
Open/closed	Abierto/cerrado	ah-bee-**er**-toh/ ser-**ah**-doh
Left/right	Izquierda/derecha	iss-key-**eh**-dah/ dare-**eh**-chah
Is it near?	¿Está cerca?	es-**tah sehr**-kah
Is it far?	¿Está lejos?	es-**tah leh**-hoss
I'd like . . .	Quisiera . . .	kee-see-**ehr**-ah
. . . a room	un cuarto/una habitación	oon **kwahr**-toh/**oo**-nah ah-bee-tah-see-**on**
. . . the key	la llave	lah **yah**-veh
. . . a newspaper	un periódico	oon pehr-ee-**oh**- dee-koh
. . . a stamp	un sello de correo	oon **seh**-yo deh korr-**eh**-oh
I'd like to buy . . .	Quisiera comprar . . .	kee-see-**ehr**-ah kohm-**prahr**
. . . soap	jabón	hah-**bohn**
. . . suntan lotion	bronceador	brohn-seh-ah-**dohr**
. . . envelopes	sobres	**so**-brehs
. . . writing paper	papel	pah-**pel**
. . . a postcard	una postal	**oo**-nah pohs-**tahl**
. . . a ticket	un billete (travel)	oon bee-**yee**-teh
	una entrada (concert etc.)	oona en-**trah**-dah
How much is it?	¿Cuánto cuesta?	**kwahn**-toh **kwes**-tah
It's expensive/ cheap	Es caro/barato	es **kah**-roh/ bah-**rah**-toh
A little/a lot	Un poquito/mucho	oon poh-**kee**-toh/ **moo**-choh
More/less	Más/menos	mahss/**men**-ohss
Enough/too (much)	Suficiente/	soo-fee-see-**en**-teh/
I am ill/sick	Estoy enfermo(a)	es-**toy** en-**fehr**-moh(mah)

Call a doctor	Llame a un medico	**ya**-meh ah oon **med**-ee-koh
Help!	Ayuda	ah-**yoo**-dah
Stop!	Pare	**pah**-reh

DINING OUT

I'd like to reserve a table . . .	Quisiera reservar una mesa . . .	kee-**syeh**-rah rreh-sehr-**bahr** oo-nah **meh**-sah . . .
. . . for two people.	para dos personas.	**pah**-rah dohs pehr-**soh**-nahs
. . . for this evening.	para esta noche.	**pah**-rah **ehs**-tah **noh**-cheh
. . . for 8 PM	para las ocho de la noche.	**pah**-rah lahs **oh**-choh deh lah **noh**-cheh
A bottle of . . .	Una botella de . . .	**oo**-nah bo-**teh**-yah deh
A cup of . . .	Una taza de . . .	**oo**-nah **tah**-sah deh
A glass of . . .	Un vaso (water, soda, etc.) de...	oon **vah**-so deh
	Una copa (wine, spirits, etc.) de...	oona **coh**-pah deh
Bill/check	La cuenta	lah **kwen**-tah
Bread	Pan	pahn
Breakfast	El desayuno	el deh-sah-**yoon**-oh
Butter	mantequilla	man-teh-**kee**-yah
Coffee	Café	kah-**feh**
Dinner	La cena	lah **seh**-nah
Fork	tenedor	ten-eh-**dor**
I don't eat meat	No como carne	noh koh-moh **kahr**-neh
I cannot eat . . .	No puedo comer . . .	noh **pweh**-doh koh-**mehr**
I'd like to order . . .	Quiero pedir . . .	**kee**-yehr-oh peh-**deer**
I'd like . . .	Me gustaría . . .	Meh goo-stah-**ee**-ah
I'm hungry/thirsty	Tengo hambre/sed	**Tehn**-goh **hahm**-breh/seth
Is service/the tip included?	¿Está incluida la propina?	es-**tah** in-cloo-ee-dah lah pro-**pee**-nah
Knife	cuchillo	koo-**chee**-yo
Lunch	La comida	lah koh-**mee**-dah
Menu	La carta, el menú	lah **cart**-ah, el meh-**noo**
Napkin	servilleta	sehr-vee-**yet**-ah
Pepper	pimienta	pee-mee-**en**-tah
Plate	plato	
Please give me . . .	Me da por favor . . .	meh dah pohr fah-**bohr**
Salt	sal	sahl
Spoon	cuchara	koo-**chah**-rah
Sugar	ázucar	ah-**su**-kar
Tea	té	teh
Water	agua	**ah**-gwah
Wine	vino	**vee**-noh

On the Calendar

February

Carnaval. Before Lent, the streets of La Paz are awash in colorful Mardi Gras–like celebrations complete with costumes and parades.

March and April

Semana Santa (Holy Week). During this week leading up to Easter Sunday, Mexico celebrates with family gatherings, religious ceremonies, and plenty of fiestas.

August

Fiestas de la Vendimia. In celebration of the grape harvest, the wine festival in Valle de Guadalupe is held the first two weeks of August, with plenty of wine and paella. ⊕ *vendimia.mendoza.gov.ar*

September

Independence Day. Each September 15 starting at 11 pm, Mexico's president rings the country's liberty bell to signal the start of celebrations for Mexico's independence. The next day, September 16, usual festivities include a parade but vary from town to town.

November

Art Walks. On Thursday from November to June, participating galleries and shops in downtown San José del Cabo stay open until 9 pm and serve drinks and snacks, and many arrange for special events or openings. There is usually music on Plaza Mijares, and it's not uncommon for the streets to be full of people, locals and tourists alike.

Dia de los Muertos (Day of the Dead). November 2 is Mexico's national day for honoring the dead and celebrating the memory of loved ones who have passed. Family altars are decorated elaborately with photos, candles, and food.

Los Cabos Film Festival. Filmmakers from around the world debut their work at this event. ⊕ *cabosfilmfestival.com*

December

Christmas festivities. On December 12 Mexico feasts on Día de Nuestra Señora de Guadalupe (Day of Our Lady of Guadalupe), to celebrate the belief that the Virgin Mary was encountered in Mexico City on December 9 and 12. Las Posadas (The Inns), taking place from December 16 to 25, commemorates the journey of Joseph and Mary traveling from Nazareth to Bethlehem.

Gastrovino Baja Food & Wine Festival. Generally held in November or December, Todos Santos celebrates its culinary standouts at this celebration of local food and wine. ⊕ *www.gastrovino.mx*

New Year's Eve. Fireworks light up the sky over Playa Médano in Cabo San Lucas, where there's always a party.

Sabor a Cabo (The Flavors of Cabo). In early December this weeklong celebration of food, drink, and music showcases the area's top restaurants. ⊕ *www.sabora-cabo.info*

Whale-watching season. From December to April humpback whales can be spotted migrating in the waters off La Paz.

Chapter 3

CABO SAN LUCAS

Updated by
Jenny Hart

 Sights
★★★★☆

 Restaurants
★★★☆☆

 Hotels
★★★★☆

 Shopping
★★★☆☆

 Nightlife
★★★★☆

NEIGHBORHOOD SNAPSHOT

TOP EXPERIENCES

■ **Land's End:** This must-see rock formation and its surrounding beautiful beaches stun. Superb snorkeling and diving is to be found, particularly in front of the iconic natural monument, El Arco (The Arch).

■ **Alfresco Dining:** Feast on Mexican specialties and fresh, local seafood at fine open-air restaurants with gorgeous ocean and sunset views.

■ **Whale-Watching:** See the biggest show on earth as migrating humpbacks splash down in spectacular fashion each winter.

■ **Rock Star Parties:** Boisterous downtown nightspots beckon, from rock royalty–approved Cabo Wabo to the lively beachfront Mango Deck.

■ **Spa Time:** Indulge yourself with pampering massages and treatments at one of the town's dizzying array of upscale resort spas.

GETTING HERE

To reach Cabo San Lucas, fly into the Los Cabos International Airport (SJD) in San José del Cabo; Cabo San Lucas International Airport (CSL) is used fairly exclusively by private and charter planes. Getting from SJD to Cabo San Lucas is easily accomplished by a variety of transportation options, with a direct ride taking about 40 minutes.

A seat on a shared shuttle (booked at the airport) will cost between $300-450 MXN (approximately $18–$27) per person, depending on the location of your hotel. If you book in advance with Transcabo (⊕ www.transcabo.com), the shared shuttle is $26 per person or $140 for a private SUV (for up to six passengers). Uber also picks up and drops off from the airport; prices fluctuate based on the time of day and traffic. Buses from the airport are available, but are rarely used by tourists.

VIEWFINDER

■ You'll run into photogenic moments around nearly every corner of downtown Cabo San Lucas, from colorful cactus and tile displays to neon signs touting catchphrases like "I♥Cabo" and "Mexico is always a great idea." Most famous are the red #CABO signs, positioned strategically around town to ensure you'll find one, whether you're at the marina or the beach. Nothing man-made compares, however, to the stunning sight of Land's End, best viewed up close by boat or from one of Playa El Médano's many rooftop bars and restaurants.

PLANNING YOUR TIME

■ Cabo San Lucas is a year-round destination, but high season is from October to May, a fact reflected in higher hotel and resort rates. These are the most temperate months of the year, with a nearly endless succession of glorious sunshine and warm (rather than hot) temperatures. Whale-watching is best between mid-December and mid-March, while marlin fishing is best from July to October.

Lively beaches, legendary nightlife, and buzzy seaside cantinas make Cabo San Lucas the rowdiest and arguably most popular destination on the Baja California peninsula, but that's just the tip of the iceberg (or should we say *arch*?) when it comes to Cabo's myriad enticements. Cabo San Lucas is also a marlin-fishing capital, water-sports wonderland, and home to world-class resorts, all wrapped into one sun-kissed destination where the Sea of Cortez meets the Pacific Ocean.

The natural attractions of Baja's south-ernmost community are on full display from the first glimpse of the half-mile headland called Land's End, complete with picturesque beaches and notable granite formations, including El Arco (The Arch). Playa El Médano, a 2-mile stretch of golden sand, serves as the center of the local social scene and is framed by resorts, restaurants, beach bars, and sou-venir shops. Médano Beach also acts as an activities rental center for kayaks, Jet Skis, stand-up paddleboards, and more.

The impressively large and well-equipped marina is headquarters for the char-ter fishing fleet, as well as tour boats offering everything from snorkeling and diving to sunset sails and seasonal whale-watching. For all the appealing activities possible at the marina, the broad, bordering boardwalk promenade offers the appeal of a different sort;

notably, open-air dining and drinking, plus shopping stops galore—from flea mar-ket–style vendors to upscale boutiques.

Although not at the level of sister city San José del Cabo in terms of trendy restaurants and art galleries, downtown Cabo San Lucas promises plenty of great shopping, dining, and nightlife choices. A favorite of celebrities and spring breakers alike, nightclub and restaurant El Squid Roe has consistently headlined Cabo's nightlife for more than 30 years. Shops can be found on every downtown street, and although jewelry stores, pharma-cies, and souvenir outlets are the most commonly encountered retail options, discerning shoppers can find everything from folk art to custom-made resort clothing. Dining is more varied; taquerías are prevalent, of course, but thanks to a large wave of immigration some genera-tions ago, so, too, are Italian restaurants.

Freshly caught local seafood is the best bet, however, and many restaurants in town offer "you hook it, we cook it" specials for visiting anglers.

Sights

Land's End is *the* must-see attraction—not only in Cabo San Lucas, but perhaps all of Baja California Sur. It is well worth buying a ticket on a boat tour (or hiring a water taxi) just to see its many distinctive features up close. Save a day or evening for the excursion; it's easy to spend hours gazing at the scene.

★ Land's End

OTHER ATTRACTION | Land's End sightseeing is at the heart of nearly every local boat tour. Everybody knows **El Arco** (The Arch), the naturally occurring granite arc that's defined the vista for millions of years, but there's more to see here, too. Granite pinnacles **Pelican Rock** and **Neptune's Finger** jut out from the sea and are home to marine life galore. Numerous beautiful beaches—most famously **Playa del Amor** (Lover's Beach) and **Playa del Divorcio** (Divorce Beach)—are dotted along the base. There's also a keyhole-shape opening known as **The Window to the Pacific**; a rock that purportedly looks like the famous cartoon canine, **Scooby Doo**; and a spade-shape opening on the Pacific side known as the **Pirate's Cave,** reputed to be the site of long-buried treasure. Sightseers will also notice the ruins of the old fish cannery, which was the center of local commerce before the age of tourism. The beaches below it are popular among Mexican tourists, separate from the hubbub of nearby Médano.

You can hike the peak at Land's End called **Mt. Solmar** (or traditionally Cerro del Vigía, which means "lookout hill"; it was a lookout point for the pirates who would attack Spanish ships) for lovely views of the Cabo San Lucas Bay. A local man named Enrique Morales, who owns the private property leading up to Mt. Solmar, leads free, dog-friendly morning hikes every day except Saturday.

⚠ **You can't walk here from town so plan to hire a car to take you there, and back.** ✉ *Cabo San Lucas.*

Marina Cabo San Lucas

PROMENADE | One of the most active marinas in the entire world (many of its 380 docked boats go in and out every day), Cabo's marina is great to stroll along, people-watch, and take in the glittering views. Lined with dining and shopping spots, you can easily spend hours here, and likely will. Expect a few tourist traps—as well as pesky solicitations from vendors—but the inflated pricing may be worth the convenience and scenery. ✉ *Blvd. Paseo de la Marina, Marina San Lucas.*

Plaza Amelia Wilkes

PLAZA/SQUARE | Cabo San Lucas' centrally located town square is a picturesque place to take a breather during an afternoon of exploration. The public space is home to colorful gardens, a gazebo, and an event every Friday evening called "Viva la Plaza" from 5 pm to 9 pm, which features local makers selling artwork and snacks. It's named for Amelia Wilkes Ceseña, a schoolteacher for 43 years, a tireless advocate for the town, and the first woman ever appointed to political office in Baja California Sur. At the edge is the Natural History Museum of Cabo San Lucas; it's modest and in serious need of a refurbishment, but admission is only $2 and it hosts a neat collection of fossils and rocks, along with placards in English. ✉ *Cabo San Lucas ✛ Av. Lázaro Cárdenas and Calles Hidalgo, Madero, and Cabo San Lucas.*

Beaches

Sandy beaches are easy to find throughout coastal Cabo San Lucas, although at many, swimming is not advised. The rule of thumb is to avoid going into the water on the Pacific Ocean side due to strong rip currents and occasional rogue waves. The beaches along the calm Bahía de Cabo San Lucas, however, are great for swimming, snorkeling, and more.

Lover's Beach (*Playa del Amor*)

BEACH | Accessible only by boat, this charming beach at the tip of the Land's End peninsula is just as lovely as its name implies. Though the towering cliffs on either side lend an air of romantic seclusion, don't expect much privacy: it's one of the area's most photographed spots. It's an excellent place to swim and snorkel, with a variety of tropical fish easily visible in the clear, shallow water. Walk through a gap in the rocks to reach the cheekily named Divorce Beach (Playa del Divorcio); while the water at Lover's Beach faces the Sea of Cortez and is calm and pleasant, Divorce Beach is on the turbulent and unpredictable Pacific. It's far too dangerous for swimming, but ideal for sunbathing. Picnics are also popular, but be sure to bring your own food and refreshments; there may be a vendor or two selling drinks, but not reliably. To get here, you can hire a water taxi (called a "panga") to bring you there and back from Playa El Médano or the marina. Prices vary and can be negotiable depending on the vendor, but typically the cost can be $10–$20; the final departure back to shore is usually 4 pm. You can also rent a kayak, Jet Ski, or paddleboard and make your way over independently. **Amenities:** none. **Best for:** swimming; snorkeling. ⊠ *Cabo San Lucas* ✛ *At Land's End.*

Playa El Médano

BEACH | **FAMILY** | Foamy plumes of water shoot from wave runners and dozens of water taxis buzz through the calm waters off Médano Beach, a 3-km (2-mile) span of grainy tan sand that's more beautiful than you might expect from such a central, touristy zone. It's always crowded, but always fun. A variety of water-sports activities and rentals are available, with swimming areas roped off to prevent accidents. The water is usually calm enough for small children, but be aware of quick shoreline drop-offs: life preservers are a good idea for the little paddlers in your group. Bars and restaurants line the Médano, their waiters delivering ice buckets filled with beer to sunbathers in lounge chairs. The busiest and buzziest spot on the beach is around Mango Deck and The Office, where beachgoers can enjoy midday revelry, but there are plenty of more relaxed oceanfront venues, too. Feel free to spread out on the sand with your own towel, drinks, and snacks, whether to save money or simply do your own thing. There's a constant stream of passing vendors offering everything from silver jewelry to T-shirts... and under their breath, smokeable substances. (The current craze is a collection of crass bandanas, the phrasing on some foul enough to make a sailor blush.) If you're not interested, just politely decline and they will respectfully continue on. **Amenities:** food concession. **Best for:** partying; beach clubs; swimming. ⊠ *Cabo San Lucas* ✛ *Near Villa Del Palmar Beach Resort & Spa.*

🍴 Restaurants

Cabo San Lucas has historically fallen short of San José and the Corridor in terms of fine dining, but the scene has grown tremendously in the last few years, with more delicious options than ever before. Between the local haunts that have been longtime favorites, the energetic eateries primed to start your night right, and the classic seaside restaurants where the sunset is a main course, you're bound to eat well no matter your craving.

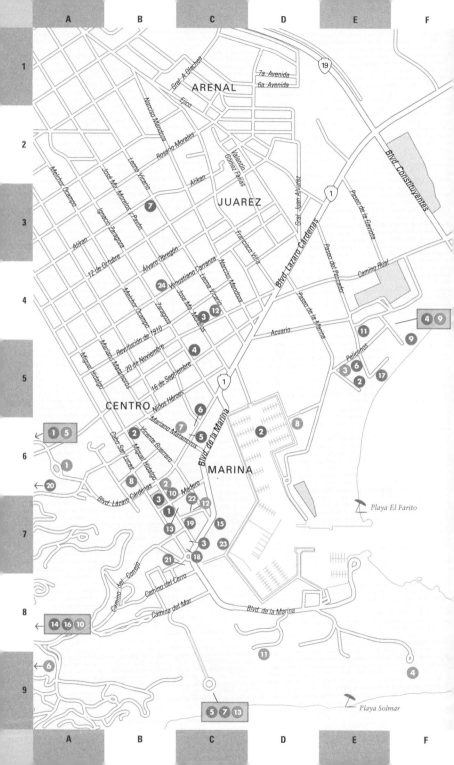

Cabo San Lucas

Viejo a San José

Playa El Médano

Bahía San Lucas

0 — 1,000 ft
0 — 200 m

Lover's Beach

El Arco (The Arch) ◆

PACIFIC OCEAN

KEY

- ① *Sights*
- ① *Restaurants*
- ① *Quick Bites*
- ① *Hotels*

Sights ▼

1 Land's End **G9**
2 Marina Cabo San Lucas **D6**
3 Plaza Amelia Wilkes.... **B7**

Restaurants ▼

1 Anica.................... **A6**
2 Baja Brewing Company................. **E5**
3 Chubby Noodle Cabo...................... **C7**
4 Craft Los Cabos **E4**
5 Don Manuel's **C9**
6 Edith's Restaurant **E5**
7 El Farallon **C9**
8 The Fish Sushi........... **B6**
9 Funky Geisha............ **F4**
10 Invita Bistro **B6**
11 La Lupita Taco & Mezcal................... **E4**
12 Los Tres Gallos........... **C4**
13 Mama's Royal Café..... **B7**
14 Muna Restaurant **A8**
15 Nicksan **C7**
16 Nobu Restaurant Los Cabos............... **A8**
17 The Office **E5**
18 Outpost **C7**
19 Pancho's Restaurant & Tequila Bar **C7**
20 Pícaro Garden Cuisine **A6**
21 Romeo y Julieta.......... **C7**
22 Salvatore G's **C7**
23 Solomon's Landing **C7**
24 Tropical Kitchen Cabo..................... **B4**

Quick Bites ▼

1 The Cabo Coffee Company................ **B7**
2 Cafe Distrito 23410...... **B6**
3 El Pollo de Oro **C4**
4 Los Claros **C5**
5 Rico Suave **C6**
6 Tacos Guss **C6**
7 Taqueria El Paisa **B3**

Hotels ▼

1 The Bungalows Hotel...................... **A6**
2 Casa Bella **B6**
3 Corazón Cabo Resort & Spa **E5**
4 Grand Solmar Land's End Resort & Spa **F9**
5 Grand Solmar Pacific Dunes **A6**
6 Hard Rock Los Cabos................ **A9**
7 Los Milagros **C6**
8 Marina Fiesta Resort & Spa **D6**
9 ME Cabo **F4**
10 Nobu Hotel Los Cabos................ **A8**
11 Sandos Finisterra **D9**
12 Siesta Suites **C7**
13 Waldorf Astoria Los Cabos Pedregal **C9**

Anica

$$$ | **MEXICAN** | If you plan to stay in a resort community to the immediate west of Cabo San Lucas (like Quivira, Diamante, or Rancho San Lucas), then Anica needs to be on your radar. Named after the first indigenous settlement in Baja California Sur, the menu—inspired by ancient tribal cooking techniques—is a delicious blend of traditional and contemporary. **Known for:** local ingredients; Mexican coffee; exceptional wine list. Ⓢ *Average main: $35* ✉ *Grand Solmar Pacific Dunes, Carretera Todos Santos (Hwy. 19), Km 120, Cabo San Lucas* ☎ *624/145–7575* ⊕ *grandsolmarpacific-dunes.mx* ⊗ *No lunch.*

Baja Brewing Company

$$ | **AMERICAN** | A branch of the established San José del Cabo microbrewery, this rooftop cantina has eight styles of beer on tap plus whichever additional seasonal brews are available—order a sampler to try a taste of each. A menu of classic pub fare is available for dining, with special emphasis on their "famous" beer pizzas; the dough is made daily from spent barley, yeast, and beer. **Known for:** local craft beer; open-air dining; views of Land's End. Ⓢ *Average main: $18* ✉ *Corazón Cabo Resort & Spa, Pelicanos 225, Playa El Médano* ☎ *624/163–7876* ⊕ *bajabrewingcompany.com.*

Chubby Noodle Cabo

$$ | **ASIAN FUSION** | This trendy, San Francisco–based restaurant decided that Cabo was missing out on quality Asian comfort food, and, honestly, they were right. The clientele is an interesting mix of hip locals and families alike, and it's the perfect spot for a hearty bowl of noodles and a refreshing cocktail, both of which will fuel you up nicely after a long day on the water. **Known for:** creative Asian fusion dishes; theme cocktails; fast service. Ⓢ *Average main: $18* ✉ *Calle Miguel Hidalgo at Blvd. Paseo de la Marina, Centro* ☎ *624/120–7449* ⊕ *chubby-noodlecabo.com.*

Craft Los Cabos

$$$$ | **STEAK HOUSE** | The initial draw of this rooftop restaurant may be its privileged overlook of Médano Beach (sunset, unsurprisingly, is the hottest hour for a reservation), but the strength of the menu would warrant a visit, regardless. Every item from this "Open Fire Kitchen" is grilled and smoked, bringing a creative technique and fresh flavor to an area mostly dominated by beach clubs. The wind can get somewhat fearsome come nightfall, but thick, cozy blankets are readily provided. **Known for:** USDA Prime steaks; "farm-to-glass" mixology; panoramic views. Ⓢ *Average main: $65* ✉ *ME Cabo by Meliá, Acuario Zona Hotelera, Playa El Médano* ☎ *624/167–1071* ⊕ *craftrestaurant.com.mx* ⊗ *No lunch.*

★ Don Manuel's

$$$ | **MODERN MEXICAN** | **FAMILY** | While the Waldorf Astoria's other restaurant, El Farallon, tends to gather universal acclaim from Cabo's visitors and residents, we'd like to boldly suggest that dining at Don Manuel's is an even better experience. Open for each meal of the day, the modern Mexican cuisine served is innovative and decadent. **Known for:** hacienda-style kitchen and wares; handcrafted cocktails; private dining on the beach. Ⓢ *Average main: $40* ✉ *Waldorf Astoria Los Cabos Pedregal, Camino del Mar 1, Pedregal* ☎ *624/163–4300* ⊕ *www.waldorfastoria-loscabospedregal.com.*

Edith's Restaurant

$$$ | **MEXICAN** | **FAMILY** | One of the more upscale choices near Médano Beach, Edith's is the sister restaurant to popular The Office. The Caesar salad and bananas flambé are prepared tableside at this colorful and much-loved restaurant, while Wally's Special, a medley of lobster, shrimp, and fish, is one of the most ordered items on the menu. **Known for:** local ingredients; wine cellar for small private parties; nice cocktails. Ⓢ *Average main: $50* ✉ *Av. del Pescador, Playa El Médano* ☎ *624/143–0801* ⊕ *www.edithscabo.com* ⊗ *No lunch.*

El Farallon

$$$$ | SEAFOOD | Perhaps the most revered reservation to score in Cabo San Lucas, cliffside El Farallon provides one of the most breathtaking vantage points in town. There's no typical menu here—rather, that day's selection of grilled entrées, featuring fish, shrimp, scallops, steak, and more, are presented on a large chalkboard, along with the available sides. **Known for:** best sunsets in Cabo; curated Champagne list; live entertainment. $ *Average main: $125* ✉ *Waldorf Astoria Los Cabos Pedregal, Camino del Mar 1, Pedregal* ☎ *624/163–4300* ⊕ *www.waldorfastorialoscabospedregal.com* ⊘ *No lunch.*

★ The Fish Sushi

$$ | SUSHI | Delivering a similar quality to their contemporaries but at a more accessible price point, this sushi spot is still a bit under the radar, but that won't be for long. If you go, don't be fooled by the nondescript exterior: you're in the right place, and it's worth going inside! **Known for:** fresh, affordable sushi; vegetarian options; box lunches. $ *Average main: $15* ✉ *Miguel Hidalgo at Cinco de Mayo, Centro* ☎ *624/143–4636* ⊕ *thefishsushi.com* ⊘ *Closed Sat. No lunch.*

Funky Geisha

$$$ | ASIAN FUSION | It's no surprise that this impossibly hip Asian fusion hot spot originated in Tulum, as it feels a bit more suited for that crowd than what's typically found in Cabo. But Funky Geisha's presence marks an exciting change in the local party scene—it's no longer limited to just spring breakers or sea dogs—and diners can enjoy a variety of sushi, curry, noodles, and rice dishes while wiggling their toes in the sand and gazing in awe at a nightly fireworks display just steps away. **Known for:** chic decor; Japanese drum show; vegan dining options. $ *Average main: $30* ✉ *ME Cabo by Meliá, Acuario Zona Hotelera, Playa El Médano* ☎ *624/167–1072* ⊕ *funkygeisha.com.mx.*

Invita Bistro

$$ | ITALIAN | Go for the delicious complimentary focaccia bread; stay for the fine wines, family-style fare, and charming views of downtown Cabo San Lucas. Chef and co-owner Antonello Lauri shows off his Roman heritage on the menu at Invita, which is overflowing with traditional Italian favorites like the filling eggplant Parmesan made from recipes passed down from his grandmother. **Known for:** views of town square; serious wine selection; traditional Italian recipes. $ *Average main: $21* ✉ *Calle Miguel Hidalgo, Cabo San Lucas* ⊹ *Across from Plaza Amelia Wilkes* ☎ *624/143–1386* ⊕ *www.invitabistro.com* ⊘ *No lunch.*

La Lupita Taco & Mezcal

$$$ | MEXICAN | After picking up somewhat of a cult following in San José del Cabo, La Lupita opened this location that's just as fun—there's a prominent stage overlooking the restaurant floor for bands to perform on and free-flowing cocktails. Just one block from Médano Beach, it feels less touristy than many of the neighboring establishments serving up gourmet tacos (the santo pastor is their specialty, but you'll want to try a variety), flights of mezcal, and an unbeatable ambience. **Known for:** elevated tacos; authentic jícara bowls for sipping mezcal; lively atmosphere. $ *Average main: $25* ✉ *Acuario at Av. del Pescador, Playa El Médano* ☎ *624/172–0398* ⊕ *lalupitatym.com* ⊘ *Closed Mon.*

★ Los Tres Gallos

$$$ | MEXICAN | Ask any Cabo local where you should get dinner, and there's a good chance they'll suggest Los Tres Gallos. Fun, festive, and flavorful, it's a must-try for anyone seeking traditional Mexican cuisine. **Known for:** old-fashioned charm; modern mariachi music; delicious margaritas. $ *Average main: $25* ✉ *Calle Leona Vicario at 20 de Noviembre, Cabo San Lucas* ☎ *624/130–7709* ⊕ *facebook.com/lostresgallos.*

Mama's Royal Café

$ | MEXICAN | This casual, open-air spot advertises themselves as "probably the best breakfast restaurant in the whole country," and they're not wrong. Everything on the menu is good (if you return multiple times on the same trip, you'll be in good company), but their claim to fame is the decadent French toast stuffed with a mix of cream cheese and ricotta topped with fresh fruit, pecans, and flambéed orange liqueur. **Known for:** "The World's Best French Toast"; homemade salsas; fresh-squeezed juices. $ *Average main: $10* ✉ *Calle Hidalgo at Zapata, Cabo San Lucas* ☎ *624/143–4290* ⊕ *facebook.com/mamascabo* ☷ *No credit cards* ⏱ *No dinner.*

★ **Muna Restaurant**

$$$$ | MEDITERRANEAN | If there's one thing for certain, Nobu knows food, and the hotel's newest restaurant, a Mediterranean masterpiece helmed by executive chef Paolo della Corte, is coming for the throne. Every bite from start to finish will melt in your mouth like warm butter, but be warned: this place is not inexpensive. **Known for:** separate kitchens for every course; confit duck gyros; rooftop sunset views. $ *Average main: $70* ✉ *Nobu Hotel Los Cabos, Polígono 1. Fracción D, Fraccionamiento Diamante, Cabo San Lucas* ☎ *624/689–0160* ⊕ *loscabos.nobuhotels.com* ⏱ *No lunch.*

Nicksan

$$$ | JAPANESE | Cabo San Lucas's original sushi restaurant, Nicksan has remained a go-to date night and celebration location for over 30 years. Owner Angel Carbajal is an artist behind the sushi counter (he also owns fishing boats that collect fish each day), having been mentored by Masayuki Niikura (one of the first-ever Japanese chefs to prepare spicy tuna), and his creative Japanese-Mexican fusion dishes, nicknamed "Nicksan style," expertly balance the culinary traditions of Japan with the unique flavors of Mexico.

Known for: tuna specialties; divine sauce on the sashimi cilantro; expensive. $ *Average main: $25* ✉ *Blvd. Marina Lote 10 Local 2, Plaza de la Danza, Cabo San Lucas* ☎ *624/128–1537* ⊕ *www.nicksan.com.*

Nobu Restaurant Los Cabos

$$$$ | JAPANESE FUSION | Sitting pretty as one of the world's most famous high-end restaurant chains, Nobu exudes luxury and cool. The Los Cabos location features the classic menu by namesake chef Nobu Matsuhisa—traditional Japanese cuisine fused with Peruvian flavors—as well as specialty plates inspired by ingredients local to the region. **Known for:** family-style sushi; trendy seaside dining; celebrity clientele. $ *Average main: $220* ✉ *Nobu Hotel Los Cabos, Polígono 1. Fracción D, Diamante, Cabo San Lucas* ☎ *624/689–0160* ⊕ *loscabos.nobuhotels.com* ⏱ *Closed Tues. No lunch.*

The Office

$$$ | MEXICAN | Based on seating availability alone, this is, without question, the most popular restaurant in Cabo San Lucas. Day and night, the place is packed, thanks to its well-prepared and well-portioned seafood-based menu and drinks, as well as its history of being the first-ever palapa to grace Médano Beach's sandy shore. **Known for:** kitschy decor; views of El Arco; Cabo breakfast staple. $ *Average main: $35* ✉ *Playa El Médano, Playa El Médano* ☎ *624/143–3464* ⊕ *theofficeonthebeach.com.*

★ **Outpost**

$$$ | CONTEMPORARY | This trendy restaurant and lounge grows most of its vegetables and herbs on its rooftop garden, sourcing any remaining ingredients from its San Jose–based sister restaurant, Flora Farms. Whether you come just for drinks or a full-course meal (both are popular options), every bite and sip will taste impossibly fresh. **Known for:** margarita mixology; live DJ music; funky decor. $ *Average main: $25* ✉ *Blvd. Paseo de la*

Marina at Calle Cabo San Lucas, Centro ☎ *624/132–2842* ⊕ *www.outpost.mx.*

Pancho's Restaurant & Tequila Bar

$$ | **MEXICAN** | **FAMILY** | Sample one or several of the more than 500 tequilas available and you'll surely appreciate the rainbow-color Oaxacan tablecloths, murals, painted chairs, and streamers even more than you did when you first arrived. Coat your stomach in the process with dishes from different states throughout Mexico: mole from Puebla, carne asada from Sonora, tamales from Oaxaca, and seafood from Baja are just some of the tasty items you can order. **Known for:** a tequila "museum" featuring rare bottles; festive decor; tequila tasting menus. ⑤ *Average main: $22* ⊠ *Calle Hidalgo, Cabo San Lucas* ✛ *Between Zapata and Camino del Conejo* ☎ *624/143–0973* ⊕ *panchos.com.*

Pícaro Garden Cuisine

$$$ | **MEXICAN FUSION** | A rustic-chic oasis overlooking the Pacific, Pícaro is not just a restaurant, but a destination in and of itself. Perched on a hilltop about a 20-minute drive from Centro, you'll forget about the schlep when you taste Chef Christian Ricci's Mexican/Mediterranean cuisine, inspired by both the local produce and his Italian upbringing. **Known for:** three- or five-course Chef's Selection tasting experience; gorgeous earthenware; signature cocktails and snacks. ⑤ *Average main: $45* ⊠ *Rancho San Lucas, Hwy. to Todos Santos, Km 120, Cabo San Lucas* ☎ *624/689–0050* ⊕ *picarogardencuisine.com* ⊘ *No lunch.*

Romeo y Julieta

$$$ | **ITALIAN** | At this longtime local establishment near the entrance to Pedregal, diners are delightfully surprised to find an elegant dining area that's open to the stars. Nightly live music and an adjacent wine bar offer a more romantic and sophisticated evening out, a reprieve from the neighborhood's rowdiness, and fresh, house-made pasta (including gluten-free options) and tableside Caesar salad are among the highlights. **Known for:** romantic courtyard; fine Italian cuisine; The Wine Bar next door. ⑤ *Average main: $25* ⊠ *Blvd. Marina at Camino del Cerro, Cabo San Lucas* ☎ *624/143–0225* ⊕ *www.restaurantromeoyjulieta.com* ⊘ *No lunch.*

Salvatore G's

$$ | **ITALIAN** | Hidden inside the lush courtyard of a local boutique hotel, this humble, family-owned eatery has been serving up a Sicilian storm for over a century, bringing the Galluzzo family's heirloom recipes and signature massive portions to the hungry people of Cabo's center. The place has gotten so popular that there are often set seating times for dinner; be sure to call ahead to make a reservation. **Known for:** large portions; reasonably priced; charming ambience. ⑤ *Average main: $18* ⊠ *Siesta Suites Hotel, Emilio Zapata s/n, Cabo San Lucas* ✛ *Between Vicente Guerrero and Miguel Hidalgo* ☎ *624/105–1044* ⊕ *salvatoregs.com* ⊘ *No lunch Sun.*

Solomon's Landing

$$ | **SEAFOOD** | **FAMILY** | Chef and owner Brian Solomon runs one of the most popular restaurants on the Cabo San Lucas Marina, supplementing waterfront views with first-class service and an enormous range of quality food and beverages. Fresh local seafood is the specialty of the house, but pastas, steaks, and traditional Mexican favorites are also staples of the lunch and dinner menus. **Known for:** fresh local seafood; busy crowds; homemade pasta. ⑤ *Average main: $22* ⊠ *Blvd. Paseo de la Marina Centro, Marina San Lucas* ✛ *Behind Tesoro Los Cabos Resort* ☎ *624/219–3228* ⊕ *www.solomonslanding.com.mx.*

Tropical Kitchen Cabo

$$ | **VEGAN** | For a light and healthy breakfast, look no further than this plant-based café. Bright, colorful, and filled with greenery, it's a can't-miss spot for vegetarian and vegan travelers looking for fresh smoothies, açai bowls, and the like. **Known for:** hosting community events;

photogenic dishes and drinks; vegan brunch. ⑤ *Average main: $13* ✉ *Venustiano Carranza Lot 3, Centro* ✛ *Between Zaragoza and Morelos* ☏ *624/264–3701* ⊕ *www.tropicalkitchencabo.com* ⊘ *No dinner.*

☕ Coffee and Quick Bites

Eating street food is synonymous with visiting Mexico—even in a posh destination like Los Cabos. There are many reasons to opt for a light bite here; perhaps to satisfy a late-night craving, to take a break from rich restaurant dining, or to save a few bucks. Or maybe you just love tacos, which might be the best reason of them all.

Beyond tasty tortillas, Cabo also has some lovely options for coffee, pastries, sandwiches, and juices.

★ The Cabo Coffee Company

$ | **CAFÉ** | The intoxicating aroma of fresh coffee (and pastries, too!) lures locals and visitors alike into this spacious café just off of Plaza Amelia Wilkes. Claiming (with little backlash) to serve the best organic coffee in town, The Cabo Coffee Company sources their beans from a private grower in the Sierra Madre Mountains of Oaxaca then roasts them fresh daily here in Cabo San Lucas. **Known for:** wide selection of drinks; space for co-working; reading nook. ⑤ *Average main: $3* ✉ *Calle Cabo San Lucas and Esquina Aquiles Serdan, Centro* ☏ *624/105–1754* ⊕ *www.cabocoffee. com.*

Cafe Distrito 23410

$ | **CAFÉ** | A few blocks away from downtown Cabo's heavy foot traffic and named after the town's zip code, this is an adorable place to grab breakfast or spend an afternoon co-working. Their slogan is "Coffee made by locals, for locals," and their beans are sourced from the Mexican state of Chiapas and are available for sale to take home with you. **Known for:** open-air seating; cold brew;

hip decor. ⑤ *Average main: $12* ✉ *Calle Miguel Hidalgo at Niños Heroes, Centro* ☏ *624/122–4533* ⊕ *www.facebook.com/ Distrito23410* ⊘ *No dinner.*

El Pollo de Oro

$ | **MEXICAN** | At "The Golden Chicken," it's best to order... well, chicken! You can try it roasted, grilled, fried, or baked, in fajitas, enchiladas, burritos, soup... a menu worthy of Forrest Gump's narration. **Known for:** generous portions; affordably priced; roast chicken. ⑤ *Average main: $8* ✉ *Morelos at 20 de Noviembre, Cabo San Lucas* ☏ *624/143–0310* ⊕ *www.facebook.com/ElPolloDeOroDeLosCabos.*

Los Claros

$ | **MEXICAN** | Come to Los Claros for seafood tacos galore! Fill your tortillas with a variety of fish and shrimp, served battered, grilled, or "crunchy." It's inexpensive, but cash-only. **Known for:** marlin tacos; ceviche; margaritas. ⑤ *Average main: $3* ✉ *Zaragoza at 16 de Septembre, Cabo San Lucas* ☏ *624/355–8278* ⊕ *www.facebook.com/tacoslosclaros* ⊟ *No credit cards.*

Rico Suave

$ | **MEXICAN** | Rico Suave boasts an impressive selection of 100% natural juices and smoothies, freshly squeezing and blending almost every fruit (and vegetable) that you can imagine. You can order breakfast or lunch here, as well; tortas (street food–style sandwiches made on *bolillo* bread, a baguette-style roll) are popular. **Known for:** delivery service; smoothies with orange; tortas especiales. ⑤ *Average main: $7* ✉ *Blvd. Lázaro Cárdenas s/n, Centro* ☏ *624/143–1043* ⊕ *www.ricosuave.com.mx* ⊘ *No dinner.*

Tacos Guss

$ | **MEXICAN** | Day or night (and especially at night), this traditional taqueria has you covered for all your taco needs. Asada (beef) and pastor (pork) are the most popular orders here, and even a single taco comes with a giant tray of

complimentary salsas and toppings—
Known for: late-night tacos; speedy
service; generous toppings delivered
to the table on a tray. ⑤ *Average main:
$3* ✉ *Blvd. Lazaro Cardenas at Melchor
Ocampo, Centro* ☎ *624/105–1961.*

Taqueria El Paisa

$ | MEXICAN | This popular taco joint is
slowly taking over the area, with two
locations in Cabo San Lucas plus out-
posts in San José, La Paz, and even Mazatlán. Their beef is 100% sirloin from the
Mexican state of Sonora, and it can be
ordered one of three ways: grilled, grilled
without fat, or fried. **Known for:** sirloin and
al pastor tacos; shrimp quesadillas; fresh
guacamole. ⑤ *Average main: $3* ✉ *Blvd.
Lázaro Cárdenas, Centro* ☎ *624/143–
1489* ⊕ *https://taqueriaelpaisa.restaurant-
webexperts.com/.*

 # Hotels

The benefits of basing yourself right in
Cabo San Lucas, over anywhere else in
the region, are clear ones: convenience
and access. Truly *anything* that you're
looking to get out of your vacation—relaxation, exploration, aquatic adventure, or
partying—is right at your fingertips, as
the entire town is walkable (or, if you prefer not to walk, a short and inexpensive
Uber ride away).

Your ideal lodging location within San
Lucas depends on your priorities. Pro-
spective early risers for fishing, scuba
diving and the like will appreciate staying
as close to the marina as possible. Those
craving both an action-packed location as
well as great views should opt for accommodations along Playa El Médano. The
hotels on the Pacific coast offer a more
tranquil setting and classic resort feel
while still being close to the best dining,
shopping, and nightlife. Just few blocks
deeper into town are a range of locally
owned boutique properties, perfect for
those on a tighter budget or simply looking for a more personal place to stay.

The Bungalows Hotel

$ | B&B/INN | If solitude and a reasonable
room rate are more important than being
in the center of the action, The Bungalows might be your place. **Pros:** oasis-like
property; excellent value; outstanding
breakfasts. **Cons:** noise from traffic and
surrounding neighborhood; a bit off the
beaten path; uphill walk from town.
⑤ *Rooms from: $115* ✉ *Blvd. Miguel
Angel Herrera, Arenal* ☎ *624/125–4426*
⊕ *www.thebungalowshotel.com* ⇥ *16
rooms* ⦿ *Free Breakfast.*

★ Casa Bella

$ | B&B/INN | The Ungson family had been
in Cabo for more than four decades
before turning their home across from
Plaza Amelia Wilkes into the classiest and
friendliest inn in the neighborhood. **Pros:**
property feels totally secluded; private
home atmosphere; extended stays are
negotiable. **Cons:** no TVs or phones in
the rooms, unreliable Wi-Fi; minimal
amenities; not kid-friendly. ⑤ *Rooms
from: $200* ✉ *Calle Hidalgo 10, Centro*
☎ *624/143–6400* ⊕ *www.casabellahotel.
com* ⇥ *11 rooms* ⦿ *No Meals.*

Corazón Cabo Resort & Spa

$$ | RESORT | Located on the most popular
stretch of Playa El Médano, families,
couples, and friends will all equally feel at
home in these chic, comfortable ocean-
front towers. **Pros:** multiple rooftop bars/
restaurants; great beach club; every room
has views of Land's End. **Cons:** disorgan-
ized front desk; small pool areas; no kids
club. ⑤ *Rooms from: $339* ✉ *Pelicanos
225, Playa El Médano* ☎ *624/980–0604*
⊕ *www.corazoncabo.com* ⇥ *305 rooms*
⦿ *No Meals.*

Grand Solmar Land's End Resort & Spa

$$$ | RESORT | FAMILY | Architecture melds
perfectly with natural surroundings as
hotel suites dramatically hug cliff and
sea and subterranean stone passages
open to infinity pools framed by cactus
gardens and raked sand. **Pros:** stunning
ocean views; one of the original Cabo
resorts; as close to El Arco as you

can get. **Cons:** 75% of rooms are for timeshares; always fully booked; dated decor. ⑤ *Rooms from: $480* ✉ *Av. Solmar 1A, Centro* ✛ *Next to Solmar Resort* ☎ *800/509–5991* ⊕ *grandsolmarresort. solmar.com* ⇗ *246 rooms* ⍟❘ *No Meals.*

Grand Solmar Pacific Dunes
$$$$ | **RESORT** | **FAMILY** | Impressive in every respect, this aptly named resort commands well over a mile (2 km) of Pacific Ocean coastline north of Cabo San Lucas, with an 18-hole golf course from Greg Norman, excellent on-site dining options, a beachfront spa, sleek swimming pools, and a small salt-water lagoon you can kayak and paddleboard in. **Pros:** spacious suites with upscale furnishings; family-friendly amenities; preferred tee times at Solmar Golf Links. **Cons:** far from downtown Cabo San Lucas; extremely windy; will be under construction for the next decade. ⑤ *Rooms from: $510* ✉ *Carretera Todos Santos (Hwy. 19), Km 120, Cabo San Lucas* ☎ *800/509–5991* ⊕ *grandsolmarpacificdunes.mx* ⇗ *145 suites* ⍟❘ *No Meals.*

Hard Rock Los Cabos
$$$$ | **RESORT** | **FAMILY** | It's likely no surprise that music is creatively incorporated throughout the Hard Rock's resort experience; there's a pool with an underwater playlist, Fender guitars can be delivered to your room, and the spa even uses sound vibrations in its treatments. **Pros:** lively pool parties; professional recording studio on-site; elevated rooms and suites. **Cons:** upcharges for the best dining; slow service when crowded; memorabilia decor is a bit kitschy. ⑤ *Rooms from: $595* ✉ *Fraccionamiento Diamante, Cabo San Lucas* ☎ *624/689–0300* ⊕ *hotel.hardrock.com/los-cabos* ⇗ *639 rooms* ⍟❘ *All-Inclusive.*

Los Milagros
$ | **HOTEL** | Tucked away on a side street in the middle of the most happening part of town, this humble but charming boutique hotel is dripping in brilliant purple bougainvillea and orange lipstick vines

that line the central patio. **Pros:** cozy, well-priced rooms; convenient location in downtown Cabo; international clientele. **Cons:** front desk is often unattended; outdated technology; modest pool. ⑤ *Rooms from: $85* ✉ *Mariano Matamoros 3738, Centro* ☎ *624/143–4566* ⊕ *www.losmilagros.com.mx* ⇗ *17 rooms* ⍟❘ *No Meals.*

Marina Fiesta Resort & Spa
$ | **RESORT** | **FAMILY** | Location, location, location: Marina Fiesta's may be the very best in town, and that, coupled with an extraordinarily reasonable nightly rate make it a top choice for an interesting mix of guests: fishermen, families, and college-age partiers. **Pros:** located right on the marina; great value for the price; close to everything. **Cons:** subpar dining; property is a little dated; pushy about tipping. ⑤ *Rooms from: $125* ✉ *Marina, Lots 37 and 38, Marina San Lucas* ☎ *844/278–6596* ⊕ *www.marinafiestaresort.com* ⇗ *155 rooms* ⍟❘ *No Meals.*

ME Cabo
$$$ | **RESORT** | Break out the bottle service: ME Cabo is the perfect base for affluent travelers looking to let loose. **Pros:** party hot spot; chic and comfortable rooms; pet-friendly. **Cons:** loud music penetrates the rooms; inattentive service; pool gets crowded quickly. ⑤ *Rooms from: $315* ✉ *Playa El Médano, Playa El Médano* ☎ *624/145–7800* ⊕ *www.melia.com* ⇗ *169 rooms* ⍟❘ *Free Breakfast.*

Nobu Hotel Los Cabos
$$$$ | **HOTEL** | Celebrities and influencers are common guests at Nobu Los Cabos, and you'll feel like one yourself moving through this stylish paradise. **Pros:** Cabo's trendiest hotel; best-in-class dining; outdoor hydrotherapy garden. **Cons:** no on-site activities or entertainment; very expensive; far from downtown Cabo San Lucas. ⑤ *Rooms from: $545* ✉ *Polígono 1. Fracción D. Fraccionamiento Diamante, Cabo San Lucas* ☎ *305/674–5575* ⊕ *loscabos.nobuhotels.com* ⇗ *260 units* ⍟❘ *No Meals.*

3

Cabo San Lucas

Sandos Finisterra

$$$$ | **RESORT** | **FAMILY** | Sandos Finisterra, whose name means "Land's End" in Latin due to its privileged location at the Baja peninsula's southernmost point, offers guests the best of both worlds: the quintessential all-inclusive experience while being just steps from downtown. **Pros:** stunning views of both the ocean and marina; short walk into town; excellent service. **Cons:** low-quality food and drinks; lounge chairs fill up quickly; thin walls between rooms. $ Rooms from: $528 ✉ Blvd. Marina, Cabo San Lucas ☎ 624/145–6700 ⊕ www.sandos.com ⤸ 265 rooms ⁑ All-Inclusive.

Siesta Suites

$ | **HOTEL** | For travelers on a budget, there's no better choice than Siesta Suites as all the rooms come with kitchenettes equipped to stock basic groceries, and a standard room (which has two queen beds and a wide couch) can easily sleep up to five adults. **Pros:** quaint, convenient, and safe; friendly staff; cheap drinks at Terrace Bar. **Cons:** Wi-Fi does not reach the bedroom; motel-style layout; curtains must remain drawn for privacy. $ Rooms from: $85 ✉ Calle Zapata at Guerrero, Cabo San Lucas ☎ 624/143–2773, 619/376–9529 ⊕ www.siestasuitescabo.com ⤸ 21 rooms ⁑ No Meals.

★ Waldorf Astoria Los Cabos Pedregal

$$$$ | **RESORT** | The majestic Waldorf Astoria Los Cabos Pedregal lies on Cabo San Lucas's most coveted parcel of land—an extraordinary, 24-acre site at the southern tip of the peninsula accessible only through the longest private tunnel in Mexico, a chandelier-lit passage through sheer granite that opens into an open-air lobby backed by gorgeous Pacific Ocean vistas. **Pros:** every room has a plunge pool and ocean view; very exclusive; exceptional service and a staff that calls you by name. **Cons:** beach is not swimmable; might be too mellow for some; extremely expensive. $ Rooms from:

$1,200 ✉ Camino del Mar 1, Pedregal ☎ 624/163–4300 ⊕ www.waldorfastorialoscabospedregal.com ⤸ 112 rooms ⁑ No Meals.

Nightlife

The start of Cabo San Lucas' party reputation can be traced back to its infancy, when the town's tourism comprised exclusively of fishermen and their families. As the fishermen's children came of age, a demand grew for entertainment near the marina; a marriage of the naughty and the nautical, if you will. This not only explains the core location of Cabo's nightlife scene—a stone's throw from where the boats are docked—but the "fishy" names of some of the town's oldest nightlife establishments. A second iteration came thanks to Sammy Hagar, the Van Halen rocker behind the infamous Cabo Wabo Cantina. The opening of the rock club brought international attention to Cabo that hasn't let up since.

Today, it's easier than ever to let loose in the way that best suits you. "Nightlife" is a limited term, as some of Cabo's best imbibing happens during the day—be that a cold beer by the marina or a round of tequila shots at the beach bars on Médano. After dark, you have your choice between checking out live music, a few craft cocktail and wine bars, and some of the most famous nightclubs in all of Mexico.

BARS

Bikini Bar

LIVE MUSIC | A chilled-out alternative to Cabo Wabo, you can listen to excellent live music play on an outdoor stage designed to look like a mound of sand. Sports games are also frequently broadcast. For a bite to accompany a beverage, try the sushi. ✉ Blvd. Paseo de la Marina at Mariano Matamoros, Centro ☎ 624/168–3651 ⊕ www.facebook.com/BikiniBarCabo/.

Cabo Wabo

LIVE MUSIC | Easily the most famous bar in Los Cabos (if not Mexico as a whole), Cabo Wabo is worth a visit for the novelty alone. There's live music every afternoon and evening, and if you're lucky, you might just witness a jam session from owner Sammy Hagar and some of his legendary musician friends, who stop by a few times a year. The club's zany design—high cavernous ceilings, zebra stripes, and psychedelic neon patterns—are as fun as ever, even if the venue is now past its prime. (The energetic crowds once featured on MTV are largely a thing of the past, save for Hagar's annual Birthday Bash, which sells out instantly.) There's a steep markup on the menu's prices, but the house Cabo Wabo Tequila still merits a taste. Grabbing a bottle or a T-shirt from the on-site souvenir shop is a must for any Van Halen fan. ⊠ *Calle Guerrero, between Madero and Av. Lázaro Cárdenas, Centro* ☎ *624/143–1188* ⊕ *www.cabowabocantina.com.*

Cock's Cantina

COCKTAIL BARS | Popular among the trendy, local crowd, this three-story bar around the corner from Médano serves up some of the very best cocktails in town, handcrafted with fresh ingredients. Thirsty patrons spill out into the street on weekend evenings, but will happily clear the way for you to order a drink. ⊠ *Av. del Pescador 1, Playa El Médano* ☎ *624/129–0293* ⊕ *www.facebook.com/ cockscantinaloscabos.*

El Squid Roe

DANCE CLUB | The epitome of Cabo San Lucas nightlife, this original and iconic three-story dance club has changed very little since its opening three decades ago, but remains as popular as ever. Revelers of all ages can be found lined outside for admission on any given night, despite a hefty cover charge and the neighboring clubs remaining empty. It's known to get wild, and that's the main draw for most—either to participate in the madness, or to people watch with amusement. At virtually every breakfast buffet in town, you'll hear *someone* remarking about "what happened last night at El Squid Roe." ⊠ *Av. Lázaro Cárdenas, Centro* ✛ *Between Zaragoza and Morelos* ☎ *624/157–4479* ⊕ *www. elsquidroe.com.*

Fenway Bar

SPORTS BARS | A unique sports bar concept—unique for Cabo San Lucas, anyway—this Red Sox–themed bar features live sporting events (from every sport) on close to a dozen TVs. Owner Ignacio "Nacho" Padilla Rivas grew up in Aguascalientes, Mexico, but is a die-hard fan of the Boston team and has furnished this funky little hole-in-the-wall with a replica Green Monster scoreboard and memorabilia galore. ⊠ *Calle Emiliano Zapata, between Guerrero and Hidalgo, Centro* ✛ *Across from Siesta Suites Hotel and Salvatore G's Restaurant* ☎ *624/355–8015* ⊕ *www.facebook.com/ fenwaybarcabo* ⊗ *Closed Sun.*

Happy Ending Cantina

BARS | Cheap drinks are the name of the game at Happy Ending, whether you're looking for an early evening pregame or a last call nightcap. They're known for housing an impressive number of beer pong tables as well as an all-hours deal of two beers and two shots for just $5. (The house tequila is unspeakably foul, however, so maybe opt for just the beer.) ⊠ *Blvd. de la Marina 22, Centro* ☎ *624/143–0404* ⊕ *happyendingcantina.com.*

Jungle Bar

BARS | If you belong to the 50 and over crowd who likes to rock out, you'll have a riot of a time at Jungle Bar. This outdoor spot is always packed, thanks to its low prices and live music. It can take forever to get your drinks, though, so take advantage of their two-for-one deals and order several at once. ⊠ *Plaza Mariachis, Blvd. Marina, Marina San Lucas* ☎ *624/143–7401* ⊕ *www.facebook.com/ JungleBarCabo.*

Mango Deck

BARS | Mango Deck is "spring break" personified, from the costumed employees pouring shots directly into partygoers' mouths to the "booty shaking" competitions held on a stage in the sand (and livestreamed to their website). It's unquestionably Cabo's most popular beachfront venue, whose music you can hear blasting from every direction. As it's also a restaurant, children are inexplicably allowed and occasionally present, but we strongly recommend limiting your party to consenting adults only. ⊠ *Playa El Médano, Playa El Médano* ☎ *624/143–0901* ⊕ *www.mangodeckcabo.com.*

The Nowhere ¿Bar?

BARS | This marina-facing hole-in-the-wall turns into a powerhouse party destination, filled to the brim with tourists and locals alike. Expect a loud but well-curated playlist of music and a hopping dance floor. ⊠ *P Dock, Blvd. Paseo de la Marina 17, Marina San Lucas* ☎ *624/157–4479* ⊕ *www.thenowherebar.com.*

Slim's Elbow Room

BARS | Slim's calls itself "the world's smallest bar," and you'll be lucky to get a seat at this kitschy four-seat space that plays honky-tonk music and serves $3 beers and tequila shots. Signed dollar bills line the walls and ceiling, and a buzzing, standing crowd loiters out the door and onto the Boulevard Marina sidewalk each evening, vibing off its energy. ⊠ *Plaza de los Mariachis, Blvd. Marina, Centro* ⊕ *www.slimscabo.com.*

Tanga Tanga

BARS | It would be easy to pass by this nonchalant sidewalk bar without a second thought, but you'd be remiss: virtually everything (the quality of the drinks, live music, general energy) is better than you'd expect. The crowd is quite diverse in terms of age and nationality, but everyone there is ready to have a good time. Bonus points if you hit the dance floor! ⊠ *Plaza de la Danza, Blvd. Marina, Centro*

☎ *624/143–1511* ⊕ *www.facebook.com/tangatangarestaurantbar.*

Uno Mas?

BARS | This tiny, cash-only palapa bar has a diehard fan following, many of whom will wear its branded merch around town and abroad. Stop by for margaritas made with fresh-squeezed juice and conversation with the friendly owners and regulars. Pace yourself, though, as these drinks have been known to pack a punch! ⊠ *Plaza del Sol, Blvd. Marina, Marina San Lucas* ☎ *624/105–1877* ⊕ *www.facebook.com/unomascabo1* ⊗ *Closed Sun.*

Vas Que Vuelas Mezcalería

COCKTAIL BARS | Though it's around the corner from the clubbing scene, the vibe at Vas Que Vuelas couldn't be more different. Come by to enjoy an artisanal cocktail or pour of small-batch mezcal; they've got the largest selection in town. Like the drinks, the food is also inspired by Oaxaca; order a tlayuda for a great late-night snack. ⊠ *Calle Niños Héroes at Ignacio Zaragoza, Centro* ☎ *624/129–1675* ⊕ *www.facebook.com/Vasquevuelasmezcaleria.*

BEACH CLUBS
Corazón Beach Club

BARS | One of the coziest places to relax on Playa El Médano is on an umbrella-covered daybed at Corazón. Attentive waiters are quick to deliver your food and drink orders, and a rope around the perimeters keeps outside vendors from disturbing your peace. It gets crowded, so reserve a space in advance and arrive early to guarantee the best experience. ⊠ *Corazón Cabo Resort & Spa, Pelicanos 225, Playa El Médano* ☎ *624/980–0604* ⊕ *www.corazoncabo.com.*

Taboo Beach Club

BARS | Although Taboo does have a handful of lounge chairs on the sand, the real party is at the beachfront pool, where a DJ spins music that gets everyone dancing. It's a place best enjoyed with a group of friends, as those in rented cabanas and ordering bottle service are given preferential treatment. Beyond food and drinks, you can also request a hookah to enjoy amid the sea breeze. ⊠ *ME Cabo, Acuario, Playa El Médano* ☎ *624/167–1073* ⊕ *www.taboobeach-club.com.mx/en.*

🛍 Shopping

Cabo San Lucas is a fun and easy place to shop; virtually anything you'd want to buy, from a simple souvenir to a special keepsake, can be found (with options to choose from!) downtown.

Classic and creative tchotchkes are available in droves throughout the stalls of the various plazas to the west of the marina. More practical items, like bathing suits and sweatshirts (should you have forgotten something necessary at home) can be easily purchased at the mall, Puerto Paraíso, from either your favorite international chain or a local boutique. A number of resident makers create and sell their handiwork in shops throughout Cabo, too; from fine art to custom clothing, these are the businesses most worth supporting.

CLOTHING

CABO The Store

CLOTHING | Looking for souvenir swag to take home with you? Feel free to skip over the made-in-China kiosks surrounding the marina and make your way to CABO The Store, instead. You'll find chic apparel stitched with the town's name, along with illustrated logos of The Arch, a fish, golf club, and cactus. It's pricey, but really high quality. ⊠ *Puerto Paraíso, Blvd. Lázaro Cárdenas Local 75, Cabo San Lucas* ☎ *624/157–6600* ⊕ *cabothestore. com.*

Cariloha

TEXTILES | Everything at this island-inspired chain, which sells bed sheets, mattresses, and apparel, is made out of sustainable bamboo. T-shirts bearing cute Cabo San Lucas designs are light, breathable, and very soft—perfect to wear on hot days of exploration. ⊠ *Blvd. Paseo de la Marina at P. Marlin 1, Marina San Lucas* ⊕ *www.cariloha.com/.*

★ Eclectic Array

CRAFTS | Eclectic Array curates an exquisite collection of handmade, artisan goods—like accessories, crafts, and home decor—from across Mexico. Their mission is to provide fair trade and sustainable opportunities to the country's Indigenous communities, and the products they sell are authentic, gorgeous, and one-of-a-kind. ⊠ *Blvd. Paseo de la Marina at P. Marlin 1, Marina San Lucas* ☎ *624/143–8877* ⊕ *eclecticarray.com.*

Enamor-Art

HATS & GLOVES | The quintessential accessory to rock in Los Cabos is a handmade *sombrero*—both to keep the sun off your face and as a fashion statement. Local artisan Víctor Orduña uses royal palm grown in his home state of Puebla to weave custom hats in three colors (tan, natural, and white), then sews in colorful designs with yarn. Visit his workshop to see a variety of premade options, or with a minimum order of four, he'll come to you and will create custom designs. ⊠ *Gral. Juan Álvarez, Ampliación Juárez, Cabo San Lucas* ☎ *624/161–2050* ⊕ *en-amor-art.com/.*

Pepita's Magic of the Moon

CLOTHING | Owner Pepita Nelson creates beautiful, original resortwear designs for mature women, including hand-painted silk dresses, blouses and skirts. With a selection of fabrics and patterns that are flattering for all figures, she can custom fit to your exact measurements. ⊠ *Francisco I Madero 7, Centro, Cabo San Lucas* ✛ *Between Guererro and Blvd. Marina, next to J&J* ☎ *624/143–3161* ⊕ *facebook. com/pepitasmagic* ⊗ *Closed Sun.*

3

Cabo San Lucas

JEWELRY

A general rule of thumb when shopping for jewelry in Mexico is to be cautious. Items usually won't have a set price and the first quote you receive from shopkeepers may be double or more what it's actually worth. That said, you can find some stunning pieces (especially made of silver, which Mexico is known for) in these shops, made by families who have been in the business for generations.

■ TIP→ **Avoid buying silver on the street or at the beach, as it likely isn't real.**

Flores Jewelry

JEWELRY & WATCHES | The Flores family has been making jewelry in Cabo San Lucas for a quarter-century and is one of the most reliable establishments in town. Locals will say they got their pieces via "Botas from Valente"; Valente Flores being the shop's owner, and his cousin, Botas (a nickname), the lead jeweler. A slew of other relatives work the counter, happy to offer you complimentary tequila if you spend long enough browsing. Ask about their pieces made with fire opal, the national gemstone of Mexico. ✉ *Francisco I Madero at Vicente Guerrero, Centro* ⊕ *www.facebook.com/flores. jewerly1.*

LOCAL ART

ambienta

HOUSEWARES | Make your home bathroom feel like a spa with these handmade stone dishes, trays, and dispensers. Made out of marble, onyx, and resin sourced from the Mexican states of Puebla, Chiapas, and Oaxaca, you can buy individual items or complete sets. ✉ *Francisco I Madero at Vicente Guerrero, Cabo San Lucas* ☎ *624/143–2059* ⊕ *ambientaloscabos.com.*

★ Auténtica

ART GALLERY | Artist Tomás Reyes owns Galeria Auténtica, the largest collection of original Mexican fine art in all of Los Cabos. A third-generation art dealer, Reyes represents and stocks the work on 18 different artists (including his own),

each of whom he visits twice annually to select which pieces he wants to bring back to sell. One of the artists, David Moreno, is a Cabo native and oil paints local scenes onto pieces of marble. ✉ *Francisco I Madero at Blvd. Paseo de la Marina, Cabo San Lucas* ☎ *624/119–7792.*

Cobalto Pottery and Tiles

CERAMICS | The biggest (and best) pottery collection in Los Cabos is at Cobalto, a colorful boutique set near the town square in Cabo San Lucas that specializes in talavera-style pottery and tiles from Puebla and Guanajuato. Owner Raquel Pantoja regularly travels the country looking for new pieces, including incredible ceramics by local artisans that were hand-painted with needles to form intricate patterns. All pottery on-site is lead-free and dishwasher safe. ✉ *Plaza Alamar, Calle Madero, between Guerrero and Hidalgo, Cabo San Lucas* ✛ *Around the corner from Cabo Wabo* ☎ *624/122– 2527* ⊕ *cobaltotiles.com.*

★ The Glass Factory (*Fábrica de Vidrio Soplado*)

GLASSWARE | Nearly every souvenir shop or boutique you visit in Los Cabos will have gorgeous glassware in stock... and it is all made here, using 100% recycled glass. Come to see the process live (more than a dozen artisans are hard at work every weekday, crushing, liquefying, then sculpting glass into exquisite figures) and shop through an incredible selection of drinking glasses, vases, ornaments, and more, created with every color and in every design imaginable. Note: it's a little far from the center of town, so you may want to visit by car. ✉ *Calle General Juan Álvarez, Cabo San Lucas* ✛ *Between Capitán Manuel Pineda and 7a Ave.* ☎ *624/143–0255* ⊕ *www. glassfactory.com.mx* ⊗ *Factory closed weekends.*

Zen-Mar Folk Art Gallery

CRAFTS | This friendly shop carries a seemingly limitless supply of traditional masks, figurines, and other pieces of Mexican folk art, like *amate* (paper made of tree bark). You'll see a lot of iconic cultural imagery, like the *sagrado corazón* (flaming sacred heart) and *calavera* (Day of the Dead skull). Owner Manuel Martínez, who passionately took the reins from his father, founder Zenon Martínez (hence the name), has a particular penchant for masks and travels the country finding the most interesting ones to stock. There's something for everyone, with prices starting at around $5 and, based on size and rarity, going up into the hundreds. ⊠ *Av. Lázaro Cárdenas, Centro* ✛ *Between Matamoros and Ocampo* ☎ *624/143–0661* ⊕ *www.zen-mar.com.*

MALLS
Luxury Avenue
MALL | This boutique mall houses a selection of luxury makeup, jewelry, and fashion brands. Most desirable for tourists may be MAC Cosmetics and Ultrafemme, where you can get done up in advance of a big event; Swarovski and Ultrajewels, should you be seeking a level of jewelry not found in the local shops; and Sunglass Hut, which offers a chic selection of sunnies to save your eyes from the harsh Cabo rays. ⊠ *Av. Lázaro Cárdenas, Cabo San Lucas* ✛ *Adjacent to Puerto Paraíso mall* ☎ *624/163–4280* ⊕ *www.luxuryavenue.com.*

Puerto Paraíso
MALL | Though you probably didn't come on vacation to go to the mall, it's quite nice to have one as conveniently located as Puerto Paraíso, which sits pretty right on the marina. There are some practical stores that may come in handy in a pinch (like an AT&T and MacStore for electronics), as well as many places to buy beachwear and accessories. There's also a bank (Scotiabank), which is a safe place to withdraw cash in pesos, and a grocery store (Selecto Súper Chedraui), should your place have a kitchen that you'd like to stock up. Or if you just need to catch your breath after disembarking

a boat, the mall is ready and waiting with its refreshing air conditioning and public restrooms. ⊠ *Av. Lázaro Cárdenas 1501, Marina San Lucas* ☎ *624/144–3000* ⊕ *www.puertoparaiso.mx.*

 ## Activities

BOATING
If there's one excursion to participate in during your trip to Cabo San Lucas, it should be a boat tour. The themes vary, but all tours follow essentially the same route: through the Cabo San Lucas Bay, pausing at El Arco, around Land's End into the Pacific Ocean, and then eastward through the Sea of Cortez along the Corridor. During the day, you'll likely have the option to swim and snorkel. In the evening, you can enjoy watching the sun set from out on the ocean. Whether you book a catamaran, sailboat, or yacht, all tours include an open bar and some light bites, if not a full meal.

Cabo Adventures
SAILING | Cabo Adventures is Los Cabos' most prolific tour company, running a variety of tours every day of the week. The benefit is that you can nearly always find availability on the day that best suits you; the disadvantage is that the experience can feel a bit manufactured.

Cruises to El Arco are their bread and butter, and you can choose between booking a spot aboard a sailboat or catamaran. (The difference? Catamarans tend to be more spacious and sturdy, while sailboats are more intimate and adventurous.) The daytime tours last four hours and include lunch, plus snorkel gear and a stand-up paddleboard. The sunset sails are 2½ hours and provide hors d'oeuvres. Both include open bar... there's always an open bar. ■ **TIP→ Don't get too excited about a 30% off sale; it's literally always there.** ⊠ *Blvd. Paseo de la Marina, Lote 7-A, Marina San Lucas* ☎ *624/173–9528, 800/916–8734* ⊕ *www. cabo-adventures.com* ⛵ *Day sail from $104; sunset sail from $76.*

Glass-bottom boats take passengers to Cabo's top attractions, including Land's End and El Arco.

Caborey

BOATING | One of the largest boats docked in Marina Cabo San Lucas, this hulking, 144' triple-deck catamaran is a floating restaurant. Caborey's Sunset Premier Dinner & Show includes a three-course meal, open bar, a performance during dinner and live band afterwards, all while sailing over a 2½ hour span. The Sunset Mexican Dinner is a tab more casual, featuring a dinner buffet, open bar, and live music. Sailings depart from the Cabo San Lucas Cruise Port. ⊠ *Hotel Tesoro Los Cabos, Blvd. Marina, Marina San Lucas* ☎ *624/143–8060, 866/460–4105* ⊕ *www. caborey.com* ✉ *Buffet dinner from $95; Dinner and show from $135.*

Cabo Sailing

SAILING | Forget the party-boat scene. The best introduction to the coastal geography and laid-back lifestyle of Cabo San Lucas is via private charters with Cabo Sailing. The company has a superb collection of boats, including both 38-foot and 42-foot Hunter sailboats perfect for group outings, family snorkeling expeditions, or romantic sunset sails for two. For a more economical deal, you can join a shared snorkeling or sunset sailing with other travelers. ⊠ *Plaza Nautica, Blvd. Marina, Local C-5, Marina San Lucas* ☎ *624/143–8485, 619/784–2745* ⊕ *www.cabosailing. com* ✉ *Private charter from $637; shared sailing from $90.*

La Isla Tour

BOATING | La Isla Tour's catamarans are easily recognizable out on the water, as they are each custom-built to look like two-story floating lounges. Owner Carlos Hudson has decked out each boat in his fleet with cozy, communal furniture, so that everyone on a charter can relax together. His smallest boats can hold up to six people, while his largest can accommodate up to 80 (and two Jacuzzis). The charters include snacks and soft drinks, served by a personal chef and bartender, but open bar is an additional cost. You can, however, BYOB. ⊠ *Marina Cabo San Lucas, Gate G, Marina San Lucas* ☎ *624/241–4843* ⊕ *laislatour.mx* ✉ *From $465 for 3½ hr charter.*

★ Seashine Adventures

BOATING | Chartering a yacht is a fantastic activity to celebrate a special occasion, like a big birthday or bachelorette party, and Seashine exceeds expectations about what the experience should be like. The boats in their fleet are absolutely stunning, but what's especially memorable are the crew (helpful, friendly, and available to meet your every whim) and the generous, flavorful dishes, prepared fresh on board by a professional chef. ✉ *Marina Cabo San Lucas, Dock H, Marina San Lucas* ⊕ *seashineadventures. com* ✉ *Starting at $900 (up to 4 guests) or $1,800 (up to 10 guests) for 3 hrs.*

FOUR-WHEELING

Riding an ATV across the desert is a thrill, and an iconic activity to do in Baja California Sur. The tours originating in Cabo San Lucas are notoriously more structured than you'll find in less populated towns, which could be ideal for cautious newbies but a little disappointing for true adventure seekers.

The most popular route passes first through Cabo San Lucas, and continues through desert cactus fields, before arriving at a big play area of large sand dunes with open expanses and specially carved trails. You can reach extremely high speeds as you descend the tall dunes. Navigating the narrow trails in the cactus fields is exciting, but not for the faint-hearted or steering-impaired. Another favorite trek travels past interesting rock formations, little creeks, and the beach on the way to a small mountain village called La Candelaria.

Be sure to wear sneakers and clothes that you don't mind getting dirty, plus a long-sleeve shirt or sweatshirt for afternoon tours in winter.

Amigos Activities

FOUR-WHEELING | With Amigos, you can ride a single, double or quadruple ATV through the desert, on the beach, and

---

Whale-Watching Tips

Whale-watching season in Los Cabos is officially from mid-December to mid-April. The best spot in Cabo San Lucas to watch humpbacks and other whales transit to their winter breeding grounds (other than on a close-up boat excursion) is the tower at the **Sandos Finisterra** resort. Day passes are usually available for nonguests and include pool access and all-inclusive food and drink. To watch whales from the shore, go to the beach at the Grand Solmar Land's End, or lookout points along the Corridor.

---

beyond. There are four daily departure times, with most tours lasting about two hours. All the safety gear (plus a bandana, to keep dust off your face) is provided. ✉ *Carretera Federal 19 Migriño, Km 106, Cabo San Lucas* ☎ *624/143–0808* ⊕ *www.amigosactivities.com* ✉ *Starting at $130/single or $160/double.*

Cactus Tours

FOUR-WHEELING | **FAMILY** | Cactus has a massive number of daily ATV tours, including one specially designed for kids. Located on a particularly safe trail, ages 7-plus can ride as a copilot and 10-plus can drive. Despite departing hourly, these tours are often full, so reserve your space at least a day in advance. Round-trip shuttle transportation from your hotel is included. ✉ *Federal Hwy. 19, Cabo San Lucas* ✛ *20 min outside Cabo San Lucas* ☎ *624/171–8790* ⊕ *www.cactusatvtours. com* ✉ *From $104.*

GOLF

Greens fee prices quoted include off- and high-season rates and are subject to frequent change.

Cabo San Lucas Country Club

GOLF | Don't let the name fool you: Cabo San Lucas Country Club has long been popular due to its public accessibility; plus, it's the only course in the area to feature Land's End views. Designed by Pete Dye's late brother Roy (and finished by *his* son Matt), this was one of the first 18-hole golf layouts ever completed in Los Cabos. A renovation by acclaimed Mexican course designer Agustín Pizá in 2018 resulted in changes on the back-nine, but the double-dogleg par-5 7th is the same, and, at 610-yards, remains one of the longest holes in Mexico. The driving range is open at night, which has made it a big hit with locals, who often stop by with friends to hit buckets of balls and share buckets of beer. ⊠ *Hwy. 1, Km 3.7, Cabo San Lucas* 🕾 *624/143–4653* ⊕ *www.cabocountry.com* ✉ *From $81* 🏌 *18 holes, 6,852 yards, par 71* ☞ *Pro shop, golf academy, lighted driving range, putting green, golf carts, rental clubs, restaurant.*

★ Solmar Golf Links

GOLF | This 7,210-yard, Greg Norman–designed course opened to acclaim in 2020 as the only links course in the area, and with a sustainability designation from Audubon, to boot. The most spectacular hole is the 161-yard, par-3 17th, which features an island green; the only one of its kind in Cabo and one of the most photographed spots on the course. Solmar Golf Links impresses with pristine fairways, Pacific Ocean views, windswept dunes, and British-style bunkering. Food stations are strategically placed, ensuring players don't have to take too many swings between refreshing food and drinks, all of which are complimentary. Baby deer live among the rugged, natural landscape, and you will occasionally see them prancing across the fairway. Guests of Solmar Hotels & Resorts receive preferred tee time rates. ⊠ *Carretera Todos Santos (Hwy. 19), Km 120, Cabo San Lucas* 🕾 *624/689–0052* ⊕ *solmargolf. com/* ✉ *From $195* 🏌 *18 holes, 7,260 yards, par 72.*

JET-SKIING AND WATERSKIING

Competition among operators in Cabo San Lucas is pretty fair, so most offer comparable, if not identical, prices. Both Jet-Skiing and waterskiing cost about $50 for a half hour and $90 for a full hour, but prices are negotiable, especially if booking for a group.

KAYAKING

In Cabo San Lucas, Playa El Médano is the best beach for kayaking. A number of companies located along El Médano offer kayak rentals, and there are guided tours that go out to Lover's Beach to view El Arco, and around the Land's End rocks. Rates are generally uniform from one operator to another.

High Tide Los Cabos

KAYAKING | High Tide uses glass-bottom kayaks, allowing you to see underwater life as you paddle. Complimentary transportation is provided within the main tourist area of Cabo San Lucas, San José del Cabo, and the Corridor, as are snorkel gear and wetsuits, if needed. ⊠ *Plaza Gali, Blvd. Paseo de la Marina 36, Cabo San Lucas* 🕾 *624/142–0424* ⊕ *hightidelos-cabos.com* ✉ *$95.*

Tio Sports

KAYAKING | Tio Sports was one of the original water-sports companies on Playa El Médano more than 30 years ago, and is still a major operator with a sports palapa located on the beach, plus stands and offices throughout Los Cabos. Their 2½-hour kayak tour cruises around the Bay and includes a snorkeling stop at Pelican Rock. ⊠ *ME Cabo, Playa El Médano, Cabo San Lucas* 🕾 *624/143–3399* ⊕ *www.tiosports.com* ✉ *$85.*

Mutual curiosity between a scuba diver and a gentle whale shark

SCUBA DIVING AND SNORKELING
There are four main dive sites in Cabo San Lucas, all located in the government-protected part of the bay called the Cabo San Lucas Marine Reserve, near Land's End. **Pelican Rock** is the most popular for snorkelers and divers, thanks to its shallow depths and clear waters; the reef, full of tropical fish, starts at just 10 feet deep. This is a calm spot where you can also look down on one of the famous "sandfalls" (what looks like a waterfall made out of sand, dropping into a 1,200 foot canyon), discovered by none other than Jacques Cousteau. **Neptune's Finger** is a striking underwater pinnacle teeming with marine life, perfect for spotting schools of fish and cool coral formations. There are two reefs here and another underwater sand cascade, as well. **The North Wall** is a dramatic vertical drop-off with stunning topography, and **Land's End Point,** which has you diving in both the Sea of Cortez and Pacific Ocean, has the ruins of a shipwreck amid its marine life.

The main issue with diving in the Bahía de Cabo San Lucas is the amount of boat traffic; the sound of motors penetrates deep into the water and can slightly mar the experience, if you let it. The dive sites can be a bit crowded, too, with groups from almost every dive shop in town passing through. But they're absolutely worth exploring, whether you're an avid diver or fledgling snorkeler.

Baja Shark Experience
SNORKELING | Have you ever jumped *into* the water when there was a shark approaching your boat? You will with Evans Baudin, founder of Baja Shark Experience, an ethical tour operator who leads safaris to snorkel in the open ocean alongside various species of Cabo's nomadic sharks, including makos, hammerheads, silkies, and blue sharks. Baudin gives swimmers a detailed briefing on how to act in the water to ensure tranquillity and safety for all beings involved, which is both educational and reassuring. The odds of crossing paths other additional animals in the wild,

like dolphins, sea turtles, or even orcas, are a likely possibility. ⊠ *Marina Cabo San Lucas, C Dock, Marina San Lucas* ☎ *624/161–7961* ⊕ *bajasharkexperience. com* ⊠ *$200.*

★ Cabo Private Guide

SCUBA DIVING | When Laura Tyrrell moved to Cabo in 2015 to work as a dive instructor, she saw a huge gap in the market: a need to "escape the crowd" of mass tourism and offer divers a more personalized experience. She opened Cabo Private Guide, a PADI five-star dive center that matches every booking with an ultra-experienced dive instructor for one-on-one attention. Snorkeling guides, too, are rescue diver certified at a minimum, and beyond Cabo San Lucas, the shop specializes in bringing advanced divers to see the hammerheads at Gordo Banks. ⊠ *Plaza Nautica, Blvd. Paseo de la Marina 1, Cabo San Lucas* ☎ *624/160–9925* ⊕ *www.caboprivateguide.com/* ⊠ *Two-tank dives from $135; equipment rental $35.*

Dive Ninja Expeditions

SCUBA DIVING | Rated the #1 best dive center for the Pacific & Indian Oceans by Scuba Diving Magazine and the first PADI eco-center in Mexico, you can't go wrong diving with Dive Ninja Expeditions. In addition to regular dives in the Cabo San Lucas Marine Reserve, Team Ninja can also take you on a night dive, where you can meet Cabo's nocturnal aquatic creatures, like white-tip sharks, lobsters, and octopus, and see biolumi-nescent plankton light up the water with green sparks. ⊠ *Ignacio Zaragoza 345 Esq, 16 de Septiembre, Cabo San Lucas* ☎ *973/619–9976, 624/247–3741* ⊕ *www. diveninjaexpeditions.com* ⊠ *Two-tank dives from $130; equipment rental $35.*

SPAS

Amura Spa

SPA | Just half a block up from the mari-na, this gold-accented, softly designed spa is the perfect place to escape to while members of your party take to the open seas. Body aches are no match for the massage therapists at Amura, unafraid to knead your muscles until tension you didn't even realize you had is released. Soak afterward in the hot tub and cold plunge for total rejuvenation. ⊠ *Marina Fiesta Resort & Spa, Paseo de la Marina, Lotes 37 and 38, Marina San Lucas* ☎ *624/145–6031* ⊕ *mghspacollec-tion.com/amura-spa* ⊠ *Massages: from $163. Facials: from $181. Hair: from $42. Mani-Pedi: from $33.*

★ KORPO Wellness Experience

SPA | Hair of the dog, but at the spa? We'll bite. KORPO's 100-minute signature treatment, the ME Tequila, is centered on the spirit and its antioxidant, antiaging and moisturizing properties. Guests start the service by sipping a shot, guaran-teed to rosy their cheeks, before being painted with an agave body wrap, meant to remove dead skin and improve the skin's texture with a glowing appearance. After showering off, a full-body massage ensues that is so positively delicious, the recipient will melt into the table like butter on a hot day. ⊠ *ME Cabo, Acuario Zona Hotelera, Playa El Médano* ☎ *551/168–9820* ⊕ *www.melia.com* ⊠ *Massages: from $165. Facials: from $225. Signature treatment: $250.*

The Sand Bar

SPA | Looking for something simple but satisfactory? The Sand Bar on Medano Beach is where all the locals go for a spur-of-the-moment massage. What started as a fun promotion—women could receive foot massages while their husbands watched football at the bar—turned into something seriously profitable; the restaurant's second floor, which looks out at Land's End, is now equipped with 30 massage tables and employs over 75 full-time thera-pists. ⊠ *Calle Cormonares s/n, Playa El Médano* ☎ *624/358–9951* ⊕ *thesandbar. mx* ⊠ *Massages: from $36.*

★ **Waldorf Astoria Spa**

SPA | Waldorf Astoria Spa does an incomparable job at marrying traditional folk healing with the highest level of luxury and service. Every square inch of the facilities has been thoughtfully designed, and every movement by a healer or therapist is done with the greatest intention. The spa's signature treatments represent the phases of the moon and how our well-being can align with nature; each 110-minute treatment includes a body scrub, wrap, and massage, but uses different scents and ingredients to evoke sensations of awakening, nourishment, calmness, and restoration. ⊠ *Waldorf Astoria Los Cabos Pedregal, Camino del Mar 1, Pedregal* ☎ *624/163–4300* ⊕ *www.waldorfastorialoscabospedregal. com* ⊠ *Massages: from $350. Facials: from $360. Signature treatments: $570. Folk healing treatments: from $360. Hair: from $105. Mani-Pedi: from $60.*

SPORTFISHING

The waters off Los Cabos are home to more than 800 species of fish—a good number of which bite all year-round. It's easy to arrange charters online, through hotels, and directly with sportfishing companies along the docks at Marina Cabo San Lucas. (Rather than book through an independent agent roaming the marina, it's best to reserve through a reputable company in an actual office.) Ships depart from sportfishing docks at the south end of the marina, near the Puerto Paraíso Mall, or from the docks at Hotel Tesoro Los Cabos. It's important to get specific directions, since it's hard to find your spot before departing at 6:30 am.

Prices range from $250 or $350 a day for a *panga* (small skiff) to $600 to $2,700 a day for a larger cruiser with a bathroom, a sunbathing deck, and a/c. The sky's the limit with the larger private yachts (think 80 feet); it's not unheard of for such vessels to cost $6,000 or $10,000 a day.

No matter what you pay, rates should include a captain and crew, tackle, bait, drinks, and sometimes lunch. If you plan to spend a full day at sea, it's best to purchase an all-inclusive package rather than a bare-bones trip lacking in services. Factor in the cost of a fishing license (about $20), required for all passengers over 18 years of age. Fishing licenses can be purchased for about half the price through the CONAPESCA website (⊕ *www.sportfishinginmexico.com*).

★ **Boats Baja**

FISHING | The team behind Boats Baja are some of the kindest in the marina, a welcome change of pace (especially for first-time visitors) from the grizzly mariners that seem to run the place. Their boats are equipped with the latest fishing gear and technology, like GPS and fish-finding equipment—that, coupled with the crew's tenacity to not give up, all but ensures you won't come home empty-handed. Seasoned fishermen are guaranteed to have a great time, but so are the aspiring anglers: particularly patient with newbies, they'll guide you every step of the way, from casting your line to reeling in the catch of a lifetime. ⊠ *Manzana 1, Lote 04, Cabo San Lucas* ☎ *624/264–4339* ⊕ *www.boatsbaja.com* ⊠ *Charters starting from $550.*

Minerva's Baja Tackle

FISHING | Renowned tackle store Minerva's Baja Tackle and Sportfishing Charters has been around for more than 40 years and has its own small fleet with two sportfishing charter boats from 31 feet to 33 feet. ⊠ *Madero between Blvd. Marina and Guerrero, Marina San Lucas* ☎ *624/143–1282, 888/480–7826* ⊕ *www. minervas.com* ⊠ *Charters from $969.*

Picante Fleet

FISHING | One of the top sportfishing fleets, Picante Fleet offers a wide selection of more than a dozen well-equipped boats, from top-of-the-line, 31-foot sport fishers to a 110-foot luxury yacht. If you

Continued on page 89

SPORTFISHING

Cabo San Lucas is called both the Marlin Mecca and Marlin Capital of the World for good reason. Thanks to the warm waters of the Sea of Cortez, the tip of the Baja Peninsula has one of the world's largest concentrations of billfish. And, no matter what time of year you visit, there's a great chance—some locals say a 90% one—you'll make a catch, too.

More than 800 species of fish swim off Los Cabos, but anglers pursue only about half a dozen types. The most sought-after are the huge blue or black marlin, which have been known to fight for hours. The largest of these fish—the so-called granders—weigh in at 1,000 pounds or more. The more numerous, though smaller (up to 200 pounds), striped marlin are also popular catches.

Those interested in putting the catch of the day on their table aim for the iridescent green and yellow dorado (also called mahi-mahi), tuna, yellowtail, and wahoo (also known as ono)—the latter a relative of the barracuda that can speed along at up to 50 mph. Also gaining popularity is light-tackle fly-fishing for roosterfish, jack crevalle, and pargo from small boats near the shore.

Something's always biting, but the greatest diversity of species inhabit Cabo's waters from June through November, when sea temperatures climb into the high 80s.

(above)Striped marlins feeding on sardines off the coast of Baja Sur.

WHAT TO EXPECT

You don't need to be experienced or physically strong to sportfish. Your boat's captain and crew will happily help you along, guiding you on how to properly handle the equipment.

Some of the larger boats have the so-called fighting chairs, which resemble a dentist's chair, firmly mounted to the deck. These rotate smoothly, allowing you to follow the movement of a hooked fish and giving you the support you need to fight with a large black or blue marlin for an extended period of time.

(top) Sportfishing in Los Cabos—one man's catch

Experienced fishermen sometimes forego chairs for the stand-up technique using a padded harness/fighting belt that has a heavy-duty plastic-and-metal rod holder connected to it. Though physically demanding—especially on the arms and lower back—this technique often speeds up the fight and is impressive to watch.

FISHING TWO WAYS

Most of Cabo's boats are equipped for the more traditional heavy-duty sportfishing using large, often cumbersome rods and reels and beautiful, colorful plastic lures with hooks. A modified form of fly-fishing is gaining popularity. This requires a finessed fly-casting technique and spot-on timing between crew and the fisherman. It utilizes ultra-lightweight rods and reels, relatively miniscule line, and a technique known as bait and switch.

You attract fish as near to the back of a boat as possible with hook-less lures. As the crew pulls in the lures, you cast your fly (with hooks) to the marlin. Fights with the lighter equipment—and with circle hooks rather than regular ones—are usually less harmful, enabling more fish to be released.

CONSERVATION IN CABO

You're strongly encouraged to use the less-harmful circle hooks (shaped like an "O"), as opposed to J-hooks, which do terrible internal damage. It's now common to release all bill-fish, as well as any dorado, wahoo, or tuna that you don't plan to eat. Folks here frown on trophy fishing unless it takes place during an official tournament. Instead, quickly take your photos with the fish, then release it.

The Cabo Sportfishing Association has a fleet-wide agreement that no more than one marlin per boat be taken per day. Usually all are released, denoted by the "T" flags flown from a boat's bridge as it enters the marina.

The few marlin that are brought in are hoisted and weighed, photographed, and then put to good use— taken to be smoked or given to needy locals. You can ask

the crew to fillet the tastier species right on your boat, and you can usually arrange for the fish to be smoked or vacuum-packed and frozen to take home. Many restaurants, especially those found marina-side in Cabo San Lucas, will gladly prepare your catch any way you like. You hook it, they cook it.

CHARTERING A BOAT

You can arrange charters at hotels—through a concierge or a charter desk—at Los Cabos tackle shops, or directly through charter companies. It's also possible to make arrangements online before you arrive. Indeed, it's good to do this up to three months in advance for the busiest months of October and November. ■ TIP→ **Don't arrange charters through time-share companies. They aren't always reliable and sometimes work with boats that aren't that well equipped.**

Rates usually include a captain and crew, tackle, bait, fishing licenses, and soft drinks. You often need to bring your own lunch; if it is included, it usually costs extra, as do alcoholic drinks. Unless you're quoted an all-inclusive charter price, confirm what is and isn't included. Also, a tip of 15% of the cost of the charter will be appreciated. Note, too, that some charter companies will try to help solo anglers hook up with a group to share a boat.

A walk along the perimeter of the Marina Cabo San Lucas demonstrates that Cabo really is all about fishing. Indeed, this is where most vendors are based and where most yachts set sail. (Departures are generally predawn—between 6 and 6:30 am—so it's not a bad idea to locate your dock and boat ahead of time, in the light of day.)

It seems as if every yacht tied to the docks is a sport fisher, and you'll see different colored flags flying from the boats' outriggers. These designate the numbers and types of fish caught during the previous day of fishing as well as the number of marlin released. The blue flags are for marlin, yellow for dorado, white for wahoo, and red for tuna. Each red and white "T"-flag means a billfish was tagged and released.

A charter boat on the Sea of Cortez.

The Original Cabeños

The indigenous inhabitants of Cabo San Lucas were the Pericú, hunter-gatherers whose territory included much of the present day Los Cabos municipality, as well as offshore islands like Cerralvo, Espíritu Santo, Partida, and San José.

Although the Pericú have been culturally extinct since the late 18th century, they were much in the news earlier this century when it was discovered they shared a genetic makeup remarkably similar to that of Australian aborigines.

Based on this discovery and mounting evidence, it is now thought that the Pericú migrated from Melanesia some 15,000 years ago, a separate and earlier migration than was previously thought (that they crossed the Bering Strait at the end of the last ice age, when much of the Americas became populated).

In 1992 a major excavation on the site of what would become Villa del Palmar Resort and Spa on Playa El Médano provided compelling evidence that the Pericú used the same primitive tools for the entirety of their existence. They were remarkable fishermen, nonetheless, a fact remarked on by all the early European visitors to the region.

prefer smaller boats, there's the Picantito fleet, with a trio of 24-foot Shamrock walk-around boats. These are primarily used for fishing close to shore. Picante offers trips and boats that vary in size and price. ⊠ *Puerto Paraíso Mall Local 39-A, Marina San Lucas* ☎ *624/143–2474, 714/442–0644* ⊕ *www.picantesportfishing.com* 🖃 *Charters from $1,020.*

Pisces Sportfishing Fleet

FISHING | Some of Cabo's top hotels use the extensive range of yachts from Pisces Sportfishing Fleet. The fleet includes the usual 31-foot Bertrams, but also has a sizable fleet of 50- to 70-foot Viking and Riviera yachts with tuna towers, air-conditioning, and multiple staterooms. Pisces also has luxury yachts up to 163 feet in length. Chartering a 31-foot Bertram is all-inclusive for up to six people, and trips last for around eight hours. ⊠ *Cabo Maritime Center, Blvd. Marina, Suite 1-D, Marina San Lucas* ☎ *624/143–1288, 877/286–7938* ⊕ *www. piscessportfishing.com* 🖃 *Charters from $695.*

WHALE-WATCHING

Long before snowbirds discovered the joys of wintering in Los Cabos, the world's largest creatures were migrating annually from their arctic summer feeding grounds to warm-water winter breeding grounds in coves and inlets around Baja California Sur. These are the longest mammalian migrations ever tracked, with the record held by a gray whale dubbed Varvara, who logged over 14,000 miles round-trip from Sakhalin Island, Russia to Cabo San Lucas in 2015. It's estimated that upwards of 5,000 whales make the journey to Southern Baja each year, with gray whales heading primarily to lagoons in San Ignacio, Ojo de Liebre, and Magdalena Bay on the Pacific Coast, 175 miles or more north of Cabo San Lucas.

Grays are commonly seen in Los Cabos, but the focus of local tours is on humpbacks; not only because of their large numbers, but also their spectacular breaches. They lift nearly their entire bodies—all 30 tons or so—out of the water for epic splashdowns, and are known for photogenic behaviors such as spyhopping (lifting their giant heads to take a gander at the surroundings) and lobtailing (a hard slap of the fluke on the surface of the water).

Other species are less prevalent, but orcas, sperm whales, fins, pilot whales, and even blue whales (the largest creature to ever exist on Earth) are sometimes spotted. Whale-watching season officially begins in Los Cabos on December 15 and ends on April 15. The best tours include hydrophones, so in addition to seeing whales you can also hear their haunting "songs."

⇨ *Nearly every tour operator in town offers whale-watching tours (from $80 depending on size of boat and length of tour) from Cabo San Lucas.*

Cabo Expeditions

RAFTING | Cabo Expeditions is a pioneer in the whale watching business and the only tour operator in Los Cabos authorized by the Mexican government to rescue whales when they get tangled in fishing line. Get up-close and personal with these majestic giants onboard a high-speed zodiac boat, which can quickly, closely and safely approach the site of any spout, fluke, froth or splash. ⊠ *Blvd. Marina s/n, Plaza de la Danza Local 6, Cabo San Lucas* ☎ *624/143–2700* ⊕ *www.caboexpeditions.com.mx* ✉ *$85.*

Whale Watch Cabo

RAFTING | Whale sightings are guaranteed with this conscious, eco-friendly tour operator; if for whatever reason none come out during your tour, you are welcome to join another one for free. A marine biologist guide leads every tour to share their knowledge and observations, and complimentary photos are included. Book a spot on a group trip or a private tour for just your family. ⊠ *Plaza Bonita, Blvd. Paseo de la Marina 17, Cabo San Lucas* ☎ *624/105–9336, 800/650–0564* ⊕ *www.whalewatchcabo.com* ✉ *Group tour: $89/person. Private tour: $499 total.*

Chapter 4

THE CORRIDOR

4

Updated by
Luis F. Dominguez

⊙ Sights	🍴 Restaurants	🛏 Hotels	🛍 Shopping	🍸 Nightlife
★★☆☆☆	★★★★★	★★★★★	★★★☆☆	★★★☆☆

NEIGHBORHOOD SNAPSHOT

TOP EXPERIENCES

■ **Luxury Resorts:** A few of the most exclusive resorts in Mexico are located here, including Esperanza, Montage, and Las Ventanas al Paraiso.

■ **Snorkeling:** For an unforgettable experience, submerge yourself in Chileno Bay. You'll spot fish close to the shore, even while standing.

■ **Fine Dining:** Home to some of the Baja Península's most spectacular restaurants, expect sophisticated dishes in stunning outdoor settings.

■ **Golf:** The number of first-class golf courses may surprise you. Designed by the best, with lush fairways, the courses suit all types of putters.

■ **Spa Time:** Treat yourself to a massage at one of the area's dizzying array of upscale resort spas.

GETTING HERE

The easiest way to arrive from the airport (SJD) is to take a shuttle, which costs about $125 for a private ride for up to six people. Taxi prices will always be higher and will depend on your negotiation skills. Renting a car is a good (and cheaper) option, as it will give you freedom to explore the region.

The Corridor runs along the four-lane Carretera Transpeninsular (Highway 1), which has more-or-less well-marked turnoffs for hotels though signage can appear at the very last minute. Drivers tend to speed along this highway, so drive with caution.

PLANNING YOUR TIME

The Corridor is quietest between June and mid-November. Snowbirds flock south and whale-watching tours take place during high season (December and May). Save a day to venture outside the resort-heavy area if you desire authentic, local experiences. If you're not staying along the Corridor, it's worth carving out time to visit one of its spas or golf courses, or book dinner at one of its top-notch restaurants with El Arco views.

BEST BEACHES

■ **Bahía Santa María:** For the area's best snorkeling, visit this gorgeous beach with calm waters and colorful fish. Get there early to grab one of the few palapas and enjoy clearer visibility below the surface. 19 km (12 miles) west of San José del Cabo, 13 km (8 miles) east of Cabo San Lucas.

■ **Chileno Bay:** Swimmable beaches aren't common in this region, and that's what sets this picturesque beach apart. Protected by a nearby coral reef, it's perfect for swimming. 17 km (10 miles) west of San José del Cabo,16 km (10 miles) east of Cabo San Lucas.

■ **Costa Azul:** This beach is home to two of the most famous surf breaks in all of Baja: La Roca and The Zipper. 1 km (½ mile) west of San José del Cabo, 28 km (17 miles) east of Cabo San Lucas.

■ **Monumentos:** Come here to enjoy surfing with a view of El Arco, Cabo San Lucas famous rock formation. Its challenging left-hand point break makes it a popular spot among expert surfers. 26 km (16 miles) west of San José del Cabo, 5 km (3 miles) east of Cabo San Lucas.

Carretera Transpeninsular dips into *arroyos* (riverbeds) and climbs onto a floodplain studded with boulders and cacti between San José del Cabo and Cabo San Lucas. This stretch of desert terrain connecting Los Cabos' sister cities, known as the Corridor, has long been the haunt of the rich and famous. In the 1950s a few fishing lodges and remote resorts with private airstrips attracted adventurers and celebrities. As the fastest developing area in Los Cabos, today the region has gated communities, resorts lining beautiful beaches, posh hotels, and championship golf courses.

Although it doesn't have the nightlife of Cabo San Lucas or local flavor of San José del Cabo, the Corridor hits a sweet spot for travelers whose top priority is a luxurious, private resort with access to top-notch restaurants, beaches, and activities. In fact, the Corridor is arguably the most action-packed location in Los Cabos. The stretch of land between the Sea of Cortez and Baja desert packs in world-famous golf courses, the biggest adventure park in the area, plus snorkeling, diving, whale-watching, sportfishing, and turtle releases along the beaches of the area's lavish hotels.

Sometimes referred to as the Tourist Corridor, the area primarily caters to out-of-towners. Travelers looking for a more profound Mexico experience will need a car (or an Uber or taxi) to travel to the sights and hopping bars of Cabo San Lucas or the authentic, colorful adobe dwellings you'll find in parts of San José del Cabo. But if you're willing to drive, or if you're content to stay put at a resort area that has plenty of its own entertainment and scenery, there is no better place than the Corridor.

■ TIP→ **For purposes of organization and mapping, we're including the residential part of Cabo San Lucas that leads into The Corridor in this chapter.**

 Beaches

The Corridor's coastline edges the Sea of Cortez, with long, secluded stretches of sand, tranquil bays, golf fairways, and huge resorts. Only a few areas are safe for swimming, but several hotels have man-made rocky breakwaters that create semisafe swimming areas when the sea is calm. Look for blue-and-white signs along Highway 1 with symbols of a snorkel mask or a swimmer and *acceso a playa* (beach access) written on them to alert you to beach turnoffs. It's worth studying a map ahead of time to get an idea of where your turnoff will be. Don't hesitate to ask around for directions, and don't lose hope if you still need to circle back around once or twice. Facilities are extremely limited and lifeguards are nonexistent, though many of the beaches now have portable toilets.

Bahía Santa María and Bahía Chileno are two beautiful strands in the Corridor. Bahía Santa María is the less busy of the two, and both beaches offer fun snorkeling and safe swimming; the docile fish will actually approach you. For seclusion, drive northeast to the stunning beaches on the dirt road northeast of San José del Cabo. Soon after leaving San José you'll see Playa Las Viudas dotted with shade palapas and surfers looking for the next big break. Don't be put off by all of the private homes or "no trespassing" signs—beaches are plentiful and public access is clearly marked. The dirt road from the highway is well maintained and fine for passenger cars (despite dire-sounding warnings from locals who will tell you that you must have a four-wheel-drive vehicle)—but the dirt roads are best avoided if it's raining.

★ **Bahía Chileno** (*Chileno Bay*)

BEACH | FAMILY | A calm enclave—with golf courses, residences, and Chileno Bay Resort—is roughly midway between San José and Cabo San Lucas. Consistently ranked one of the cleanest beaches in Mexico, Chileno has been awarded "Blue Flag" certification, meaning 32 criteria for safety, services, water quality, and other standards have been met. The beach skirts a small, crescent-shape cove with aquamarine waters and an outside reef that are perfect for snorkeling and swimming (there are even restrooms, showers, and handicap access). To the east are tide pools great for exploring with the kids. Getting here is easy, thanks to the well-marked access ramps on both sides of the road. Along the western edge of Bahía Chileno, some 200 yards away, are some good-size boulders that you can scramble up. In winter this part of the Sea of Cortez gets chilly—refreshing for a dip, but most snorkelers don't spend too much time in the water. On weekends get to the bay early if you want to claim shade under a palapa. **Amenities:** toilets; showers; parking lot. **Best for:** swimming; snorkeling; sunset. ⊠ *Bahía Chileno, The Corridor* ⊹ *The turnoff for beach is at Km 14.5 on Hwy. 1. Look for signs whether driving west from San José or at Km 16 when driving east from Cabo San Lucas.*

★ **Bahía Santa María** (*Santa Maria Beach*)

BEACH | FAMILY | This wide, sloping, horseshoe-shape beach is surrounded by cactus-covered rocky cliffs; the placid waters here are a protected fish sanctuary. The bay is part of an underwater reserve and is a great place to snorkel: brightly colored fish swarm through chunks of white coral and golden sea fans. Unfortunately, this little slice of paradise has limited palapas for shade, so arrive early or bring a beach umbrella. In high season, from November to May, there's usually someone renting snorkeling gear or selling sarongs, straw hats, and soft drinks. It's best to bring your own supplies, though, including lots of drinking water, snacks, and sunscreen. Snorkel and booze-cruise boats from Cabo San Lucas visit the bay in midmorning through about 1 pm. Arrive midafternoon if you want to get that total Robinson Crusoe feel. The parking lot is a quarter mile or so off the highway and is sometimes guarded; be sure to tip the guard. The bay is roughly 19 km (12 miles) west of San José and 13 km (8 miles) east of Cabo San Lucas. Heading east, look for the sign saying "playa santa maría." **Amenities:** toilets; free parking; showers; lifeguards. **Best for:** snorkeling; swimming; surfing; walking. ⊠ *The Corridor* ✢ *19 km (12 miles) west of San José del Cabo, 13 km (8 miles) east of Cabo San Lucas.*

Playa Buenos Aires

BEACH | This wide, lengthy, and accessible stretch of beach is one of the longest along the Cabo Corridor, but is rapidly developing with new resorts. Reef breaks for surfers can be good, but the beach is also known for its riptides, making it unswimmable. It's a great beach for long, quiet runs or walks, and it's not uncommon to find locals with horses to rent for a beachside ride. Whales can easily be spotted from the beach from January through March. The small, man-made "Tequila Cove" between Hilton and Paradisus has calm waters, excellent for swimming. Here you'll find a tiny shack renting bodyboards and other water-sports equipment. **Amenities:** toilets; water sports; free parking. **Best for:** surfers; walking. ⊠ *The Corridor* ✢ *Near Secrets Marquis Hotel Los Cabos/Hilton and stretching down to Meliá Cabo Real.*

Playa Costa Azul

BEACH | Cabo's best surfing beach runs 3 km (2 miles) south from San José's hotel zone along Highway 1. The Zipper and La Roca breaks are world famous. Playa Costa Azul connects to neighboring Playa Acapulquito in front of the Cabo Surf Hotel. Surfers gather at both beaches year-round, but most come in

summer, when hurricanes and tropical storms create the year's largest waves, and when the ocean is at its warmest. This condo-lined beach is popular with joggers and walkers, but swimming isn't advised. When getting in and out of the water in front of Cabo Surf Hotel (where surf lessons take place), watch out for the sea urchins that cling to the shallow rocks. Beginner surfers should ask locals to point out the mound of hidden rocks near the break closest to the cliffs; this means it's much safer to take "rights" than "lefts" at this break. Although not overly common, jellyfish can also be a problem here. The turnoff to this beach is sudden and only available to drivers coming from Cabo San Lucas (not from San José del Cabo). It's on the beach side of the highway, at Zipper's restaurant, which is on the sand by the surf breaks. If coming from San José del Cabo, you have to exit at Costa Azul Surf Shop and drive under the highway to the parking area. Food and drinks are available at Zipper's restaurant or at 7 Seas restaurant. Surfboards can be rented at Costa Azul Surf Shop or at Cabo Surf Hotel. **Amenities:** toilets; food and drink; free parking. **Best for:** surfing; walking; sunset. ⊠ *The Corridor* ✢ *Just over 1 km (½ mi) southwest of San José del Cabo.*

Playa Las Viudas (*Widow's Beach*)

BEACH | Just west of Santa María Bay, this small public beach is often referred to as Twin Dolphin Beach after the Twin Dolphin Hotel, a longtime landmark that was demolished in mid-2007 to make room for Chileno Bay Club. The reef makes it a great place for snorkeling (bring your own gear), but it is open to the ocean and all the inherent dangers that entails, so swimming is not recommended. Low tides reveal great tidal pools filled with anemone, starfish, and other sea creatures (please leave these creatures in the sea). Rock outcroppings create private areas and natural tabletops in the sand for beach picnics. The waters are also popular for kayaking and paddleboarding.

4

The Corridor

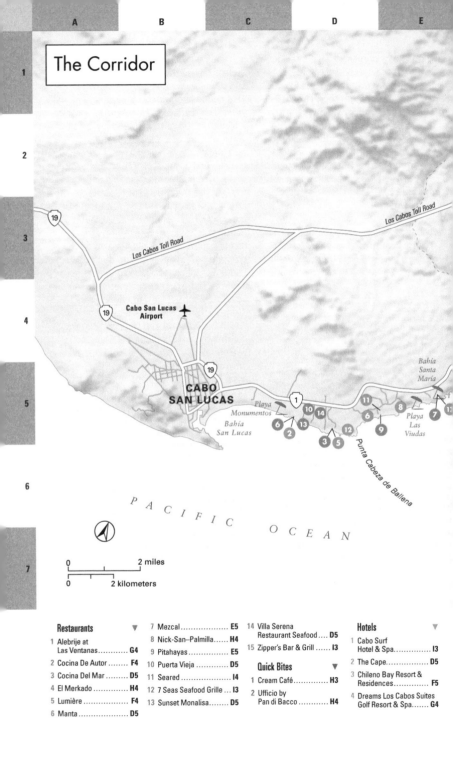

The Corridor

PACIFIC OCEAN

0 — 2 miles
0 — 2 kilometers

| F | G | H | I | J |

1

↑ TO LOS CABOS
INTERNATIONAL AIRPORT

10

1

2

Los Cabos Toll Road

10

SAN JOSÉ
DEL CABO

3

15

Bahía
San José del Cabo

8

1

1 12

Playa Costa Azul

4 2

Playa Palmilla

PALMILLA

11

9 7

1 14

1

2 10

5

4

16

21 19 13

20

Playa
Buenos Aires

18

Punta Palmilla

4

Bahía Chileno

3

Punta Chileno

KEY

1 *Restaurants*

1 *Quick Bites*

1 *Hotels*

5

6

7

Amenities: toilets; showers; free parking. **Best for:** snorkeling; walking; sunrise. ✉ *Hwy. 1, Km 12, Santa Maria Bay, The Corridor* ✛ *Turnoff sign after El Tule bridge.*

Playa Monumentos

BEACH | A left-hand point break put this small beach on the map and made it a favorite of expert surfers who love dealing with the challenges it presents. However, Playa Monumentos isn't only for surfers, as snorkeling and kayaking are also practiced on its waters. The location of this beach is one of its main assets, as it's quite close to Cabo San Lucas, and even the famous El Arco can be seen from its shores. Actually, one could say that The Corridor area starts with this beach, as it's the first one to the East after the famous Medano Beach in Cabo San Lucas. Turn right on the Misiones del Cabo entrance, as if you were going to the Sunset Monalisa and park wherever you find a spot between this restaurant and The Cape hotel. **Amenities:** food and drink; free parking; water sports. **Best for:** surfing; snorkeling; kayaking; sunset. ✉ *The Corridor* ✛ *5 km (3 miles) east of Cabo San Lucas, right by Sunset Monalisa restaurant.*

Playa Palmilla

BEACH | FAMILY | Check out the impressive multimillion-dollar villas on the road to Playa Palmilla, the best swimming beach near San José. Turn off the highway as if you're going to the One&Only Palmilla and then cross over the highway on an overpass. Continue about half a mile. The entrance is from the side road through the ritzy Palmilla development; take a left before you reach the guardhouse of the One&Only hotel. There are signs, but they're not exactly large. The beach is protected by a rocky point and the water is almost always calm; Punta Palmilla, farther out, is popular with surfers during huge swells (20 feet or more). A few thatched-roof palapas on the sand provide shade; there are trash cans but no

restrooms. Guards patrol the exclusive section known as Pelican Beach fronting the hotel, discouraging nonguests from entering—although the public legally has access to cross the beach in front of the resort property. Guests of One&Only have access to beachfront cabañas, surf instruction, beach equipment, toilets, and a restaurant. **Amenities:** toilets; showers; lifeguards; free parking. **Best for:** walking; swimming; snorkeling. ✉ *Entrance on Hwy. 1, at Km 27, The Corridor* ✛ *8 km (5 miles) southwest of San José del Cabo.*

🍴 Restaurants

Dining along the Corridor between San José del Cabo and Cabo San Lucas used to be restricted to the ever-improving hotel restaurants. But with the addition of The Shoppes at Palmilla shopping center, just across from the One&Only Palmilla resort, top-notch eateries are establishing a new dining energy along this stretch of highway, giving drivers along the Corridor a tasty reason to slow down, and maybe even stop.

Alebrije at Las Ventanas

$$$ | MEXICAN | It's well known that Las Ventanas is one of the best hotels in Mexico, and the on-site dining likewise does not disappoint. A diverse Mexican menu pays homage to Oaxaca, a southern Mexican state with an extraordinarily rich culinary tradition, and a focus on family recipes. **Known for:** Oaxacan cuisine; wide variety of moles; nightly live music. ⑤ *Average main: $50* ✉ *Carretera Transpeninsular, Km 19.5, The Corridor* ☎ *624/144–2800* ⊕ *rosewoodhotels.com/en/lasventanas.*

★ Cocina De Autor

$$$$ | CONTEMPORARY | Led by two-Michelin-starred chef Sidney Schutte, the signature restaurant at Grand Velas is turning heads for its 10-course tasting menu that's as impressive on presentation as it is on taste. Each bite is a mini-explosion in your mouth—not to be confused with

molecular gastronomy (according to the chef himself). **Known for:** 10-course tasting menu; European techniques; reservations required. ⑤ *Average main: MP4500* ✉ *Grand Velas, Carretera Transpeninsular, Km 17.3, The Corridor* ☏ *624/104–9826* ⊕ *loscabos.grandvelas.com* ⊗ *No lunch.*

★ **Cocina del Mar**

$$$ | SEAFOOD | Baja Californian chef Raul Soto delivers an elevated culinary experience at Cocina del Mar, the elegant restaurant in the exquisite Esperanza Resort. Using daily market ingredients and focusing on simple seafood, Soto presents inventive dishes such as charred octopus, grilled Kumiai oysters, or the zarandeado-style blue colossal shrimp. **Known for:** romantic location on the cliff; delicious mango and passion fruit sorbet; whole fish encased in salt and herbs. ⑤ *Average main: $50* ✉ *Esperanza Resort, Carretera Transpeninsular, Km 7, The Corridor* ☏ *624/145–6400* ⊕ *aubergeresorts.com/esperanza.*

El Merkado

$ | MODERN MEXICAN | FAMILY | At this glorified food court, more than 20 culinary offerings are at your disposal, ranging from Mexican and Greek to Spanish and Italian. Savor wine, cheese, or tapas while the little ones dig into gourmet hot dogs, creamy gelato, or treats from the candy shop. **Known for:** multitude of choices; reasonable prices; great sushi. ⑤ *Average main: $10* ✉ *Koral Center, Blvd. Cerro Colorado, Carretera Transpeninsular, Km 24.5, The Corridor* ☏ *624/191–4476* ⊕ *facebook.com/elmerkadocabo.*

Lumière

$$$ | FRENCH FUSION | For refined dining in an intimate atmosphere, head to this modern French restaurant that serves refreshingly original dishes. The setting is sophisticated without excess, while the cuisine is bold and authentic. **Known for:** extraordinary seven-course tasting menu; delicious seared scallops; organic, local ingredients. ⑤ *Average main: $40* ✉ *Le Blanc Spa Resort, Carretera Transpeninsular, Km 18.4, The Corridor* ☏ *624/163–0100* ⊕ *leblancsparesorts.com/los-cabos* ⊗ *No lunch.*

★ **Manta**

$$$ | MEXICAN FUSION | Dine with ubercool people at Manta, The Cape's culinary centerpiece by chef Enrique Olvera. Sip a cocktail in the sunken lounge bar, and move on over to the terrace with views of El Arco and surfers in action. **Known for:** globally inspired Mexican cuisine; remarkable sunset views of El Arco; local ingredients from Baja Califonia Sur. ⑤ *Average main: $35* ✉ *The Cape, Carretera Transpeninsular, Km 5, Misiones del Cabo, The Corridor* ☏ *624/163–0010* ⊕ *mantarestaurant.com* ⊗ *No lunch.*

Mezcal

$$$ | MEXICAN | FAMILY | You'll be hard-pressed to find a better Mexican restaurant in the area than this stylish establishment. Modern gastronomic techniques and sophisticated dishes highlight organic ingredients from local farmers. **Known for:** confit octopus taco; signature mezcal and tequila tastings; wake up cocktails for breakfast. ⑤ *Average main: MP635* ✉ *Montage Los Cabos, Carretera Transpeninsular, Km 12.5, The Corridor* ☏ *624/163–2035, 800/772–2226 from U.S.* ⊕ *montagehotels.com/loscabos.*

Nicksan–Palmilla

$$ | JAPANESE | FAMILY | For fresh, inventive sushi, there's no question that the Nicksan franchise corners the market, and this outpost in The Shoppes at Palmilla shopping mall wins the prize. Pair wine or sake with each of your selections, perhaps the lobster roll (with cilantro, mango, mustard, and curry oil), lobster *sambal* (marinated in sake with soy, ginger, and garlic), or tuna tostadas served on rice crackers with avocado. **Known for:** great lobster roll and ahi tostada; sushi with a Mexican twist; sashimi with chili pepper sauce. ⑤ *Average main: $20* ✉ *The Shoppes at Palmilla L-116, Hwy. 1, Km 27.5, The Corridor* ☏ *624/144–6262* ⊕ *nicksan.com.*

Boat tours from Cabo San Lucas often stop at Bahía Santa María for snorkeling.

★ Pitahayas

$$$ | ASIAN | Set under a soaring palapa overlooking the rollicking surf, this restaurant above the beach in the Hacienda del Mar Los Cabos blends Asian and Polynesian ingredients with local products for a menu that showcases well-executed Pacific Rim fusion. Seafood-heavy dishes are the specialty. **Known for:** Mexican-Asian fusion; outstanding wine cellar; a classic of Los Cabos dining scene. ⑤ *Average main: $35 ⊠ Hacienda del Mar Los Cabos, Carretera Transpeninsular, Km 10, The Corridor* ☎ *624/145–6113* ⊕ *www.pitahayas.com.*

Puerta Vieja

$$$ | INTERNATIONAL | Puerta Vieja translates into "Old Door," and the beautiful door you enter through, imported from India, is indeed over 160 years old. Though Puerta Vieja serves lunch, we suggest dinner at sunset, when the view of El Arco is the most impressive. **Known for:** tasty lobster thermidor; interesting seafood and steak combos; savory chocolate cheesecake. ⑤ *Average main:*

MP485 ⊠ Carretera Transpeninsular, Km 6.3, The Corridor ☎ *624/104–3252* ⊕ *puertavieja.com.*

★ Seared

$$$$ | STEAK HOUSE | Opened by three-Michelin-starred chef Jean-Georges Vongerichten, this signature restaurant at One&Only Palmilla is one of the priciest spots in Los Cabos, but it's also one of the best. Boasting hand-selected cuts of steak and freshly caught Pacific seafood, the menu showcases everything from caviar to Kobe beef. **Known for:** fine cuts of beef; elaborate wine list; remarkable appetizers. ⑤ *Average main: $100 ⊠ One&Only Palmilla, Carretera Transpeninsular, Km 7.5, The Corridor* ☎ *624/146–7000* ⊕ *www.oneandonlyresorts.com* ⑪ *Elegant resort attire.*

7 Seas Seafood Grille

$$$ | ECLECTIC | FAMILY | It's quite soothing to sit in this restaurant at the ocean's edge under the shade of a palapa while watching the surfers. For breakfast munch on their *machaca con huevos* (eggs scrambled with shredded beef) washed down with a fresh-fruit smoothie, but later in the day, grab some blue shrimp tacos or a grilled marinated octopus accompanied by a blueberry mojito. **Known for:** gluten-free and vegetarian options; inventive seafood cuisine with eclectic style; regional organic vegetables. $ *Average main: $35* ✉ *Cabo Surf Hotel, Carretera Transpeninsular, Km 28, at Acapulquito Beach, The Corridor* ☎ *624/142–2666* ⊕ *7seasrestaurant.com.*

Sunset Monalisa

$$$$ | **ITALIAN** | Stunning views of El Arco from cocktail tables along the cliffs make this restaurant just outside Cabo San Lucas the best place to toast the sunset. Chef Hector Morales' menu offers a variety of dishes including beef tenderloin delivered on a hot stone and grilled table-side, but portions are on the smaller side, so it's worth splurging for the Mona Lisa signature five-course menu, which includes truffle fettuccine and Australian Wagyu. **Known for:** chef's tasting menu; sunset views of El Arco; live jazz sessions. $ *Average main: $70* ✉ *Carretera Transpeninsular, Km 5.5, Misiones del Cabo, The Corridor* ☎ *624/105–8970* ⊕ *www.sunsetmonalisa.com* ⊙ *No lunch.*

Villa Serena Restaurant Seafood

$$ | **SEAFOOD** | **FAMILY** | Open for more than 30 years in the Villa Serena neighborhood along the main highway, this quiet, open-air, palapa-covered restaurant offers standard fare, from beef and shrimp kebab to baby back BBQ ribs and lobster tail, with some Mexican specialties thrown in. If you grab an ocean-facing table, you can watch the cruise ships glide past. **Known for:** Sunday special paella; unique lobster's tail; outstanding ocean views. $ *Average main: $25* ✉ *Hwy. 1, Km 7.5, The Corridor* ☎ *624/145–8244* ⊕ *villaserenarestaurant. com.*

Zipper's Bar & Grill

$$ | **AMERICAN** | **FAMILY** | Popular with the surfing crowd, this palapa-covered joint is right on Costa Azul beach, just south of San José del Cabo. Though their burger is the reason to come, the aroma of grilling lobster and tacos, and a soundtrack of surf tunes are why many return. **Known for:** fried fish and large portions; live bands playing rock classics; incredible burger. $ *Average main: $15* ✉ *Carretera Transpeninsular, Km 28.5, The Corridor* ☎ *624/172–6162* ⊕ *www.facebook.com/ zippersbargrill.*

☕ Coffee and Quick Bites

Cream Café

$$ | **CAFÉ** | **FAMILY** | The go-to place for brunch outside of the big resort restaurants, this European-style café and bakery is the perfect stop for a quick coffee, pastry, or a slice of pizza. Vegetarian and vegan dishes are available, as well as nonalcoholic cocktails. **Known for:** delicious smoothies; great breakfast options; variety of crepes. $ *Average main: MP360* ✉ *The Shoppes at Palmilla, Carretera Transpeninsular, Km 19.5, The Corridor* ☎ *624/172–6160* ⊕ *creamcafeloscabos.com.*

Ufficio by Pan di Bacco

$$ | **CAFÉ** | **FAMILY** | Refuel with a coffee and pizza of Neapolitan roots at the Koral Center food hall. Order a takeaway tiramisu and choose your coffee beans for a premium espresso. **Known for:** great frappuccinos; delicious Neapolitan pizzas; free Wi-Fi. $ *Average main: MP450* ✉ *Koral Center, Carretera Transpeninsular, Km 7.55, The Corridor* ☎ *624/688–6753* ⊕ *www.pandibacco.com/ufficio.*

Hotels

Even before the Corridor had an official name or even a paved road, the few hotels here were ritzy and elite; one even had its own private airstrip. As the saying goes, the more things change, the more they stay the same—developers have deliberately kept this area high-end and private. The Corridor is the most valuable strip of real estate in the region, with

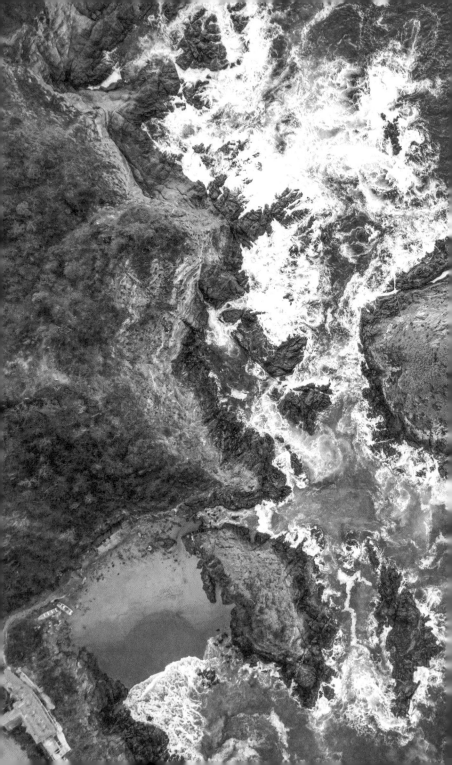

Did You Know?

Fascinating rock forma-
tions abound along the
beaches of Los Cabos.
Seismologists say that
about 30 million years
ago, a major seismic
event tore a long finger
of land—now called Baja
California Peninsula—
away from mainland
Mexico.

guard-gated exclusivity, golf courses, luxury developments, and unsurpassed views of the Sea of Cortez.

★ Cabo Surf Hotel & Spa

$$$ | HOTEL | FAMILY | Professional and amateur surfers alike claim the prime ocean-view rooms in this small hotel on the cliffs above Playa Costa Azul that has successfully blended surfing and pampering into one property. **Pros:** blends surfing and pampering; hotel guests receive discount on surf lessons and rental; free yoga on weekends. **Cons:** traffic from the highway can be noisy; usually full, as wedding parties tend to book the entire hotel; service charge added per night. ⑤ *Rooms from: $400* ✉ *Playa Acapulquito, Km 28, The Corridor* ☎ *624/142–2666, 858/964–5117 in U.S.* ⊕ *cabosurfhotel. com* ⤴ *36 rooms* ⦿⧀ *No Meals.*

The Cape

$$$$ | RESORT | Of all the draws of this Thompson Hotel—from the architectural masterpiece by Javier Sanchez to the breathtaking views of El Arco—perhaps the greatest appeal is the integration of nature, such as the spa set in natural rock formation or the boulders, cacti, and native plants that dot the grounds where two black buildings house sleek, modern rooms. **Pros:** great surf spot out front; unbelievable view of the arch; beautifully designed. **Cons:** not ideal for children; pool area can get loud on weekends; rocky beach. ⑤ *Rooms from: $650* ✉ *Carretera Transpeninsular, Km 5, The Corridor* ☎ *624/163–0000, 844/778–4322 from U.S.* ⊕ *www.hyatt.com/thompson-hotels* ⤴ *157 rooms* ⦿⧀ *No Meals.*

Chileno Bay Resort & Residences

$$$$ | RESORT | FAMILY | Set on the protected cove of Chileno Bay, one of the best spots for snorkeling and swimming in Los Cabos, this hotel hits the mark with families seeking personalized, informal service. **Pros:** ideal for families; pristine beaches with tranquil waters; infinity pool and oceanfront hot tubs. **Cons:** beach can get crowded with nonguests;

far from both Cabos, San Lucas and San José; no meal plans. ⑤ *Rooms from: $1,000* ✉ *Carretera Transpeninsular, Km 15, The Corridor* ☎ *884/207–9354 US Toll Free, 624/104–9600* ⊕ *aubergeresorts. com/chilenobay* ⤴ *99 rooms, 60 villas* ⦿⧀ *No Meals.*

Dreams Los Cabos Suites Golf Resort & Spa

$$$ | RESORT | FAMILY | This casual, unfussy resort is touted as a romantic getaway, but with an average of five weddings a week, it's more a destination for families and wedding parties with guests of all ages in attendance. **Pros:** Explorers Club for kids; golf concierge; plenty to entertain. **Cons:** resort can sometimes feel overrun with children; food is abundant but cuisine is only average; nonswimmable beach. ⑤ *Rooms from: $400* ✉ *Carretera Transpeninsular, Km 18.5, The Corridor* ☎ *866/237–3267 from U.S., 624/145–7600* ⊕ *dreamsresorts.com* ⤴ *272 rooms* ⦿⧀ *All-Inclusive.*

★ Esperanza

$$$$ | RESORT | One of the most exquisite resorts in Los Cabos, focused on privacy and impeccable service, and home to one of the best spas in the region, Esperanza is true luxury. **Pros:** most private property in Los Cabos; two secluded white-sand beaches; casitas have ocean views and renovated interiors. **Cons:** the high cost of incidentals can get exhausting; wind can be fierce on the rocky cliffs; nonswimmable beach. ⑤ *Rooms from: $1,050* ✉ *Carretera Transpeninsular, Km 7, Punta Ballena, The Corridor* ☎ *624/145–6400, 866/311–2226 in U.S.* ⊕ *aubergeresorts.com/esperanza* ⤴ *123 villas* ⦿⧀ *Free Breakfast.*

Four Seasons Resort and Residences Cabo San Lucas at Cabo del Sol

$$$$ | RESORT | FAMILY | One of the most recent additions to Cabo's resort landscape, this place delivers what its guests have come to expect from the Four Seasons luxury brand—a unique experience with top-quality services all around. **Pros:** all rooms are oceanfront

The Esperanza Resort boasts two secluded white-sand beaches.

or enjoy ocean views; rare swimmable beach in Cabo; great activities program for kids. **Cons:** golf course is shared with other resorts and developments; pricey accommodations; sprawling facilities mean long walks. ⑤ *Rooms from: $1,200* ✉ *Four Seasons Resort and Residences, Carretera Transpeninsular, Km 10.3, The Corridor* ☎ *800/819–5053* ⊕ *www.four-seasons.com* ⤴ *96 suites* ⍟ *No Meals.*

Garza Blanca Resort & Spa Los Cabos

$$$ | RESORT | FAMILY | This family-friendly, optional all-inclusive resort is a standout in every sense of the word and every aspect of the experience offered to guests; it's luxury mixed with class and upscale service. **Pros:** state-of-the-art spa; outstanding kids' club; amazing rooftop terrace with infinity swimming pool. **Cons:** far from both Cabo San Lucas and San José del Cabo; all-inclusive guests have to wear bracelets; restaurant reservations are recommended to be made 30 days in advance. ⑤ *Rooms from: $445* ✉ *Carretera Transpeninsular, Km 17.5, The Corridor* ☎ *800/931–6023 toll-free in U.S. and Canada, 624/105–4460* ⊕ *cabo. garzablancaresort.com* ⤴ *315 suites* ⍟ *All-Inclusive.*

Grand Fiesta Americana Los Cabos All Inclusive Golf & Spa

$$$$ | RESORT | FAMILY | The dramatic lobby of this all-inclusive resort is eight stories above the beach, and every room looks out onto the Sea of Cortez. **Pros:** every room has an ocean view; discounts to the spa and golf course; complimentary minibar and free Kids' Club. **Cons:** rocky beach; service is notoriously spotty; slow elevators. ⑤ *Rooms from: $500* ✉ *Cabo del Sol, Carretera Transpeninsular, Km 10.3, The Corridor* ☎ *443/310–8137* ⊕ *grandfiestamericana.com* ⤴ *525 rooms* ⍟ *All-Inclusive.*

★ Grand Velas Boutique Los Cabos

$$$$ | RESORT | Opening its doors in 2024, this brand-new, adults-only, all-inclusive boutique resort has 79 suites, two gourmet restaurants, and one swimming pool, differentiating itself from the massive resorts of the area and providing truly personalized service.

Pros: access to next door Grand Velas Resort restaurants; stylish agave tasting room; all suites include either Jacuzzi or plunge pool. **Cons:** beach not suitable for swimming; plunge pools are too cold in winter months; far from both Cabo San Lucas and San José del Cabo. ⑤ *Rooms from: $1,098* ✉ *Carretera Transpeninsular, Km 17.3, The Corridor* ☎ *866/707–5690* ⊕ *loscabosboutique.grandvelas.com* ⇗ *79 suites* ⊚ *All-Inclusive.*

★ **Grand Velas Los Cabos**

$$$$ | **RESORT** | **FAMILY** | With a curved, half-moon layout that ensures ocean views for all rooms, this luxury resort does not cut the usual "all-inclusive" corners: instead the Grand Velas offers an excess of everything, from its spacious rooms (1,180-square-feet), each with an outdoor Jacuzzi, minibar, walk-in closet, and views of the ocean and three pools, to top-notch dining options, premium drinks, and excellent service. **Pros:** coolest Kids-and-Teens' clubs in Cabo; two-Michelin-star chef at Cocina de Autor; tequila and mezcal tasting room. **Cons:** restaurants require reservations; rocky beach; extra charge for hydrotherapy treatments. ⑤ *Rooms from: $1,200* ✉ *Carretera Transpeninsular, Km 17.3, The Corridor* ☎ *624/104–9800, 877/418–3059 in U.S.* ⊕ *loscabos.grandvelas.com* ⇗ *307 suites* ⊚ *All-Inclusive.*

Hacienda del Mar Los Cabos, Autograph Collection

$$$ | **RESORT** | **FAMILY** | Small domes and barrel tile roofs top eight buildings at this lovely, hacienda-style resort in the Cabo Del Sol development. **Pros:** rooms are serene and quiet; extraordinary dining options; great for families with kids. **Cons:** beach is not usually good for swimming; minibars in rooms aren't stocked; large size of resort means long walks. ⑤ *Rooms from: $420* ✉ *Carretera Transpeninsular, Km 10, The Corridor* ☎ *624/145–6110, 844/323–2625 in U.S.* ⊕ *www.haciendadelmar.com.mx* ⇗ *270 suites* ⊚ *No Meals.*

Hacienda Encantada Resort & Residences

$$ | **RESORT** | **FAMILY** | Despite the enormous size of this timeshare-resort hybrid, there are only 205 rooms and 35 residences, meaning guests are treated to 1,400-square-foot hacienda-style suites. **Pros:** outstanding views; excellent taco bar; all-inclusive package includes dining at marina restaurants. **Cons:** beach not swimmable; extra charge for premium alcohol, certain menu items, and room service; noisy golf carts putt around the property. ⑤ *Rooms from: $200* ✉ *Carretera Transpeninsular, Km 7.3, The Corridor* ☎ *624/163–5550, 844/289–6318 toll-free in U.S.* ⊕ *haciendaencantada.com* ⇗ *238 rooms* ⊚ *All-Inclusive.*

Hilton Los Cabos

$$$$ | **RESORT** | **FAMILY** | Rooms are spacious at this hacienda-style Hilton built on one of the Corridor's few swim-friendly beaches. **Pros:** 24-hour gym; minigolf at kids' club; great cocktail bar. **Cons:** spa services are not up to par with the rest of the resort; obstructed ocean views from some rooms. ⑤ *Rooms from: $550* ✉ *Carretera Transpeninsular, Km 19.5, The Corridor* ☎ *877/354–1399* ⊕ *www.hiltonloscabos.com* ⇗ *375 rooms* ⊚ *No Meals.*

★ **Las Ventanas al Paraíso**

$$$$ | **RESORT** | From the moment your private butler greets you with a foamy margarita and escorts you to the spa for a welcome massage, you know you're in for some serious pampering and a special experience. **Pros:** exceptional service; stellar dining and wine/tequila selection; experiences include whale safaris, magic show dinners, and more. **Cons:** nonswimmable beach; tax and gratuity added to every bill; dangerous riptides. ⑤ *Rooms from: $1,200* ✉ *Hwy. 1, Km 19.5, The Corridor* ☎ *624/144–2800, 833/224–1926 in U.S.* ⊕ *lasventanas.com* ⇗ *84 rooms* ⊚ *No Meals.*

★ **Le Blanc Spa Resort Los Cabos**

$$$$ | **RESORT** | One of the truly all-inclusive luxury resorts in the area, Le Blanc

One&Only Palmilla is a stunning seaside resort.

distinguishes itself by being adults-only and providing outstanding dining and wellness options. **Pros:** adults only; personalized butler service; à la carte and buffet dining options included. **Cons:** far from Cabo and from San José; vibe isn't exactly Mexican; nonswimmable beach. ⑤ *Rooms from: $1,200* ✉ *Carretera Transpeninsular, Km 18, The Corridor* ☎ *624/163–0100* ⊕ *los-cabos. leblancsparesorts.com* ⇆ *373 rooms* ¶⊙¶ *All-Inclusive.*

Marquis Los Cabos

$$$$ | RESORT | Stunning architecture, a property-wide art collection of unique pieces, noticeable attention to detail, and loads of luxurious touches make the Marquis a standout. **Pros:** tranquillity prevails for complete escape; exceptional full-service spa; five on-site restaurants. **Cons:** busy wedding venue; surf is unswimmable; limited hours in some restaurants. ⑤ *Rooms from: $950* ✉ *Carretera Transpeninsular, Km 21.5, The Corridor* ☎ *800/690–0102, 877/238–9399 in U.S.* ⊕ *www.marquisloscabos.com* ⇆ *234 rooms* ¶⊙¶ *All-Inclusive.*

★ Montage Los Cabos

$$$$ | RESORT | FAMILY | Set in a beautiful natural location that blends perfectly with its design, Montage is an idyllic desert-beach retreat that pampers with lavish luxury; plus, there's a touch of local authenticity missed in other properties in the area. **Pros:** semi-private beach; fitness lessons and water sports equipment included; unlike other Corridor beaches, you can actually swim here. **Cons:** far from Cabo and from San José; luxury comes at a price; no adults-only section. ⑤ *Rooms from: $1,100* ✉ *Carretera Transpeninsular, Km 12.5, The Corridor* ☎ *624/163–2000, 800/772–2226* ⊕ *www. montagehotels.com/loscabos* ⇆ *174 rooms* ¶⊙¶ *No Meals.*

★ One&Only Palmilla

$$$$ | RESORT | Built in 1956 by the son of the then-president of Mexico, the One&Only was the first resort in Los Cabos area, and it retains an old-world atmosphere and elegance, superior attention to detail and service, and its position as one of the most exclusive luxury resorts in the region. **Pros:** flawless service and amenities; complimentary tequila and snacks delivered daily by personal butler; notable dining options. **Cons:** prices are high; often boisterous groups mar the otherwise genteel atmosphere; far from both San José and Cabo San Lucas. Ⓢ *Rooms from: $1,100* ✉ *Carretera Transpeninsular, Km 27.5, The Corridor* ☎ *624/146–7000, 888/691–8081 in U.S.* ⊕ *www.oneandonlyresorts.com/palmilla* ⤴ *176 rooms* ⍾ *No Meals.*

Paradisus Los Cabos - Adults Only
$$$ | **RESORT** | This beachside all-inclusive adults-only resort has fabulous rooms decorated in beachy tones of turquoise and gold, with private terraces overlooking the ocean or gardens as well as swim-up rooms, part of The Reserve upgrade section. **Pros:** near golf courses; decent rates; swimmable beach with man-made cove. **Cons:** Gastro Bar not part of all-inclusive plan; slippery pool area; loud music at pool carries into some rooms. Ⓢ *Rooms from: $395* ✉ *Carretera Transpeninsular, Km 19.5, The Corridor* ☎ *624/144–0000* ⊕ *www.melia.com* ⤴ *350 rooms* ⍾ *All-Inclusive.*

The Westin Los Cabos Resort Villas
$$$ | **RESORT** | **FAMILY** | Built by prominent Mexican artist Javier Sordo Madaleno, the colorful design and architecture reflecting the famous Arco (arch) make this Westin more memorable than some of the others in the Corridor. **Pros:** good children's center; great gym with yoga and Pilates classes; multiple pools including an adults-only option. **Cons:** it's a trek from the parking lot and lobby to the rooms and pools; on-site parking daily fee; nonswimmable beach. Ⓢ *Rooms from: $390* ✉ *Carretera Transpeninsular, Km 22.5, The Corridor* ☎ *624/142–9000, 800/845–5279 in U.S.* ⊕ *www.marriott.com* ⤴ *235 rooms* ⍾ *No Meals.*

Zoëtry Casa del Mar Los Cabos
$$$$ | **RESORT** | Set within the upscale Cabo Real gated community this hacienda-style resort has guest rooms with white marble floors, dark beamed ceilings, and teak furnishings along with views of the sea and a beautiful white-sand beach. **Pros:** generous complimentary perks; great breakfast buffet and poolside service; intimate and peaceful atmosphere. **Cons:** extra fee for use of kayaks; undertow at beach; pushy timeshare pitch. Ⓢ *Rooms from: $650* ✉ *Carretera Transpeninsular, Km 19.5, The Corridor* ☎ *624/145–7700* ⊕ *www.hyattinclusivecollection.com* ⤴ *57 rooms* ⍾ *All-Inclusive.*

Nightlife

Nightlife along Carretera Transpeninsular (Highway 1) between San José del Cabo and Cabos San Lucas historically consists of hotel bars in big resorts, most of which are frequented only by their guests. A few stand-alone places have sprung up in recent years, including the popular Latitude 22 The Roadhouse. A taxi or car is the best way to reach these places. Because walking home is generally not an option unless you're staying in-house or next door, nightlife ends early out here, with most bars turning off the lights around 10 or 11 pm. Head to Cabo San Lucas if you want to party later.

BARS
★ **Jazz on the Rocks Sunset Point**
LIVE MUSIC | This casual gastro pub is a colorful rooftop hot spot that shares the same stunning view of the famous Los Cabos Arch as its downstairs counterpart, Sunset Monalisa. With live jazz music every day and a selection of more than 140 wines and champagnes, this is the place to watch the sun set over light bites and cocktails. ✉ *Sunset Monalisa Restaurant, Carretera Transpeninsular, Km 5.5, The Corridor* ☎ *624/105–8970* ⊕ *sunsetmonalisa.com.*

La Biblioteca

COCKTAIL BARS | As far as posh hotel bars go, it's hard to top the Hilton Los Cabos La Biblioteca (meaning "The Library"), a fancy little bar completely dedicated to the celebration of tequila and mezcal. There's nothing raucous here, just intimate conversation over a Margarita or other agave-based cocktails. Mexican *antojitos* (small appetizers) and raw snacks provide the perfect complement or you can choose to pair your cocktails with an intimate five-course dinner. ⊠ *Hilton Los Cabos, Carretera Transpeninsular, Km 19.5, The Corridor* ☎ *624/145–6500, 877/354–1399* ⊕ *hiltonloscabos. com* ☞ *Reservation required.*

Latitude 22 The Roadhouse

LIVE MUSIC | This noisy, friendly roadhouse always attracts those looking to down a shot of tequila, sip cold beer, and mingle with old or new friends. The menu features good, dependable, and mostly American fare. From October to June they host live music, ranging in style from pop to blues to country. ⊠ *Carretera Transpeninsular, Km 4.5, The Corridor* ☎ *624/143–1516* ⊕ *www.facebook.com/ latitude22roadhouse.*

★ The Lounge Bar at Cocina del Mar

LOUNGES | The name sounds rather utilitarian, but the dim lighting and intimate setting here are anything but. Enjoy stunning views of El Arco—you are, after all, on the Cabo San Lucas end of the Corridor—at this elegant bar and lounge that's part of Esperanza's signature restaurant Cocina del Mar. Linger over quiet drinks or smoke a cigar as you listen to the sounds of the ocean and live music from Thursday to Sunday. ⊠ *Esperanza Resort, Carretera Transpeninsular, Km 7, Manzana 10, Punta Ballena, The Corridor* ☎ *624/145–6400* ⊕ *aubergeresorts.com/ esperanza.*

★ The Rooftop

LIVE MUSIC | For drinks with a view of El Arco, head to The Rooftop bar and lounge at The Cape hotel. The sleek setting boasts a beer garden, handcrafted cocktails, and live music at sunset. If it gets too breezy, move to their Glass Box boutique hotel bar specializing in tequilas and mezcals. ⊠ *The Cape, Carretera Transpeninsular, Km 5, The Corridor* ☎ *624/315–7502* ⊕ *thompsonhotels.com.*

Zipper's

LIVE MUSIC | Named for the nearby surf break, beachfront Zipper's attracts a mixed crowd of surfers and nonsurfers alike. A good selection of beer, as well as ribs and burgers, is always on hand, with live music weekdays and Sunday. ⊠ *Carretera Transpeninsular, Km 28.5, The Corridor* ☎ *624/172–6162* ⊕ *www. facebook.com/zippersbargrill.*

Shopping

There are shopping options along the Corridor—the stretch of land between San José del Cabo to the east and Cabo San Lucas to the west—but the shops cater more to resort guests and American expats than to travelers looking to experience Los Cabos. The closest thing you'll find to a shopping mall here is The Shoppes at Palmilla, across from the One&Only Palmilla Resort, with fewer than a dozen shops, galleries, and restaurants. Unless you're in search of something specific at one of the shops on the Corridor, you'll have much more fun shopping in San José del Cabo, Cabo San Lucas, or Todos Santos.

GROCERY STORES

California Ranch Market

MARKET | At this farmers' market in the middle of the Corridor, you can find organic food, plus kosher and imported products. You can also enjoy a fresh, healthy meal at their next-door sister restaurant Baja Fresh Kitchen. ⊠ *The Shoppes at Palmilla, Carretera Transpeninsular, Km 27.5, The Corridor* ☎ *624/104–0154* ⊕ *californiaranchmarket.com.*

MALLS

★ Koral Center (*El Merkado*)

MALL | FAMILY | Conveniently located in the Corridor, the Koral Center houses stores, medical facilities, a day spa, and El Merkado—a gourmet food court that converges 20 culinary offerings and the latest in Mexican gastronomy. You'll find everything from tacos and tapas to sushi and an organic market selling local products. ✉ *Blvd. Cerro Colorado, Carretera Transpeninsular, Km 24.5, The Corridor* ☎ *624/688–6724* ⊕ *www.facebook.com/ KoralCenter*.

The Shoppes at Palmilla

MALL | FAMILY | Located across from the posh One& Only Palmilla Resort, here you'll find a smattering of shops and galleries, a couple of restaurants, a coffee shop, a nice terrace with a peaceful fountain, and a view of the Palmilla development with the Sea of Cortez beyond. Pez Gordo Art Gallery is artist Dana Leib's second location and offers her pieces, as well as those by other artists. If you need to fuel up during your time here, there's an outpost of the popular Nicksan franchise as well as the Cream Cafe. These days, even a U.S. Consulate can be found here. ✉ *Carretera Transpeninsular, Km 27.5, The Corridor* ☎ *624/144–6999* ⊕ *theshoppesatpalmilla.com*.

Activities

Although there's plenty of snorkeling, diving, and surfing to be done at beaches along the Corridor, most of the tours—including popular ones from Surf in Cabo and Costa Azul Surf Shop—depart from Cabo San Lucas or San José del Cabo. Thanks to the plentiful luxury resorts in the area, spas and golf are also top activities. The Wild Canyon adventure park, too, has grown in popularity.

DIVING

The Corridor has several popular diving sites. Bahía Santa Maria (20–60 feet) has water clear enough to see hard and soft corals, octopuses, eels, and many tropical fish. Chileno Reef (10–80 feet) is a protected finger reef 1 km (½ mile) from Chileno Bay, with many invertebrates, including starfish, flower urchins, and hydroids. The Blowhole (60–100 feet) is known for diverse terrain—massive boulders, rugged tunnels, shallow caverns, and deep rock cuts—which house manta rays, sea turtles, and large schools of amberjacks and grouper.

GOLF

★ Cabo del Sol Golf

GOLF | Home to two outstanding 18-hole courses set between the mountains and the ocean, Cabo del Sol has been the region's standard-bearer since 1994. The Cove Club Golf Course designed by Jack Nicklaus has consistently been considered among the best in the world. The Desert Course, designed by Tom Weiskopf, offers amazing ocean views from every hole. Clinics and one-on-one lessons are available upon request. ✉ *Carretera Transpeninsular, Km 10.3, The Corridor* ☎ *624/145–6300, 866/231– 4677 from U.S.* ⊕ *cabodelsol.com/golf* 🏌 *Green fee $350, two–four players* ⛳ *Cove Club Course 7,091 yards, 18 holes, par 72; Desert Course 7,049 yards, 18 holes, par 72*.

Cabo Real Golf Course

GOLF | This visually attractive layout features spectacular views of the mountains and sea, as well as a challenging test. Designed by Robert Trent Jones Jr., Cabo Real has straight and narrow fairways, difficult slopes, and strategically placed bunkers. A recent reversal of the club's nines have completely refashioned the course's design, which now starts with stunning ocean views and moves through the desert and into rugged mountain peaks. Recovering from mistakes here can be quite difficult. Greens fee includes cart (walking is not permitted), water, and towel. Balls are not included. ✉ *Carretera Transpeninsular, Km 19.5, The Corridor* ☎ *624/144–0040*

⊕ *questrogolf.com/cabo-real* ⊠ *$275; $205 after 2:10 pm* ⚲ *18 holes, 6,848 yards, par 71.*

Palmilla Golf Course

GOLF | At the first course crafted by Jack Nicklaus in Latin America, you will encounter 27 holes of some of the best resort golf that Mexico has to offer. The Mountain and Arroyo Nines came first, with the Ocean Nine finished later. Generous target-style fairways wind their way through rugged mountainous desert terrain that is beautifully landscaped. The Ocean Nine drops 600 feet in elevation as you visit the edge of the Sea of Cortez, while the Mountain and Arroyo Nines are positioned higher and farther back from the water. Many will remark that the stretch of 6 to 8 holes on the Arroyo Course is one of the best anywhere, while the 3rd through 5th holes really get your attention on the Mountain Course. No matter the combination of Nines, you won't feel cheated; the conditioning is excellent though expensive. Five sets of tees on every hole accommodate various skill levels. ⊠ *Carretera Transpeninsular, Km 7.5, The Corridor* ☎ *624/144–5250* ⊕ *palmillagc.com* ⊠ *From $156* ⚲ *27 holes. Mountain Nine, 3,602 yards; Ocean Nine, 3,527 yards; Arroyo Nine, 3,337 yards. All nines are par 36.*

GUIDED TOURS

Wild Canyon Adventures

ADVENTURE SPORTS | FAMILY | It's all in the name at this outdoor adventure company that offers ziplining, camel rides, bungee jumping, ATV tours, a giant swing, and a glass-bottom gondola—all of which enter vast El Tule Canyon. ATV tours (and brave hikers) can cross Los Cabos Canyon Bridge, the longest wooden pedestrian bridge in the world, measuring 1,082 feet long. Free transportation is offered from your hotel, but be sure to time your activities properly since the shuttle only runs every 3½ hours. ⊠ *El Tule Bridge, The Corridor* ☎ *624/144–4433, 866/230–5253* ⊕ *www.wildcanyon.com.mx* ⊠ *Tours from $72.*

HORSEBACK RIDING

Cuadra San Francisco Equestrian Center

HORSEBACK RIDING | FAMILY | The Cuadra San Francisco Equestrian Center offers trail rides and lessons on 50 beautiful and extremely well-trained horses. Trail rides go on the beach, into the fields, or exploring the nearby canyon. Cuadra also specializes in private trail rides, photo sessions, and equestrian courses. Note that you must query them for rates, but expect to pay close to $70 per hour. ⊠ *Carretera Transpeninsular, Km 19.5, The Corridor* ⊕ *Across from Casa del Mar and Las Ventanas al Paraíso hotels* ☎ *624/191–4777* ⊕ *www.loscaboshorses.com.*

SPAS

★ **Blanc Spa**

SPA | While the concept of wellness permeates every square foot of Le Blanc Spa Resort, it finds its pinnacle at Blanc Spa. Its outstanding facilities include 25 treatment suites, 9 indoor couples suites, 15 singles suites, and 1 Le Blanc D'Or suite. With a wide range of treatments, from a signature four-hand Pericú massage to a series of beauty services and hydrotherapy, this is a spa that never disappoints. ⊠ *Carretera Transpeninsular, Km 18, The Corridor* ☎ *624/163-0100* ⊕ *leblancsparesorts.com/los-cabos* ⊠ *Body treatments: from $173. Facials: from $166. Mani-Pedi: from $40.*

Cactus Spa

SPA | Less opulent than some of the other spas in the region, Cactus Spa makes up for it with attention to detail and great service. A full menu of rejuvenating massages and postsun body treatments make up for any lack of vanity in spa design. Try a Baja Mango, Energy Wrap, or Signature Cactus massage, which uses the healing properties of tequila. If you're feeling sweet, the Chocolate Experience and the Damiana & Coffee engage all the senses. A variety of facials for women, as well as facials specifically designed for men, round out the therapy list. An on-site salon helps with last-minute hair and makeup emergencies. ⊠ *Hacienda del Mar Los Cabos, Carretera Transpeninsular, Km 10, The Corridor* ☎ *624/145–8000* ⊕ *www.haciendadelmar.com.mx/amenities/cactus-spa* ✉ *Body treatments: from $3,320 MXN. Facials: from $4,320 MXN. Mani-Pedi: from $1,120 MXN.*

★ One&Only Palmilla Spa

SPA | Therapists lead you through a locked gate into peaceful palm-filled gardens with a bubbling hot tub and a daybed covered with plump pillows. There are 13 private treatment villas for up to two people; seven are equipped with an outdoor shower, bathtub, and thatched-roof daybed for relaxing in between or after treatments. Each treatment begins with a Floral Footbath, including the signature Secret Garden Remedy, using oil infused with herbs grown on-site. Achy athletes can opt for the surfers or golfers massage. The spa also boasts a yoga pavilion, juice bar, hair salon, and a 1920s-style barber shop for men. For the ultimate in relaxation, try the Baja Deep Tissue Pindas Ritual—two hours that combine a scalp massage, hot stones, and deep pressure. ⊠ *Carretera Transpeninsular, Km 27.5, The Corridor* ☎ *624/146–7000, 888/691–8081 from U.S. and Canada* ⊕ *oneandonlyresorts.com/palmilla* ✉ *Body treatments: from $6,840 MXN. Facials: from $6,780 MXN. Mani-Pedi: from $1,050 MXN. Parking: valet (free).*

SE Spa

SPA | With only four total treatment rooms—two individual chambers and two for couples—this cute little spa underlines the boutique personality of the resort, it's not about size but quality service. The wet areas have been designed with class, re-creating a relaxing atmosphere of intimacy that allows guests to let themselves go and enjoy the magnesium pool, the emotive tunnel, or the interesting ice room. The products used here are top-shelf and include renowned brands such as EviDenS de Beauté, Bissé, and Babor. For a connection with Mexican culture, try pampering yourself with a Tequila Cream Massage or a Blue Agave Candle Massage, both excellent options that you won't find anywhere else. ⊠ *Grand Velas Boutique Hotel, Carretera Transpeninsular, Km 17.3, The Corridor* ☎ *866/707–5690* ⊕ *loscabosboutique.grandvelas.com* ✉ *Massages: from $236. Facials: from $236. Mani-Pedi: from $55.*

SOMMA WineSpa

SPA | SOMMA is the only spa of its kind in Mexico, with only seven others throughout the world basing their treatments on wine. This concept spa uses grapes from the up-and-coming Valle de Guadalupe wine region just outside Ensenada. It's an unusual experience blended with classical treatments, focusing on the calming, cosmetic, and antioxidant properties of grapes and wine, or vinotherapy. It towers high above the Sea of Cortez with 14 treatment rooms, both indoor and open-air, and offers a geothermal hot spring and more than 41 facial and body treatments from a Champagne Wrap to a Merlot Exfoliation. ⊠ *Grand Fiesta Americana Los Cabos, Carretera Transpeninsular, Km 10.3, Cabo del Sol, The Corridor* ☎ *443/310–8137* ⊕ *grandfiestamericana.com* ✉ *Body treatments: from $80. Facials: from $170. Mani-Pedi: from $40. Parking: valet and self-parking.*

★ The Spa at Esperanza

SPA | At the exclusive, 17-acre Esperanza Resort between Cabo San Lucas and San José del Cabo, the beautiful spa is reached by way of a stone path over a koi pond. At check-in you're presented with an *agua fresca*, a healthy drink made with papaya or mango, or other fruits and herbs. Treatments incorporate local ingredients, tropical fruits, and ocean-based

Continued on page 119

Los Cabos' perfect waves

SURFING CABO STYLE

From the gentlest of beginner waves at Old Man's surf spot to the gnarliest winter waves at Los Cerritos, Los Cabos has surf for everyone. The tip of the Baja Peninsula has three key areas: the Pacific coast (often called "the Pacific side"), the East Cape, and the Cabo Corridor between them. This means that there are east-, west- and south-facing beaches taking waves from just about every direction.

There are also warm, crystalline seas and great surf schools. Friendly instructors make lessons fun and are more than willing to tailor them to the needs of anyone—from groms to retirees, aspiring surfers to experts. Schools also offer surf tours so you can benefit from insider knowledge of the local waves and quirky surf spots before heading out on your own.

LOS CABOS SURF FINDER

Heavy shore break in San Jose Del Cabo Baja California

Gentle waves during summer time.

Punta Conejo
Todos Santo
Pacific
Coast
Punta Lobos
Play San Pe
El Pesca
El Pesce
P Ce
WEST CAPE
19

PACIFIC SIDE

In winter, the Pacific from Cabo San Lucas town north to Todos Santos, often roils with rough, thundering swells. Surf spots here are only for the most accomplished although Los Cerritos, home to the Costa Azul Surf Shop and school, can have gentle waves in summer. Pacific-side beaches face essentially west and slightly north. Hence, winter swells coming from these directions (thanks to Alaskan storms) make landfall head on, creating great waves.

Punta Conejo: a rocky point break north of Todos Santos; unique in that it's surfable on both north and south swells. Has good right and left breaks. *11 km (7 miles) north of Todos Santos; turn off Hwy. 19 near Km 80.*

Punta Lobos: big point breaks with south swells. *South of Todos Santos; turn off Hwy. 19 at Km 54 onto dirt road, and continue for about 2.5 km (1.5 miles).*

Playa San Pedrito: a beautiful, broad, curved, sandy beach break, surfable on both west and

Surfing at Playa los Cerritos

Perfect waves in Baja California

north swells. *From Cabo San Lucas take Hwy. 19 until Km. 58; turn right onto the dirt road after the Campo Experimental agriculture station and continue about 2 km (1.3 miles).*

El Pescadero: fast, consistent, right reef and beach breaks; watch out for painful sea urchins in shallow water! *Hwy. 19 at Km 59.*

Playa Los Cerritos: highly versatile beach—in summer, good for beginners, with gentle breaks and a safe, sandy bottom; winter waves are gnarly. Best ones are on northwest swells, though south swells aren't bad. Both left and right beach breaks. Home to Costa Azul Surf Shop; can get crowded. *Less than a km (half a mile) south of Todos Santos; Hwy. 19 at Km 66.*

CABO CORRIDOR

The 20-mile stretch of beautiful beaches and bays between the towns of Cabo San Lucas and San José del Cabo has no less than

a dozen surf spots, including some that are hard to find and access. Opportunities range from the expert-only Monuments break just outside of Cabo to the beginner-friendly Old Man's spot. For experts, surfing in the Corridor is generally best in the summer and fall, when storms as far away as New Zealand and Antarctica can send south swells all the way up here.

Playa Monumentos: powerful left point break, offering great gut-wrenching waves on south and west swells. Dangerously shallow at low tide; many sea urchins. Great surf and sunset watching from bluff near parking area. *Far south end of Cabo's El Medano Beach, east of Cabo San Lucas on Hwy 1 at Km. 5.5; pull off at Misiones del Cabo, drive to gate.*

Playa El Tule: long wide beach with great right reef break in El Tule Arroyo, near highway bridge of same name. One of few places you can still camp; need 4WD to get here. *Midway btw. Cabo San Lucas and San José. East on Hwy. 1 at Km. 16.2, look for EL TULE sign, pull off road and drive toward ocean on sandy road.*

Costa Azul: beach of choice in summer. World-famous, experts-only Zippers break often tops 12 feet. Has two other popular breaks: Acapulquito (Old Man's) in front of Cabo Surf Hotel—forgiving with a gentle surf break

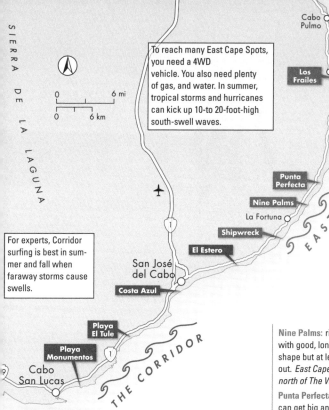

SIERRA DE LA LAGUNA

Sea of Cortez

Cabo Pulmo

Los Frailes

To reach many East Cape Spots, you need a 4WD vehicle. You also need plenty of gas, and water. In summer, tropical storms and hurricanes can kick up 10-to 20-foot-high south-swell waves.

Punta Perfecta

Nine Palms

La Fortuna

EAST CAPE

Shipwreck

El Estero

San José del Cabo

Costa Azul

For experts, Corridor surfing is best in summer and fall when faraway storms cause swells.

Playa El Tule

Playa Monumentos

Cabo San Lucas

THE CORRIDOR

and good for beginners—and The Rock, a more challenging reef break to the east. The rocks are near the surface; quite shallow at low tide. There's a restaurant and a branch of the Costa Azul Surf Shop here. *Between Km. 28 and 29 on Hwy 1.*

El Estero: freshwater estuary with a river mouth beach break (i.e., giant barrels break upon sand bars created by runoff sand deposited here after powerful summer rains). Both left and right rides. *Hwy. 1, south of Hilton Cabo Azul Resort.*

EAST CAPE

North and east of San José, up the rough, unpaved East Cape Road, there are many breaks with good waves that are perpetually empty—with good reason. To get

here, you need a 4WD vehicle. You also need plenty of gas, sufficient water, an umbrella, and mucho sun block. Waves here aren't for beginners, and some of the coast is on private property. Note, too, that locals (both Mexican and gringo) can be protective of their spots. East Cape beaches face south and east, and, in summer, tropical storms and hurricanes can kick up 10-, 15-, and even 20-foot-high south-swell waves— exciting for beginners to watch from the shore.

Shipwreck: fast, right reef break with south swells in summer. Considered the second-best summer surfing spot. Need 4WD to get here. *Off East Cape Rd., about 16 km (10 miles) up a rough, washboard road.*

Nine Palms: right point break with good, long waves and great shape but at least an hour's drive out. *East Cape Rd., 1 km (0.6 miles) north of The White Lodge hotel.*

Punta Perfecta: right point break; can get big and hollow (i.e., "tubular") during summer's south swells. Out of the way (4WD required) and hard to find; territorial local surfers get testy when asked for directions. *East Cape Rd., near Crossroads Country Club and Vinorama.*

Los Frailes: Waves get big on a south swell. Down a long, dusty, pounding drive (need 4WD). Beautiful white sand beach and tranquil desert surroundings. *East Cape Rd.*

Stand-up paddleboarding (SUP)

LEARNING TO SURF

There are numerous opportunities to learn to surf in Baja Sur.

WHAT TO EXPECT

Expect introductory classes to cover how to lie on the board, paddle properly, pop up into a surf stance, and handle riding white wash (inside waves)

GEARING UP

Both surf shops and schools offer a wide selection of lessons, gear, and boards—sometimes including "skegs," soft, stable beginners's boards with plastic fins. Novices will want to use longboards, which offer the most stability. Rash guards (form-fitting polyester vests) protect you from board chafing and sunburn. Booties, rubberized watershoes, protect your feet from rocks, coral and sea urchins.

GETTING OUT THERE

Most agree that the best place for beginners is San José del Cabo's Acapulquito Beach, home to Old Man's surf spot. It has gently breaking, "feathering" (very forgiving) waves and the region's most understanding surfers. Acapulquito Beach is also home to the Cabo Surf Hotel, with a top school. The **Mike Doyle Surf School** (⊕ *www.mikedoylesurf-school.com*) has all its full-time teachers certified by the NSSIA, the National Surf Schools and Instructor's Association (U.S.) and a great selection of more than 100 boards—short, long, "soft" boards for novices, and even a couple of SUP boards.

Costa Azul Surf Shop (⊕ *costaazulsurf-shop.com*), with branches in San José del Cabo (near Zipper's Restaurant) and south of Todos Santos, near Los Cerritos Beach, is another option for lessons. Staff here can arrange tours to breaks so far off the path that roads to them aren't always marked on maps, let alone paved. The shop's website also has good interactive surfing maps.

Costa Azul's three-hour surf excursions include two boards per person, rash guards, and surf shoes. The cost is US$180 per person.

SURF'S DOWN?

If the surf's flat, no problema! SUP, or stand-up paddleboarding, is done on flat waters using broad, long, lightweight boards that are comfortable to stand on. You paddle along, alternating sides for balance, using what resembles a single-bladed kayak paddle. SUP is easy to master, great exercise, and highly enjoyable.

Accomplished surfers have pushed the SUPing envelope, paddling their boards into the lineup (or surf zone) and right into the waves, be they small or large. The paddle is then used to steer, almost like a boat's rudder. One step at a time, though—this type of SUP is not as easy as the masters make it look!

BOARD SHAPES

Longboard: Lengthier (about 2.5–3 m/9–10.5 feet), wider, thicker, and more buoyant than the often-miniscule shortboards. Offers more flotation and speedier paddling, which makes it easier to get into waves. Great for beginners and those with relaxed surf styles. **Skill level:** Beginner to Intermediate.

Funboard: A little shorter than the longboard with a slightly more acute nose and blunt tail, the funboard combines the best attributes of the longboards with some similar characteristics of the shorter boards. Good for beginners or surfers looking for a board more maneuverable and faster than a longboard. **Skill level:** Beginner to Intermediate.

Fishboard: A stumpy, blunt-nosed, twin-finned board that features a "V" tail (giving it a "fish" like look, hence the name) and is fast and maneuverable. Good for catching small, steep slow waves and pulling tricks. At one point this was the world's best-selling surfboard. **Skill level:** Intermediate to Expert.

Shortboard: Shortboards came on the scene in the late '60s when the average board length dropped from 9'6" to 6'6" (3m to 2m) and changed wave riding forever. This short, light, high-performance board is designed for carving the wave with a high amount of maneuverability. These boards need a fast steep wave, completely different from a "longboard" break, which tends to be slower with shallower wave faces. **Skill level:** Expert.

Beginner   **Expert**

Funboards

Fish

Longboards

Shortboards

Shallow wave faces, easiest surfing   Steeper wave faces, difficult surfing

SURF SLANG

A surfer rips it up in Mexico

Barrel: The area created when a wave breaks onto itself in a curl, creating a tube that's the surfer's nirvana. Also called the green room.

Barreled: becoming totally enclosed inside the wave's barrel during a ride. The ultimate "stoke!" Getting "barreled" is also sometimes known as spending time inside the "green room" or getting "tubed."

Beach break: The safest, best type for beginners. Waves break over sandy beaches. Found at Acapulquito (Old Man's), San Pedrito, and Los Cerritos.

Close out: When a wave or a section of a wave breaks all at once, rather than steadily in one direction. A frustrating situation for surfers; there's nowhere to go as the wave crashes down.

Ding: A hole, dent, crack or other damage to a board.

Drop in: To stand up and drop down in the face of a wave. Also used when one surfer cuts another off: "Hey, don't drop in on that guy!"

Duck dive: Maneuver where the surfer first pushes his or her board underwater and then dives with it, ducking under waves that have broken or are about to break. Difficult with a longboard.

Goofy foot: Having a right-foot-forward stance on the surfboard. The opposite is known as regular.

Outside: The area farther out from where waves break most regularly. Surfers line up here, and begin their paddling to catch waves.

Point break: Created as waves hit a point jutting into the ocean. With the right conditions, this can create very consistent waves and very long rides. Punta Lobos, Punta Conejo, and Monumentos are examples.

Reef break: Waves break as they pass over reefs and create great (but sometimes dangerous) surf. There's always the chance of being scraped over extremely sharp coral or rocks. Found at El Tule, Shipwreck, and The Rock in Costa Azul.

Right/Left break: Terms for which direction the surfer actually travels on the wave, as seen from his or her perspective. Think of break direction in terms of when you're actually surfing the wave.

Set: waves often come in as sets, or groups of three to seven, sometimes more, in a row.

Stick: A surfboard.

Stoked: really, totally excited—usually about the surf conditions or your fantastic wave ride.

Swells: created by wind currents blowing over the sea's surface. The harder and the longer the winds blow, the larger the waves, and the longer the swell lasts.

Turtle roll: the surfer rolls over on the surfboard, going underwater and holding the board upside down. Used by longboarders and beginners to keep from being swept back toward shore by breaking waves.

Wipeout: a nasty crash off your board, usually having the wave crash down upon you.

Baja California Sur sunset

products. Look for such pampering as the papaya-mango body polish, the grated-coconut-and-lime exfoliation, and the four-hands massage. Yoga classes are held at 7:15 and 9 each morning for $35 (free for hotel guests). Guests can also book an evening Starlight Spa experience for exclusive after-hours access. ☒ Esperanza Resort, Carretera Transpeninsular, Km 7, The Corridor ☎ 624/145–6406 ⊕ aubergeresorts.com/esperanza ☑ Body treatments: from $250. Facials: from $250. Mani-Pedi: from $45. Parking: valet (free).

★ **The Spa at Las Ventanas al Paraíso**

SPA | Known for its innovative treatments—nopal (cactus) anticellulite and detox wrap, crystal healing massages, and raindrop therapy, the Spa at Las Ventanas has both indoor and outdoor facilities. Some of the eight treatment rooms have private patios, and the two couples' suites come with a private butler. The elemental journey Las Ventanas Collection even includes lunch from La Cocina del Spa. Salt glows and massages are available in a pavilion by the sea. There are also pampering treatments for kids (Mommy and Me) and couples (Sea and Stars). ☒ Las Ventanas al Paraíso Resort, Carretera Transpeninsular, Km 19.5, The Corridor ☎ 624/144–2800 ⊕ rosewoodhotels.com ☑ Body treatments: from $5,280 MXN. Facials: from $4,400 MXN. Mani-Pedi: $1,080 MXN. Parking: valet (free).

Spa Marquis

SPA | With its holistic approach to wellness, this spa at Marquis Los Cabos has three categories of treatment: anima (massages), corpus (wraps), and mente (facials). The spa includes a complete hydrotherapy circuit and 10 treatment cabins with 4 enjoying spectacular

ocean views and 2 reserved for couples. The resort's all-inclusive package now includes access to the hydrotherapy circuit and a 20% discount at the spa. Treatments are also available for nonguest visitors. ☒ Marquis Los Cabos, Carretera Transpeninsular, Km 21.5, The Corridor ☎ 800/690–0102, 877/238–9399 Toll Free in U.S. ⊕ marquisloscabos.com ☑ Body treatments: from $121. Facials: from $138. Mani-Pedi: from $83. Waxing: from $39. Parking: valet (free).

Spa Montage Los Cabos

SPA | Extending over 40,000 square feet of state-of-the-art wellness facilities, Spa Montage is without a doubt one of the largest and best-equipped spas in Baja. A diverse array of holistic massages, facials, and beauty treatments await, including a must-try hydrotherapy circuit and a pampering, three-hour couples massage. Its outdoor, adults-only serenity pool and jetted pool area are standouts. ☒ Carretera Transpeninsular, Km 12.5, The Corridor ☎ 624/163–2000, 800/772–2226 ⊕ montagehotels.com/loscabos ☑ Body treatments: from $290. Facials: from $335. Mani-Pedi: from $90.

Surfing in Style

One&Only Palmilla offers guests a range of five-star surf tours with the acclaimed company Tropic Surf—the pioneer in "luxury surfing." Regardless of age or ability, guests can paddle into Cabo's best breaks in style, all with an emphasis on service, luxury, water safety, and improvement.

Spa Otomí at Westin Los Cabos

SPA | Massages and wraps are the specialties provided in seven treatment rooms at the Spa Otomí. The most popular is the Otomí Signature massage, which takes guests to the peak of relaxation. The Blue Agave Candlelight massage is also a top seller. An on-site salon, barbershop, and fitness center round out the amenities. ⊠ *Westin Los Cabos, Carretera Transpeninsular, Km 22.5, The Corridor* ☎ *624/142–9000, 800/845–5279 toll-free in U.S.* ⊕ *mariott. com* ⊠ *Body treatments: from $128. Facials: from $75.*

SPORTFISHING

All the Corridor hotels work with fishing fleets anchored at the Cabo San Lucas marina (most vendors are stationed there) and a few with boats in Puerto Los Cabos, so any one of them can help you set up your fishing trips. Note that some hotels send customers to the company with the highest commission, so double-check recommendations and do your research. The major drawback of arranging a fishing trip from one of the Corridor hotels is the travel time involved in getting down to the water. It takes up to half an hour or more to reach the docks from Corridor hotels, and most boats depart at 6:30 am.

Gordo Banks Pangas

FISHING | The *pangas* (small fishing boats) of Gordo Banks Pangas are near some of the hottest fishing spots in the Sea of Cortez: the Outer and Inner Gordo banks. The smaller pangas accommodate up to three people, while their 33-foot cruisers accommodate up to six anglers per boat. ⊠ *Puerto Los Cabos, San José del Cabo, The Corridor* ☎ *624/142–1147, 619/488–1859 in U.S.* ⊕ *www.gordobanks.com* ⊠ *Pangas from $250; cruisers from $400 for a 6–7 hr trip.*

SURFING

The waves and undercurrent along the Corridor are notoriously strong, making much of the beach here unfavorable for swimming but great for surfing.

Mike Doyle Surf School

SURFING | FAMILY | The Mike Doyle Surf School is the top "surfer-friendly" location in all of Los Cabos. If you stay at the Cabo Surf Hotel where Mike Doyle is located, you can check the surf conditions from the restaurant, bar, pool, or even from your balcony. The school has more than 100 rental boards, from foam boards and short boards to longboards and stand-up paddleboards. There are five surf instructors available at the shop for lessons. ⊠ *Cabo Surf Hotel, Carretera Transpeninsular, Km 28, Playa Acapulquito, The Corridor* ☎ *624/142–2666, 858/964–5117 in U.S.* ⊕ *mikedoylesurfschool.com* ⊠ *Lessons from $118.*

★ Surf in Cabo

SURFING | FAMILY | Surf in Cabo has provided surf and SUP lessons for all levels, tours (half- and full-day), and rentals for more than a decade. They're located at Playa Costa Azul, where they organize well-rounded surfing camps, "surfaris," and "supfaris." Another bonus: they're open every day and accept credit cards. ⊠ *Carretera Transpeninsular, Km 28.5, The Corridor* ⊕ *Next to Zipper's* ☎ *624/224–2110* ⊕ *surfincabo. com* ⊠ *Surf lesson: from $1,400 MXN; Surfari: from $2,100 MXN; Supfari: from $2,100 MXN.*

Chapter 5

SAN JOSÉ DEL CABO

Updated by
Luis F. Dominguez

👁 Sights 🍴 Restaurants 🛏 Hotels 🛍 Shopping 🍸 Nightlife

★★★★☆   ★★★★★   ★★★★★   ★★★★☆   ★★★☆☆

NEIGHBORHOOD SNAPSHOT

TOP EXPERIENCES

■ **Gallery Hopping:** Visit the charming Art District during a Thursday Art Walk, when artists open their galleries and invite visitors to mingle, purchase art, and sample local food and drinks.

■ **Farm-to-Table Dining:** There are several opportunities to dine right in the picturesque farms that produce the fresh ingredients for your organic meal.

■ **Surfing:** If surfing is on your bucket list, this is the place to cross it off and simply a must when visiting San José. For something a tad easier, try paddleboarding.

■ **Strolling Downtown:** Walk the quaint streets of San José's historic center, and discover its collection of centuries-old buildings, a vibrant community plaza, and food stalls full of local flavor.

■ **Shopping:** Whether you're in the market for art, jewelry, or fresh produce from the stellar Farmer's Market (Mercado Organico), you'll find it here.

GETTING HERE

Since this is the closest neighborhood to the SJD airport, shuttle prices are slightly cheaper than to other neighborhoods ($25 for a shared ride and $80 for a private ride). Taxis charge around $75. Note that ride-share services like Uber are not allowed to pick up customers at the airport. Once in San José, the best way to move around is by taxi or Uber. There's no need to rent a car, unless you plan to go on an excursion far from town.

PLANNING YOUR TIME

May to June is the best time to visit, right after spring break and before the rainy season starts. Summer is best for surfing, and December through April is best for whale watching (and is most expensive). Plan at least a day to explore, prioritizing the art galleries and eateries downtown. Make it a Thursday, if you can, to catch the weekly Art Walk between 5 and 9 pm.

BEST BEACHES

■ **Playa Hotelera:** San José's main beach and the one that most visitors enjoy day in and day out. Although the scenery is outstanding, swimming is not recommended due to a strong undertow. Horseback riding, beach volleyball, and romantic walks at sunset are viable options, though.

■ **La Playita:** One of the rare beaches where swimming isn't too risky in Los Cabos, this "little beach" is perfect for families with small kids who enjoy its zero-wave shallow waters, while their parents relax under the tranquil palapas ($5) distributed across the shoreline. There are well-appointed bathrooms and a few nearby eateries.

■ **El Estero:** This narrow stretch of sand connects Playa Hotelera with the Marina Puerto Los Cabos area. One side of the beach is on the Pacific Ocean, while the other side is a freshwater lagoon with lush vegetation and vibrant wildlife. Sadly, you can't swim here, but it's great for kayak lovers and bird-watching enthusiasts.

If being in Mexico (and not in the thick of a hopping resort scene) sounds like the ideal setting for your vacation, San José del Cabo is the place to be. San José is the quieter, more artistic of Los Cabos' two main towns; its sister across the corridor, Cabo San Lucas, has the more exciting nightlife and rowdy beaches. What you get here is a lovely downtown that's retained much of its traditional charm, with adobe houses fronted by jacaranda trees, and a peaceful, more down-to-earth experience.

With century-old buildings and many elevated sidewalks, the Centro Histórico (historic center) is a delight to explore on foot. Plaza Mijares, the open and popular *zócalo*, is graced by a fountain, lighted at night, and a stage where live music takes place frequently for the crowds who gather to stroll to nearby art galleries, enjoy ice cream, and relax after the heat of the day has let up. Several streets fronting the square are pedestrian-only, giving this historic downtown a lush and leisurely feel.

Entrepreneurs have converted many of the old homes into stylish restaurants, and new and inventive cuisine abounds—fitting for a town with an art district that is burgeoning as well. A marina, two golf courses, and a residential community are south of Centro (town center) in Puerto Los Cabos; farther south the ever-expanding Zona Hotelera (Hotel Zone) faces a long beach on the Sea of Cortez.

Just outside San José in the lush Ánimas Bajas, farm-to-table dining concepts like Acre and Flora Farms are drawing an increasing number of visitors for fresh-as-can-be organic meals and stunning views.

◉ Sights

Many of San José's sights are located in the Centro Histórico, or historic center, a charming downtown anchored by the central Plaza Mijares. Surrounding it are a historic mission, art galleries, and colorful, pedestrian-only streets that invite you to take a relaxed stroll.

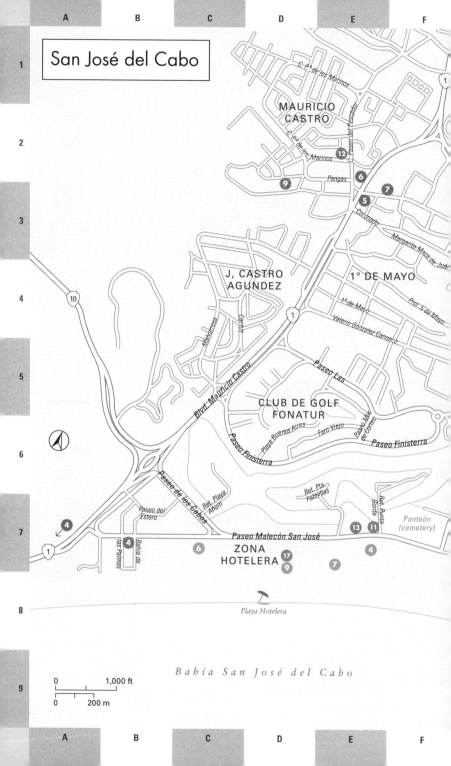

San José del Cabo

Bahía San José del Cabo

Playa Hotelera

TO
LOS CABOS
INTERNATIONAL AIRPORT

Ave. Centenario

Comonfort

C. Ignacio Zaragoza

C. Manuel Doblado

Mauricio Castro

CENTRO

Obregon

Coronado

Josefa Ma. Morelos

Miguel Hidalgo

Ave. Centenario

Blvd. Antonio Mijares

LA CHOYA

TO
LA PLAYITA
BEACH →

Benito Juarez

Estero San José

Playa Estero

Sights ▼

1 Art District.............. **G3**
2 Misión San José del Cabo..................... **G3**
3 Plaza Mijares........... **H3**

Restaurants ▼

1 Acre **I5**
2 Baja Brewing Company...... **G3**
3 Café des Artistes Los Cabos................. **I5**
4 Cynthia Fresh Organic Restaurant..... **B7**
5 Don Sanchez............ **H4**
6 El Marinero Borracho.... **I5**
7 Flora's Field Kitchen at Flora Farms............... **I5**
8 Habanero's Mexican Fusion Bistro **G6**
9 The Hangman Surf & Tacos **D2**
10 La Dolce **H3**
11 La Forchetta............. **E7**
12 Las Guacamayas Taqueria **E2**
13 Latino 8................... **E7**
14 Lolita Café **G3**
15 Los Tamarindos **H3**
16 Mi Cocina............... **H3**
17 NIDO **D7**
18 Tequila Restaurant...... **H4**

Quick Bites ▼

1 Claro Fish Jr. **G5**
2 Coffee LAB **G4**
3 French Riviera Restaurant............... **H3**
4 La Carreta Sabores de Oaxaca **A7**
5 La Michoacana **E3**
6 Tacos Rossy............. **E3**
7 Taqueria El Fogon........ **E3**
8 Taquería El Paisa **G2**

Hotels ▼

1 Casa Maat at JW Marriott Los Cabos.......**I5**
2 Casa Natalia............. **H3**
3 Encanto Inn & Suites... **H3**
4 Hilton Vacation Club Cabo Azul Los Cabos.... **E7**
5 Hotel El Ganzo............. **I5**
6 Hyatt Ziva Los Cabos....**C7**
7 Royal Solaris Los Cabos................. **E7**
8 Secrets Puerto Los Cabos Golf & Spa Resort................. **I5**
9 Viceroy Los Cabos...... **D7**
10 Zadún, a Ritz-Carlton Reserve **I5**

KEY
1 Sights
1 Restaurants
1 Quick Bites
1 Hotels

★ Art District

ART GALLERY | Within San José's historic center are four blocks packed with 14 high-quality art galleries, collectively known as the Art or Gallery District. You can walk around any time, but it's worth planning your visit on Thursday afternoon to enjoy San José's popular weekly Art Walk from 5 pm through 9 pm. During this time, gallery owners open their doors and invite you to socialize with local artists and art enthusiasts from around the globe, discovering thought-provoking artwork along the way. ⊠ *Álvaro Obregón and Morelos, Distrito del Arte* ☎ *624/168–7063* ⊕ *artcabo.com.*

Misión San José del Cabo

CHURCH | **FAMILY** | One of the most magical experiences in San José is strolling past this historic mission as its bells chime. Originally founded in 1730 near the local estuary, it was the southernmost Jesuit mission established in the Vieja California territory during Mexico's colonial days. The mission walked a tightrope between baptizing the area's indigenous Pericú and being locked in battle with them. In the 19th century the mission was destroyed by an attack, and it wasn't until 1940 that the mission was rebuilt on its current site. The mission is currently the head of a parish comprising six churches and more than 45,000 parishioners. It holds English mass every Sunday at noon. ⊠ *Parroquia de San José del Cabo, Calle Zaragoza and Miguel Hidalgo, Centro* ☎ *624/142–0064* ⊕ *facebook.com/misionsanjosedelcabo.*

Plaza Mijares

PLAZA/SQUARE | **FAMILY** | This *zócalo* (main square) and community gathering space is the heart and soul of San José del Cabo. Surrounded by city hall and the Misión de San José, it's where all manner of events and happenings take place. The nearby streets are filled with all kinds of shops, restaurants, and art galleries, but it's here that locals gather to spend their weekend afternoons eating *antojitos* (appetizers) and enjoying performances of local street artists. ⊠ *Plaza Mijares, Centro.*

 Beaches

Oh, the madness of it all. Here you are in a beach destination with gorgeous weather and miles of clear blue water, yet you dare not dive into the sea. Most of San José's hotels line Playa Hotelera on Paseo Malecón San José, and brochures and websites gleefully mention beach access. But here's the rub— though the long, level stretch of coarse brown sand is beautiful, the currents can be dangerously rough, the drop-offs are steep and close to shore, and the waves can be fierce. Although surfers love this type of water and flock here in droves, it's extremely dangerous for the casual swimmer. Warning signs are posted up and down the beach, just in case you happen to forget. Feel free to walk along the beach to the Estero San José, play some beach volleyball, or enjoy a horseback ride along the shore. For swimming head to protected Playa Palmilla just a few miles southwest, in the Corridor.

La Playita

BEACH | **FAMILY** | Located at the harbor entrance of the Puerto Los Cabos Marina, *La Playita* (meaning "The Little Beach") is one of the most popular beaches among local families due to its shallow waters and an almost complete lack of waves. Kids can run, swim, and splash around, while parents (if they so choose) will enjoy the tranquillity of the beach, the small palapas available for rent, and the convenience of having shops and small food stalls in the area. Some locals (and a few expats) also come here to fish from the shore. **Amenities:** toilets; free parking; food and drink. **Best for:** swimming; walking; sunrise. ⊠ *La Playita, La Playita.*

Playa Estero (*Estuary Beach*)

BEACH | FAMILY | A sandy beach can be enjoyed at the mouth of the Estero San José, the lush estuary that starts at the north end of Hotel Zone. This oasis is home to more than 350 species of wildlife and vegetation (200-plus species of birds alone), and can be explored on foot, or via kayaks rentable at El Ganzo Beach Club. Horses are available for hire at the end of the waterfront at Bonanza Horseback Riding. Bring bug spray, as the wetlands attract lots of mosquitoes. Not recommended for swimming, it is nevertheless a worthwhile trip in an area that is otherwise not known for its lushness. **Amenities:** free parking. **Best for:** walking; sunrise. ⊠ *Zona Hotelera.*

Playa Hotelera

BEACH | FAMILY | The long, wide stretch of beach running in front of the hotels on the coast of San José del Cabo might be stunning, but the riptides and undertows make it deceivingly dangerous for swimmers. There are no public services on the beach, but you can always duck into one of the hotels for a snack, or head across the street to Plaza Del Pescador for a meal at one of the restaurants. This beach often has locals with horses to rent for a beachside ride. Due to the line of resorts, there are only a few access points to reach the sand. **Amenities:** free parking. **Best for:** walking; surfing; sunrise. ⊠ *Zona Hotelera.*

Restaurants

Boulevard Mijares is San José's Restaurant Row, so simply meander down the main boulevard to find one that will thrill your taste buds and delight your senses. New, organic-focused restaurants are pushing the culinary scene to the outskirts of San José del Cabo in Animas Bajas. These farm-to-table finds are tucked into green valleys, creating an oasis just beyond the cactus-lined dusty roads of Puerto Los Cabos.

★ **Acre**

$$$ | MODERN MEXICAN | Twenty-five acres are what you'll find at this farmland dining experience where design, sustainability, and modern cuisine intersect. Fried Brussels sprouts with candied pumpkin seed, white Bolognese pappardelle, and cauliflower steaks that make you wonder why you don't eat more of the remarkable vegetable at home are a few of the menu offerings. **Known for:** farm-to-table experience; global cuisine with Mexican fusion; award-winning mezcal of the house. ⑤ *Average main: $29* ⊠ *Calle Rincon De Las Ánimas s/n, Las Animas Bajas* ☎ *624/172–1021* ⊕ *acrebaja.com.*

Baja Brewing Company

$$ | AMERICAN | Baja's popular brewery is right in the middle of San José del Cabo's Art District. Fun and upbeat, this brewpub has great music and serves filling pub meals. **Known for:** wood-fired pizza; customers watching behind-the-scenes brewing while enjoying beers at the bar; Baja beer on tap. ⑤ *Average main: $15* ⊠ *Morelos 1227, Distrito del Arte* ⊕ *Between Comonfort and Obregón* ☎ *624/142–5294* ⊕ *bajabrewingcompany. com.*

★ **Café des Artistes Los Cabos**

$$$$ | FRENCH FUSION | The signature restaurant of Casa Maat boutique hotel brings the refined cuisine of award-winning Chef Thierry Blouet to Los Cabos. The striking indoor-outdoor setting offers magnificent ocean- and sunset views. **Known for:** award-winning celebrity chef; stunning sunset views; tempting six-course set menu. ⑤ *Average main: $60* ⊠ *Casa Maat at JW Marriott Los Cabos, Fracción Hotelera FH5-C1, La Playita* ☎ *624/163–7600* ⊕ *cafedesartistescabos. com* ⊗ *Closed Mon. No lunch.*

Cynthia Fresh Organic Restaurant

$ | SANDWICHES | FAMILY | A hidden gem in the wide array of dining options in San José, this small restaurant and organic market serves fresh vegan and nonvegan dishes. Buy at the market and take out,

or dine-in and enjoy live music and fresh margaritas. **Known for:** fresh, organic vegan food; live music and margaritas; delicious salads. $ *Average main: $12* ✉ *Paseo Malecón San José, Plaza Caracol, Fonatur* ☎ *624/155–5874* ▭ *No credit cards* ⊘ *Closed Sun.*

★ Don Sanchez

$$$ | **MODERN MEXICAN** | Award-winning chef Edgar Roman brings contemporary Mexican cuisine from farm to table at Don Sanchez. Brick pillars, white linens, and a wine wall comprised of nearly 100 blends make up the more formal dining area, but dinner on the patio is a must. **Known for:** creamy rice with lobster tail; fine wine and hospitality; modern Mexican menu. $ *Average main: $35* ✉ *Blvd. Mijares 27, Centro* ☎ *624/142–2444* ⊕ *donsanchezrestaurant.com.*

El Marinero Borracho

$ | **SEAFOOD** | **FAMILY** | This two-story palapa restaurant, named "The Drunken Sailor," is always packed with locals and tourists alike. It's no wonder: the location across from the marina is the perfect spot to watch the sunset while enjoying a ginger mint mojito or tamarind margarita. **Known for:** unique ceviches menu; best Los Cabos dessert: avocado-lime chocolate cream pie; sunset view. $ *Average main: $11* ✉ *Near Hotel El Ganzo, Blvd. Tiburon s/n, Marina* ⊹ *Puerto Los Cabos* ☎ *624/688–5816* ⊕ *facebook.com/elmarineroborracholaplayita* ⊘ *Closed Mon.*

★ Flora's Field Kitchen at Flora Farms

$$$ | **AMERICAN** | **FAMILY** | This alfresco dining experience is built right in the center of the self-sustaining Flora Farms. It's a charming oasis featuring a farm-to-table restaurant, spa, gift shop, cooking school, organic market, and culinary cottages (private homes), all under the Flora Farms brand. **Known for:** wood-fired pizzas; wildly popular Sunday brunch; produce raised on-site. $ *Average main: $45* ✉ *Carretera Transpeninsular San José del Cabo, Km 30, Las Animas Bajas*

☎ *624/142–1000, 949/200–7342 U.S. phone* ⊕ *www.flora-farms.com* ⊘ *Closed Mon. and daily 1:30–5 pm.*

Habanero's Mexican Fusion Bistro

$$ | **MEXICAN FUSION** | **FAMILY** | Celebrity chef Tadd Chapman and partner Miguel Guerrero joined forces to relaunch this traditional Mexican restaurant in its new location and with fresh new culinary techniques. Opt for lunch specialties of Baja fish tacos and black scallop ceviche, and for dinner, try the seafood risotto, or the grilled NY strip with habanero chimichurri. **Known for:** favorite of locals; unique Mexican fusion cuisine; gorgeous courtyard setting. $ *Average main: $20* ✉ *Hotel Encanto Inn, José Maria Morelos 134, Centro* ☎ *624/142–2626* ⊕ *habanerosbistro.com.*

The Hangman Surf & Tacos

$ | **MEXICAN** | **FAMILY** | By day it looks like a hole-in-the-wall, but when the sun goes down, the rummage-sale-meets-taco-stand atmosphere of this open-air local favorite truly comes to life. Get beyond the ghoulish silhouette logo—*ahorcado* means "hangman" in Spanish—and you'll find that the food is pretty good. **Known for:** outstanding tacos; reasonable prices; authentic Mexican experience. $ *Average main: $5* ✉ *Calle Panga 30, San José del Cabo* ☎ *624/152–3989* ⊕ *facebook.com/thehangmansurfandtacos* ▭ *No credit cards* ⊘ *Closed Mon. No lunch.*

La Dolce

$$ | **ITALIAN** | **FAMILY** | This popular Italian restaurant right in the center of San José on the town's *zócalo* (square) is known for authentic and affordable Italian fare. Locals and visitors alike flock to this reasonably priced perennial favorite for antipasti and wood-fired-oven pizzas, a never-ending selection of pastas, and steaks and seafood dishes. **Known for:** authentic Northern Italian cuisine; hand-made pizza baked with mesquite wood; great Caesar salad. $ *Average main: $22* ✉ *Av. Zaragoza at Av. Hidalgo, Plaza*

Farm-fresh ingredients are served in a beautiful garden at Flora's Field Kitchen at Flora Farms.

Jardin Mijares, Centro ☎ *624/142–6621* ⊕ *restauranteladolce.com* ⊗ *Closed Mon.*

La Forchetta

$$$ | **ITALIAN** | **FAMILY** | A favorite of locals, this Italian-Mexican restaurant is the place to get Roman-style, hand-stretched pizzas. Even those who aren't fans of pizza will find something on the diverse menu, with a balanced offering of pasta, antipasti, and main courses. **Known for:** 12-inch hand-stretched pizzas; signature sfera di cioccolato dessert; sophisticated but family-friendly atmosphere. **$** *Average main: $25* ⊠ *Paseo Malecón San José, Plaza del Pescador, Lot 24, San José del Cabo* ☎ *624/130–7723* ⊕ *la-forchetta.mx* ⊗ *No lunch.*

Las Guacamayas Taqueria

$ | **MEXICAN** | **FAMILY** | Massive globes of 15 types of margaritas and a Mexican guitarist singing American covers make this a magnet for tourists, but it also draws locals. If you're looking for cheap and delicious Mexican food, you've come to the right place. **Known for:** outstanding marinated pork tacos; great prices; live

music and outdoor seating. **$** *Average main: $11* ⊠ *Calle Paseo de los Marinos, Centro* ✛ *Near corner of Pescadores* ☎ *624/189–5284* ⊕ *facebook.com/tacosguacamayas.*

Latino 8

$$ | **LATIN AMERICAN** | **FAMILY** | For a taste of Latin America's deliciously spicy cuisine and exuberant attitude toward life, visit this laid-back place where everything is colorful and everyone is happy. Order dishes of Mexican, Argentinian, Cuban, and Peruvian origins, among others, and try their exquisite cocktails while listening to live Latin music. **Known for:** Pan-Latin American menu; live salsa and bachata music; original cocktails. **$** *Average main: $20* ⊠ *Paseo Malecón San José, Plaza del Pescador, Lot 8, Fonatur* ☎ *624/130–7267* ⊕ *latino8.com.*

★ Lolita Café

$ | **CAFÉ** | In a relaxing garden filled with retro decor, waiters in mesh trucker hats and black T-shirts deliver remarkable urban Mexican cuisine with a dash of Grandma's secret recipes. Under the shade of a mango tree, start with the trio of salsas infused with orange and chipotle, served with a basket of freshly fried tortilla chips. **Known for:** delightful breakfast under the shade of a mango tree; yummy churros and gourmet coffees; fresh squeezed juices and healthy smoothies. ⑤ *Average main: $10* ⊠ *Manuel Doblado 24, Centro* ✛ *Between Hidalgo and Morelos* ☎ *624/130–7786* ⊕ *cafedelolita.com* ⊗ *Closed Mon. No dinner.*

Los Tamarindos

$$$ | MEXICAN | FAMILY | A former sugarcane mill dating back to 1888, this quaint restaurant is surrounded by farmland that provides organic fruits and vegetables to many of Cabo's top eateries. Wildflowers in Mason jars and hand-painted clay dishes set the scene at this rustic spot where the menu is based on the season's harvest. **Known for:** four-hour cooking classes ($160); true farm-to-table dining experience; homemade herbal oil on breads and meats. ⑤ *Average main: $30* ⊠ *Calle de las Ánimas s/n, Ánimas Bajas, Las Animas Bajas* ☎ *624/317–0142* ⊕ *lostamarindos.mx.*

Mi Cocina

$$$ | ECLECTIC | At this outdoor restaurant at Casa Natalia boutique hotel, fire bowls glow on the dining terrace, which is surrounded by palm trees and gentle waterfalls, blending the four elements: earth, wind, fire, and water. Tables are spaced far enough apart so that you don't have to share your whispered sweet nothings with neighbors. **Known for:** Mexican dishes with a European twist; adjoining oyster and martini bar; exceptional chicken with chocolate salsa. ⑤ *Average main: $30* ⊠ *Casa Natalia, Blvd. Mijares 4, Centro* ☎ *624/182–3709, 888/277–3814 from U.S.* ⊕ *casanatalia. com* ⊗ *Closed Tues.*

More on Tequila

The real stuff comes from the Tequila region in mainland Mexico, but Los Cabos folks are producing their own spirits; look for the labels from private local distilleries. Tequila brands offered with Los Cabos labels are Cabo Wabo, Hotel California tequila, Mexita, and Las Varitas brand.

NIDO

$$$ | JAPANESE FUSION | Covered by a nestlike dome and surrounded by *espejos de agua* (water mirrors), the Viceroy's sophisticated, design-forward restaurant impresses with its truly unique setting. The menu is equally original, with an eclectic mix of Japanese delicacies, Mexican fusion creations, and a gourmet raw bar. **Known for:** mesmerizing architectural style; raw bar and robatayaki (tableside Japanese grill); providing "love nest" for private dinners. ⑤ *Average main: $36* ⊠ *Viceroy Los Cabos, Paseo Malecón San José, Lote 8, San José del Cabo* ☎ *624/104–9999, 844/222–6987 U.S. toll-free* ⊕ *viceroyhotelsandresorts. com/los-cabos* ⊗ *No lunch.*

Tequila Restaurant

$$ | MODERN MEXICAN | A beautifully redone adobe home sets the stage for this classy dining experience on an open courtyard under the stars. A lengthy tequila list tempts diners to savor the finer brands of Mexico's national drink, and an extensive wine cellar will give you plenty of choices for what to sip as you sup. **Known for:** succulent seafood chile relleno; live music every Thursday; beautiful garden setting. ⑤ *Average main: $22* ⊠ *Manuel Doblado 1911, Centro* ☎ *624/122–2091* ⊕ *tequilarestloscabos. com* ⊗ *Close Tues. No lunch.*

☕ Coffee and Quick Bites

Claros Fish Jr.

$ | **SEAFOOD** | **FAMILY** | This is the place for a quick taco fix; $2 (fish and shrimp) or $3 (grilled scallop) gets you some serious tacos, while $8 will buy you a killer aguachile. This is the locals' go-to spot for quality seafood and affordable cold beer. **Known for:** rare stingray tacos; wide variety of ceviches; favorite of locals. $ *Average main: $8* ⊠ *Blvd. Antonio Mijares 1092, San José del Cabo* ☎ *624/146–9887* ⊕ *facebook.com/clarofishjrsjc.*

Coffee LAB

$ | **INTERNATIONAL** | **FAMILY** | Loved by locals and visitors alike, this beautiful place is a good spot to grab home-roasted specialty coffee (starting at $2.50), fresh juices (starting at $3), and paninis ($10). Check their calendar online for concerts and other events. **Known for:** specialty coffee roasted in-house; engaging cultural events; co-working area. $ *Average main: $10* ⊠ *Juarez 1717, San José del Cabo* ☎ *624/164–2941* ⊕ *lab-baja.mx* ⊗ *Closed Sun. No dinner.*

French Riviera Restaurant

$ | **CAFÉ** | **FAMILY** | The scent of fresh-baked French baguettes and a picture-perfect display of croissants, éclairs, colorful candies, and ice creams greet you at this café-bistro just off San José del Cabo's main square. In the creperie area, the cook tucks delicate crepes around eggs and cheese, ground beef and onions, or shrimp and pesto. **Known for:** organic local coffee; chocolate truffles; scrumptious breakfast crepes. $ *Average main: $10* ⊠ *Manuel Doblado at Av. Hidalgo, Centro* ☎ *624/105–2624* ⊕ *www.facebook.com/FrenchRivieraRestaurant.*

La Carreta Sabores de Oaxaca

$ | **MEXICAN** | **FAMILY** | For authentic Mexican food visit this spot serving traditional dishes from the southern state of Oaxaca. Try the enchiladas, the memelas, or the amazing guacamole with *chapulines* (grasshoppers). **Known for:** wide variety of tlayudas; authentic moles from Oaxaca; great catering services. $ *Average main: $7* ⊠ *Carretera Transpeninsular, Km 24.5, Rancho Cerro Colorado, San José del Cabo* ☎ *624/164–0260* ⊕ *lacarretamx.com.*

La Michoacana

$ | **ICE CREAM** | **FAMILY** | It may be small, but La Michoacana has a grand history of providing frozen fruit-based refreshments all over Mexico. The huge selection of *paletas* (popsicles), frozen fruit bars, and ice cream is so tantalizing, it's difficult to choose just one from the colorful display. **Known for:** best popsicles in San José; authentic Mexican ice cream; dairy-free frozen fruit bars. $ *Average main: $2* ⊠ *Ignacio Zaragoza 24, Centro* ☎ *624/177–3079* ⊕ *michoacana.com.*

Tacos Rossy

$ | **MEXICAN** | **FAMILY** | Don't be fooled by the bare-bones atmosphere: Tacos Rossy serves some of the best tacos in San José. Fish tacos are the thing at this no-frills joint brimming with local families who munch on everything from peel-and-eat shrimp to ceviche and chocolate clams. **Known for:** $3 tacos and $3 beers; large condiment bar for dress-your-own taco; best taqueria in town. $ *Average main: $11* ⊠ *Carretera Transpeninsular, Km 33, Centro* ☎ *624/142–6755.*

Taqueria El Fogon

$ | **MEXICAN** | **FAMILY** | If your to-do list includes trying authentic Mexican tacos at a local hole-in-the-wall, this is the place for you. Get your Spanish ready to order arguably the best tacos in town, plus *frijoles charros* (spicy beans) with chorizo, melted cheese, and grilled onions. **Known for:** delicious tacos al pastor; pozole on Thursday and Saturday; generously served stuffed potatoes. $ *Average main: $10* ⊠ *Manuel Doblado, Centro* ☎ *624/108–5730* ⊕ *facebook.com/el.fogon.sjc.*

Hilton Vacation Club Cabo Azul Los Cabos boasts huge villas and a tranquil pool.

Taquería El Paisa

$ | **MEXICAN** | **FAMILY** | This place is widely recognized as having "the best tacos in Cabo" ($3); you'll be surprised by how many of them you can eat at one sitting. The *al pastor* grilled pork taco is a star alongside the customary *agua de Jamaica* (hibiscus iced tea) ($2). **Known for:** quality meat from Sonora; original taco macho served in stuffed pepper instead of tortilla; delicious aguas frescas. ⑤ *Average main: $9* ✉ *Lázaro Cárdenas, Ildefonso Green, Centro* ☎ *624/191–7409.*

 ## Hotels

If you're looking for an authentic, local place to stay in Los Cabos, San José del Cabo may be it. The historic center is home to centuries-old buildings and pedestrian-only streets, a quaint town square in Plaza Mijares, and a historic church. Just beyond the center of town, and a bit farther south, is the ever-expanding Zona Hotelera, where a dozen or so hotels, timeshares, and condo projects face the long stretch of beach on the Sea of Cortez. Closer to the marina at Puerto los Cabos, the boutique El Ganzo Hotel and chain resorts like Secrets have staked their claim, with plans for further development past La Playita.

★ Casa Maat at JW Marriott Los Cabos

$$$$ | **RESORT** | A recent addition to Los Cabos resort scene, this ultra-exclusive boutique hotel designed by renowned archtect Jim Olson is a wonder of luxury. **Pros:** extraordinary design; movie theater available for private screenings; access to all facilities of next-door sister resort. **Cons:** nonswimmable beach; some rooms don't enjoy ocean views; caters to corporate, but is kid-friendly. ⑤ *Rooms from: $560* ✉ *Fraccion Hotelera FH5-C1, La Playita* ☎ *624/163–7630* ⊕ *www.marriott.com* ⤴ *45 suites* ⦿ *Free Breakfast.*

★ Casa Natalia

$ | **HOTEL** | An intimate, graceful boutique hotel, Casa Natalia is in the heart of San José's downtown and opens onto the zócalo. **Pros:** oasis in the heart of downtown; fantastic complimentary breakfast for superior rooms; lovely pool area.

Cons: no bathtubs in the standard rooms; occasional noise from music and fiestas on Plaza Mijares; no children under 13. $ *Rooms from: $235* ⊠ *Blvd. Mijares 4, Centro* ☎ *624/182–3709, 888/277–3814 from U.S.* ⊕ *casanatalia.com* 🛏 *18 rooms* ⊚ *Free Breakfast.*

Encanto Inn & Suites
$ | HOTEL | In the heart of San José's historic Art District, this gorgeous and comfortable inn has two separate buildings—one looks onto the verdant gardens and pool; the other one, across the street, is in a charming, historic building with a narrow courtyard. **Pros:** Mexican-hacienda feeling; centric location; pet-friendly. **Cons:** staffing is minimal; spotty Wi-Fi; some rooms get street noise. $ *Rooms from: $189* ⊠ *Calle Morelos 133, Centro* ☎ *624/142–0388, 210/858–5912 from U.S.* 🛏 *27 rooms* ⊚ *No Meals.*

Hilton Vacation Club Cabo Azul Los Cabos
$$ | RESORT | FAMILY | On the beach in San José del Cabo, this chic, whitewashed property is peaceful from the moment you walk through the 20-foot antique door to a waterfall wall and marble floors that lead to a breathtaking lobby centered on a circular rope structure that drops 1,200 feet from the ceiling. **Pros:** huge villas; sophisticated and elegant property; Kids' Club and designated pool for children. **Cons:** spotty Internet; beach not safe for swimming; not all rooms have ocean views. $ *Rooms from: $285* ⊠ *Paseo Malecón, Zona Hotelera* ☎ *800/438–2929 from U.S., 624/163–5100* ⊕ *caboazulresort.com* 🛏 *326 rooms* ⊚ *No Meals.*

Hotel El Ganzo
$$$ | HOTEL | At this boutique hotel with an uberchic vibe, guests can interact with artists-in-residence, musicians, and filmmakers in a creative and luxurious setting. **Pros:** an outlet for artists; free beach cruisers to explore the cactus gardens; horseback riding and estuary kayak tours. **Cons:** must spend a minimum of $40 to use the beach club; service does not match the price; no children under

18. $ *Rooms from: $480* ⊠ *Tiburón s/n, La Playita, Marina* ☎ *624/104–9000, 855/835–4269 toll-free U.S.* ⊕ *elganzo. com* 🛏 *70 rooms* ⊚ *No Meals.*

★ Hyatt Ziva Los Cabos
$$$$ | RESORT | FAMILY | This resort is great for both families and couples looking for a complete getaway, featuring 591 suites, eight restaurants ranging from French to Italian and Spanish to Japanese, seven bars, four pools (including an adults-only option), and a Kids' Club. **Pros:** great à la carte restaurant selection; spacious suites; Kids' Club and adjacent water park offer diversion for little ones. **Cons:** resort's size is a bit overwhelming; slow elevator; 30% of rooms lack ocean views. $ *Rooms from: $700* ⊠ *Paseo Malecón, Lote 5, Zona Hotelera* ☎ *624/163–7730* ⊕ *hyatt.com* 🛏 *591 rooms* ⊚ *All-Inclusive.*

Royal Solaris Los Cabos
$ | RESORT | FAMILY | Royal Solaris was the first all-inclusive in Los Cabos, and it runs smoothly like the established property it is, with plenty of entertainment options and sports activities offered. **Pros:** Kids' Club 9–5; climbing wall and mini water park; best value of the all-inclusives. **Cons:** the accommodations and food only adequate; not romantic; timeshare salespeople are pushy. $ *Rooms from: $240* ⊠ *Paseo Malecón, Lote 10, Colonia Campo de Golf, Zona Hotelera* ☎ *624/145–6800* ⊕ *hotelessolaris.com* 🛏 *390 rooms* ⊚ *All-Inclusive.*

Secrets Puerto Los Cabos Golf & Spa Resort
$$$$ | RESORT | The first of the all-inclusive chains to reach La Playita, this adults-only resort has swim-up rooms, ocean views, seven restaurants, and a 13,000-square-foot spa by Pevonia. **Pros:** nightly entertainment shows; plenty of activities; caters to adults. **Cons:** beach not swimmable; annoying timeshare pitches; no kids under 18. $ *Rooms from: $693* ⊠ *Av. Paseo de los Pescadores s/n, La Playita* ☎ *624/144–2600* ⊕ *hyatt.com* 🛏 *500 rooms* ⊚ *All-Inclusive.*

★ Viceroy Los Cabos

$$$$ | **RESORT** | Stunning architecture, top-notch facilities, and outstanding service make this luxury resort in the heart of the Zona Hotelera arguably the best resort in San José. **Pros:** stylish rooftop restaurant with outstanding ocean views; suites include large dining areas; cool in-house cinema. **Cons:** not all rooms enjoy ocean views; not the best beach for swimming or privacy; kid-friendly policy contrasts with style of resort. ⑤ *Rooms from: $647* ✉ *Paseo Malecón San José, Zona Hotelera* ☎ *624/104–9999, 844/222–6987 U.S. toll-free* ⊕ *viceroyhotelsandresorts.com/los-cabos* ⌁ *198 rooms* ⦿ *No Meals.*

Zadún, a Ritz-Carlton Reserve

$$$$ | **RESORT** | Located in the heart of the exclusive Puerto Los Cabos development, this spectacular luxury resort is everything you'd expect from Mexico's first Ritz-Carlton Reserve property. **Pros:** extraordinary dining experiences; stunning 30,000-square-foot spa; own personal "tosoani" (butler) for each room. **Cons:** nonswimmable beach; some rooms only feature resort views; luxurious but pricey. ⑤ *Rooms from: $1,039* ✉ *Blvd. Mar de Cortez, San José del Cabo* ☎ *624/172–9000* ⊕ *www.ritzcarlton.com* ⌁ *113 rooms* ⦿ *No Meals.*

Nightlife

After-dark action in San José del Cabo caters mostly to locals and tourists seeking tranquillity and seclusion. There are no big dance clubs or discos in San José. What little nightlife there is revolves around restaurants, casual bars, and large hotels. A pre- or postdinner stroll makes a wonderful addition to any San José evening. When night falls, people begin to fill the streets, many of them hurrying off to evening Mass when they hear the church bells peal from the central plaza.

A number of galleries hold court in central San José del Cabo, creating the San José del Cabo Art District. It's just north and east of the town's cathedral, primarily along Obregón, Morelos, and Guerrero streets. On Thursday night (5–9 pm) from November to June, visit the Art Walk, where you can meander around about 15 galleries, sampling wine and cheese as you go.

BARS

Baja Brewing Co.

BREWPUBS | The Baja Brewing Co. serves cold, on-site–microbrewed cerveza and international pub fare. You'll find entrées ranging from ahi tuna quesadillas to basil-and-blue-cheese burgers. Our favorite of the eight beers is the Baja Razz Ale; the BBC also brews Oatmeal Stout, a gluten-free honey mead, an Indian pale ale, and experimental brews served the first Friday of every month. If you can't make up your mind, order the sampler. ✉ *Morelos 1277 at Obregón, San José del Cabo* ☎ *624/142–5294* ⊕ *bajabrewingcompany.com.*

Cantina29 at Casa Don Rodrigo

BARS | Come here for the ambience and cocktails (the food has mixed reviews) like the blackberry mojito or house margarita. Once the home of the owner's grandparents, the building dates back to 1927 and its original brick walls are still intact, adorned with historic family photographs. The courtyard, strung with lanterns and fairy lights, is a pleasant place to enjoy the live mariachi. Happy hour from 4 to 5 pm on mojitos, margaritas and sangrias. ✉ *Blvd. Antonio Mijares 29, Centro* ☎ *624/142–0418* ⊕ *casadonrodrigo.com* ⊗ *Closed Sun.*

★ Cielomar Rooftop

LOUNGES | This sophisticated rooftop restaurant and bar serves exquisite seafood and stylish cocktails with a side of fantastic ocean views. It's a great place to have dinner at sunset and enjoy music from international DJs at night. ⊠ *Viceroy Los Cabos, Paseo Malecón San José, Zona Hotelera* ☎ *624/104–9999* ⊕ *viceroyhotelsandresorts.com/los-cabos* ⊗ *Closed Tues.*

La Osteria
LIVE MUSIC | Live music on Thursday and Friday coupled with the refreshing cocktails make this one of the best spots to grab a drink in San José del Cabo. Acoustic guitars add to the quaint atmosphere you'll find in the lantern-lit, stone courtyard. Tapas make a tasty accompaniment to the house sangrias. ⊠ *Paseo del Estero, Zona Hotelera* ☎ *624/146–9696* ⊕ *facebook.com/laosteriacabo* ⊗ *Closed Sun.*

Shooters Sports Bar & Grill
LIVE MUSIC | FAMILY | For a family-friendly atmosphere where you can order in English your choice of food and beverage and watch sports on big-screen TVs, head to Shooters, a rooftop bar overlooking the main square. It's open daily from 10 am to 11 pm, for breakfast, lunch, and dinner. ⊠ *Manuel Doblado at Blvd. Mijares, Centro* ☎ *624/146–9900* ⊕ *facebook.com/ShootersSportsBar.*

🛍 Shopping

Cabo San Lucas's sister city has a refined air, with many shops in old colonial buildings just a short walk from the town's *zócalo* (central plaza). Jewelry and art are great buys—this is where you'll find the best shopping for high-quality Mexican folk art. Many of the most worthwhile shops are clustered within a few of blocks around Plaza Mijares, where Boulevard Mijares and Avenida Zaragoza both end at the zócalo at the center of San José. Thursday nights from November to June are designated Art Nights, when galleries stay open until 9 serving drinks and snacks, with various performances, demonstrations, and dancing.

ART GALLERIES
Casa Paulina
DESIGN | More than just an art gallery, Casa Paulina inspires decorating ideas with items for the home. Candles, lamps, chairs, throws, and enormous clay pots are a few of the treasures you might find. ⊠ *Plaza Paulina, Morelos at Comonfort, San José del Cabo* ☎ *624/142–5555* ⊕ *casapaulina.com* ⊗ *Closed Sun.*

★ Frank Arnold Gallery
ART GALLERY | Frank Arnold Gallery has two big draws: it's arguably the best gallery space in town, in a modern building by local architect Alfredo Gomez; and it holds Frank Arnold's dramatic, widely acclaimed contemporary paintings that have been compared to de Kooning, Gorky, and Hans Hofmann. The gallery also features bronze sculptures and fine-art prints. ⊠ *1137 Calle Comonfort, San José del Cabo* ☎ *624/142–4422, 559/301–1148 in U.S.* ⊕ *frankarnoldart. com.*

Galería Corsica Los Cabos
ART GALLERY | Galería Corsica is in a spectacularly dramatic space. The gallery, which has two sister galleries in Puerto Vallarta and one in Mexico City, shows museum-quality fine art with an emphasis on paintings and large, impressive sculpture pieces. ⊠ *Álvaro Obregón 10, San José del Cabo* ☎ *624/146–9177* ⊕ *corsicacabo.com* ⊗ *Closed Sun.*

Galería de Ida Victoria
ART GALLERY | Galería de Ida Victoria has been designed with skylights and domes to show off the international art contained within its three floors, which includes paintings, sculpture, photography, and prints. ⊠ *Guerrero 1128, San José del Cabo* ✛ *Between Zaragoza and Obregón* ☎ *624/142–5772* ⊕ *idavictoriagallery.com* ⊗ *Closed Sun.*

Colorful colonial buildings line the historic downtown of San José.

Patricia Mendoza Art Gallery

ART GALLERY | Explore works of art by Mexico's top contemporary artists such as Eduardo Mejorada, Javier Guadarrama, Laura Aprile, Luis Filcer, and Cristina Samsa, among others. All of the artists represented here are known nationally and internationally in important collections and museums. ⊠ *Álvaro Obregón and Plaza Mijares s/n, Col. Centro, San José del Cabo* ☎ *624/158–6497, 624/105–2270* ⊕ *patriciamendozagallery. com* ⊙ *Closed Sun.*

★ Silvermoon Gallery

ART GALLERY | This gallery is remarkable in the Los Cabos region both for the assortment and the quality of art contained within its walls. Mexican folk art makes up most of the inventory here. Treasures include Carlos Albert's whimsical papier-mâché sculptures, Mata Ortiz pottery from the Quezada family, Huichol yarn "paintings," Alebrijes (colorful wooden animal sculptures) from Oaxaca, and fine jewelry. Owner Armando Sanchez Icaza is gracious and knowledgeable; he knows volumes about the artists whose work he carries. His silversmiths can also make custom jewelry for you within a day or two. ⊠ *Miguel Hidalgo, Local 2, Centro* ☎ *624/142–6077* ⊕ *www.facebook.com/ SilvermoonGalleryFolkArt* ⊙ *Closed Sun.*

FOLK ART AND CERAMICS

El Armario Art & Coffee

ART GALLERY | **FAMILY** | Calling itself "the cutest shop in town," El Armario offers a selection of Mexican folk art, ceramic pottery, candles, clay figurines, and papier-mâché—plus fresh coffee out on the patio. ⊠ *Obregón at Morelos, San José del Cabo* ☎ *624/105–2989* ⊕ *facebook. com/armarioartandcoffee* ⊙ *Closed Sun.*

La Sacristia Art & History

ART GALLERY | La Sacristia has a fine selection of Talavera pottery, traditional and contemporary Mexican jewelry, blown glass, and contemporary paintings. The glassware is incredible. ⊠ *Hidalgo 9, at Álvaro Obregón, San José del Cabo* ☎ *624/142–4007* ⊕ *facebook.com/ lasacristiart.*

JEWELRY
Artwalk Shop
CRAFTS | FAMILY | This small boutique at Casa Natalia has jewelry, handbags, and art made from recycled metals. Artwalk also has a good selection of brass jewelry from Mexico City. ⊠ *Blvd. Mijares 4, at Casa Natalia, San José del Cabo* ☎ *624/182–3709, 888/277–3814 from U.S.* ⊕ *casanatalia.com/artwalkshop* ⊗ *Closed Tues.*

MALLS
Plaza Artesanos
CRAFTS | FAMILY | With a block of 75 stalls, Plaza Artesanos has a wide selection of handmade crafts and souvenirs, including pottery, jewelry, blankets, clothing, hammocks, leather bags, and even pure Mexican vanilla extract. Don't be afraid to barter by starting at half the asking price and then meeting somewhere in the middle. ⊠ *Paseo de Las Misiones 1942, Fonatur* ☎ *624/117–6235.*

Plaza del Pescador
SHOPPING CENTER | FAMILY | An outdoor mall conveniently located across the street from San José del Cabo's string of resorts, Plaza del Pescador offers guests an alternative to hotel dining. You'll find everything from sushi and gelato to tapas and a wine bar. Among the 25 shops and restaurants are a bookstore, jewelry store, fitness gym, and coffee shop. ⊠ *Paseo Malecón, Local 21A, San José del Cabo* ⊹ *Across from Cabo Azul Resort* ☎ *624/142–3436* ⊕ *plazadelpescador.com.*

MARKETS
★ Farmers' Market (*San José del Cabo Mercado Orgánico*)
MARKET | FAMILY | Get your organic fix at the *Mercado Orgánico* every Saturday 9–3 between November and April. Jewelry, artwork, flowers, soaps, fruit, and vegetables are a few of the goodies you'll find here. Food stalls serve everything from tacos to pizza, and entertainment is offered for kids. You will surely leave with a bag full of fresh veggies and local art. ⊠ *Comonfort 6, Centro* ☎ *624/245–0059* ⊕ *facebook.com/Sanjomo* ⊗ *Closed May–Oct.*

The Shops at Flora Farms
SHOPPING CENTER | Located within the Flora Farms grounds, The Shops is a series of (wait for it) shops that sell all kinds of things from organic produce from the farm to soap and body care products, including clothes, wines, and even jewelry. It's a great place to grab a healthy snack or stock up on produce delivered daily from Flora's local farm. ⊠ *Ánimas Bajas, Las Animas Bajas* ☎ *624/142–1000* ⊕ *flora-farms.com* ⊗ *Closed Mon.*

SUNDRIES AND LIQUOR
Los Barriles de Don Malaquias
WINE/SPIRITS | Go beyond Cuervo and Patrón at Los Barriles de Don Malaquias, which specializes in rare tequilas. The tequila selection is complemented by a good collection of Cuban cigars. Owner Rigoberto Cuervo Rosales is often on-site to offer tequila tastings. ⊠ *Blvd. Mijares at Juárez, San José del Cabo* ☎ *624/130–7800.*

 Activities

GOLF
Greens fees quoted include off- and high-season rates and are subject to frequent change.

Los Cabos has become one of the world's top golf destinations thanks to two factors: the 9-hole course opened by Mexico's tourism development agency Fonatur in San José in 1988, and the area's year-round mild to warm weather—Los Cabos never experiences even the occasional frigid winter possible in the southern United States. Green fairways dot the arid landscape like multiple oases in the desert. You'll encounter many sublime views of the Sea of Cortez, and

Continued on page 145

THE ART OF THE HUICHOL

The intricately woven and beaded designs of the Huichols' art are as vibrant and fascinating as the traditions of its people, best known as the "Peyote People" for their traditional and ceremonial use of the hallucinogenic drug. Peyote-inspired visions are thought to be messages from God and are reflected in the art.

Like the Lacandon Maya, the Huichol resisted assimilation by Spanish invaders, fleeing to inhospitable mountains and remote valleys. There they retained their pantheistic religion in which shamans lead the community in spiritual matters and the use of peyote facilitates communication directly with God.

Roads didn't reach larger Huichol communities until the mid-20th century, bringing electricity and other modern distractions. The collision with the outside world has had pros and cons, but art lovers have only benefited from their increased access to intricately patterned woven and beaded goods. Today the traditional souls that remain on the land—a significant population of perhaps 6,000 to 8,000—still create votive bowls, prayer arrows, jewelry, and bags, and sell them to finance elaborate religious ceremonies. The pieces go for as little as $5 or as much as $5,000, depending on the skill and fame of the artist and quality of materials.

(left) Huichol yarn painting, National Museum of Anthropology, (top) Huichol artisan.

UNDERSTANDING THE HUICHOL

When Spanish conquistadors arrived in the early 16th century, the Huichol, unwilling to work as slaves on the haciendas of the Spanish or to adopt their religion, fled to the Sierra Madre. They lived there, disconnected from society, for nearly 500 years. Beginning in the 1970s, roads and electricity made their way to tiny Huichol towns. Today, about half of the population of perhaps 7,000 continues to live in ancestral villages and rancherías (tiny individual farms).

THE POWER OF PRAYER

They believe that without their prayers and offerings the sun wouldn't rise, the earth would cease spinning. It is hard, then, for them to reconcile their poverty with the relative easy living of "free-riders" (Huichol term for nonspiritual freeloaders) who enjoy fine cars and expensive houses thanks to the Huichols' efforts to sustain the planet. But rather than hold our reckless materialism against us, the Huichol add us to their prayers.

THE PEYOTE PEOPLE

Visions inspired by the hallucinogenic peyote cactus are considered by the Huichol to be messages from God and to help in solving personal and communal problems. Indirectly, they provide inspiration for their almost psychedelic art. Just a generation or two ago, annual peyote-gathering pilgrimages were done on foot. Today the journey is still a man's chief obligation, but they now drive to the holy site at Wiricuta, in San Luis Potosi State.

SHAMANISM

A Huichol man has a lifelong calling as a shaman. There are two shamanic paths: the path of the wolf, which is more aggressive, demanding, and powerful (wolf shamans profess the ability to morph into wolves); and the path of the deer, which is playful. A shaman chooses his own path.

BEADED ITEMS

The smaller the beads, the more delicate and expensive the piece. Items made with iridescent beads from Japan are the priciest. Look for good-quality glass beads, definition, symmetry, and artful use of color. Beads should fit together tightly in straight lines, with no gaps.

YARN PAINTINGS

Symmetry is not necessary, although there should be an overall sense of unity. Thinner thread results in finer, more costly work. Look for tightness, with no visible gaps or broken threads. Paintings should have a stamp of authenticity on the back, including artist's name and tribal affiliation.

PRAYER ARROWS

Collectors and purists should look for the traditionally made arrows of brazilwood inserted into a bamboo shaft. The most interesting ones contain embroidery work, or tiny carved icons, or are painted with copal symbols indicative of their original intended purpose, for example protecting a child or ensuring a successful corn crop.

HOW TO READ THE SYMBOLS

Spiders that come out at dawn are thought to welcome the rising sun.

The deer is the animal manifestation of the god Kahumari, who intercedes in heaven on earthlings' behalf.

Anything with horns or antlers symbolizes communion and oneness with God.

Yarn painting

■ The trilogy of corn, peyote, and deer represents three aspects of God. According to Huichol mythology, peyote sprang up in the footprints of the deer. Depicted like stylized flowers, peyote represents communication with God. Corn, the Huichol's staple

Corn symbol

food, symbolizes health and prosperity. An image drawn inside the root ball depicts the essence of God within it.

■ The double-headed eagle is the emblem of the omnipresent sky god.

Peyote

■ A nierika is a portal between the spirit world and our own. Often in the form of a yarn painting, a nierika can be round or square.

■ Salamanders and turtles are associated with rain; the former provoke the clouds. Turtles maintain underground springs and purify water.

Scorpion

■ A scorpion is the soldier of the sun.

■ The Huichol depict raindrops as tiny snakes; in yarn paintings they descend to enrich the fields.

Snakes

Jose Beníctez Sánchez, (1938—2009) may be the elder statesman of yarn painters and has shown in Japan, Spain, the U.S., and at the Museum of Modern Art in Mexico City.

144

TRADITION TRANSFORMED

The art of the Huichol was, for centuries, made from undyed wool, shells, stones, and other natural materials. It was not until the 1970s that the Huichol began incorporating bright, zingy colors, without sacrificing the intricate patterns and symbols used for centuries. The result is strenuously colorful, yet dignified.

YARN PAINTINGS
Dramatic and vivid yarn paintings are highly symbolic, stylized visions of life.

VOTIVE BOWLS
Ceremonial votive bowls, made from gourds, are decorated with bright, stylized beadwork.

MASKS AND ANIMAL STATUETTES
Bead-covered wooden or ceramic masks and animal statuettes are other adaptations made for outsiders.

PRAYER ARROWS
Made for every ceremony, prayer arrows send petitions winging to God.

WOVEN SHOULDER BAGS
Carried by men, the bags are decorated with traditional Huichol icons.

For years, Huichol men as well as women wore **BEADED BRACELETS**; today earrings and necklaces are also made.

Diamond-shape **GOD'S EYES** of sticks and yarn protect children from harm.

Desert, sea, and putting greens converge at San José's popular golf clubs.

on a few courses, play alongside it. Otherwise the motif is desert golf. Architects and designers like Jack Nicklaus, Robert Trent Jones II, Tom Weiskopf, Roy Dye, and Greg Norman have all applied their talents to courses in the area.

Club Campestre San José

GOLF | Here you are greeted by panoramic views stretching to the Sea of Cortez, canyons, and mountains on a Jack Nicklaus design. This public course also features dramatic elevation changes and undulating tricky multilevel putting surfaces. Attractive bunkering requires well-placed tee shots and very accurate iron play. They have used paspalum grass throughout the course that sets Club Campestre among the best manicured in the region. The only downfall is that there are no holes on the water. ⊠ *Libramiento Aeropuerto, Km 119, San José del Cabo* 🕾 *624/172–6500* ⊕ *questrogolf.com* 🕸 *From $120, depending on season and hrs* 🏌 *18 holes, 6,966 yards, par 71.*

The Course at Vidanta Los Cabos

GOLF | Los Cabos' original course opened in 1987 as Punta Sur Golf Course. Of all the golf courses in the area, this one would be the "starter" golf course. The layout has wide fairways and few obstacles or slopes. It's fairly flat and good for beginners or as a warm-up. The 9-hole course is lined with residential properties (broken windows are not unusual). Some holes (particularly the 7th) have nice ocean views. Beware, you will find the three par-3s to be long and testing. It was designed by Mario Schjetnan and Joe Finger. Greens fee includes cart. There's a swimming pool, tennis, and gym on-site. ⊠ *Paseo Finisterra 1, San José del Cabo* 🕾 *624/142–1134 pro shop, 866/231–4423* ⊕ *vidantagolf.com* 🕸 *9 holes twice from $149* 🏌 *9 holes, 3,153 yards, par 35.*

★ Puerto Los Cabos Golf Course

GOLF | This course, one of the area's most popular for visitors, features an unusual combination: two Nines were designed by Jack Nicklaus and the other by Greg

Norman. The Ocean Course features more expansive driving areas, whereas the Mission Course puts more of a premium on driving accuracy. Both feature attractive bunkering and paspalum putting surfaces. The Vista Course is the most recent addition to Puerto Los Cabos and has quickly become a favorite of visitors as it affords views of the Sea of Cortez surrounded by sand dunes. ⊠ *Paseo de los Pescadores, San José del Cabo* ☎ *624/105–6441* ⊕ *questrogolf.com* ⊠ *From $200, depending on season and hrs* ⅃. *27 holes, 3 18-hole combinations: Mission-Ocean 7,166 yards, 18 holes, par 72; Ocean-Vista 7,199 yards, 18 holes, par 72; Vista-Mission 7,213 yards, 18 holes, par 72.*

GUIDED ADVENTURE TOURS
Baja Outback
ADVENTURE SPORTS | FAMILY | Baja Outback offers a variety of guided tours that range from four hours to several days long. The routes run through Baja backcountry, where you have the opportunity to explore the Cape's rarely seen back roads while learning desert lore from a knowledgeable guide-cum-biologist. Day trips may include anything from hiking and snorkeling to city tours and turtle release programs (August to November). Baja Outback also offers multiday tour packages designed specially for kids, with bodyboarding and sand castle building. For adventure-driven vacationers, tours include kayaking and stand-up paddleboarding near El Arco. ⊠ *Campo de Golf Fonatur, Paseo de las Misiones Mzna. 1, Lote 3, San José del Cabo* ☎ *624/142–9214, 855/408–3772 from U.S. and Canada* ⊕ *bajaoutback.com* ⊠ *From $74.*

Baja Wild
ADVENTURE SPORTS | FAMILY | Baja Wild has a number of adventure packages that include hiking, biking, kayaking, snorkeling, surfing, and whale-watching adventures. You'll see the natural side of Cabo, with hikes to canyons, hot springs, fossil beds, and caves with rock paintings. They offer backcountry jeep tours, full-day kayak tours at Cabo Pulmo, and ATV tours in the desert. Private tours are available. ⊠ *Carretera Transpeninsular, Km 28, Plaza Costa Azul, San José del Cabo* ☎ *624/122–0107, 310/860–6979 from U.S.* ⊕ *bajawild.com* ⊠ *Tours from $75.*

HIKING
Baja Wild
HIKING & WALKING | FAMILY | Trips with Baja Wild include hikes to canyons, small waterfalls, hot springs, a fossil-rich area, and caves with rock paintings. An all-day group hiking trip includes lunch, a guide, equipment, and transfer. ⊠ *Carretera Transpeninsular, Km 28, Plaza Costa Azul, San José del Cabo* ☎ *624/122–0107* ⊕ *bajawild.com* ⊠ *From $150.*

HORSEBACK RIDING
Cantering down an isolated beach or up a desert trail is one of the great pleasures of Los Cabos (as long as the sun isn't beating down too heavily). The following places have well-fed and well-trained horses.

Bonanza Horseback Riding
HORSEBACK RIDING | FAMILY | One of the best ways to explore the San José estuary, marina, and beach is by horseback. One- or two-hour tours are led by two professional guides who take you to the most beautiful spots around. ⊠ *Blvd. Antonio Mijares, Zona Hotelera* ☎ *624/132–3480* ⊕ *facebook.com/bonanzahorse* ⊠ *From $50.*

KAYAKING
One of the most popular, practical, and eco-friendly ways to explore the pristine coves that dot Los Cabos' western shoreline is by kayak. Daylong package tours that combine kayaking with snorkeling cost anywhere from $70 to $150. Single or double kayaks can be rented by the hour for $20 to $25.

Baja Wild

KAYAKING | FAMILY | For a combined kayak and snorkeling trip, try Baja Wild. Daylong outdoor trips include surfing; hiking; ATV; and whale-watching trips (November through April), as well as baby sea turtle release excursions (September through November). All trips include transportation, equipment, and lunch; you can substitute scuba diving for snorkeling. ⊠ *Carretera Transpeninsular, Km 28, Plaza Costa Azul, San José del Cabo* ☎ *624/122–0107* ⊕ *bajawild.com* ⊠ *From $75.*

SCUBA DIVING

Expert divers head to the **Gordo Banks** (100–130 feet, also known as the Wahoo Banks), which are 13 km (8 miles) off the coast of San José. The currents here are too strong for less experienced divers. This is the spot for hammerhead sharks—which are not generally aggressive with divers—plus many species of tropical fish and rays, and, if you're lucky, dolphins. Fall is the best time to go.

SPAS

Farm Spa

SPA | As with every offering from the Flora Farms brand (including its popular Flora's Field Kitchen restaurant), the farm's natural surroundings play a big role in the unique indoor-outdoor space. Relaxing energy flows from the farm's own herbs, flowers, and trees. On offer are various skin therapies, a wide range of massages, and beauty treatments for men and women. ⊠ *Flora Farms, San José del Cabo* ☎ *624/182–5200, 949/200–7342 U.S. phone* ⊕ *flora-farms.com/spa* ⊠ *Massages: from $73. Facials: from $99. Mani-Pedi: from $58* ⊗ *Closed Mon.*

Jasha Spa & Salon

SPA | This 21,000 square foot spa offers a unique design inspired by ancient Mexican cultures and state-of-the-art facilities at the interior of the exclusive boutique hotel Casa Maat. The spa boasts 12 private rooms for massages and body

treatments, an outdoor tranquillity patio, and a Zen-like botanical garden. The spaces are huge and imposing, while the wet areas are well appointed and fully equipped with indoor and outdoor pools and private whirlpools. The temazcal (sweat lodge) is the spa's crown jewel and a favorite of guests. ⊠ *Casa Maat at JW Marriott, Fraccion Hotelera FH5-C1, La Playita, San José del Cabo* ☎ *624/163-7600* ⊕ *marriott.com* ⊠ *Massages: from $105. Facials: from $87. Mani-Pedi: from $70.*

Paz Body & Mind Spa

SPA | Surrounded by natural stone walls, all the treatment rooms at Cabo Azul's Paz Spa are named after semiprecious stones such as onyx, pearl, opal, lapis, jade, and amber. Specialties include 50-minute massages to 210-minute complete experiences, as well as exfoliations, wraps, facials, manicure, and pedicure. A terrace suite can accommodate up to four treatments at one time for those looking for group relaxation. Seven other rooms round out the spa itself, and two double cabanas on the beach are available for those seeking the sound of the waves as backdrop to their treatment. Popular therapies include a Papaya Sugar Polish and Shea Butter Massage, as well as an Aloe Cooling Massage. An on-site salon is open Monday to Saturday 9–5. ⊠ *Cabo Azul Resort, Paseo Malecón s/n, Lote 11 Fonatur, San José del Cabo* ☎ *624/163–5170* ⊕ *caboazulresort.com* ⊠ *Massages: from $75.*

The Spa at Viceroy Los Cabos

SPA | This serene, well-equipped spa extends more than 11,000 square feet and offers everything from customary massages and beauty treatments to signature vitality pools, thermal chambers, ice fountains, and even canine massage therapy. You read that right: they will massage your dog's stress away, too. If you have to choose just one treatment, go for a Viceroy ritual or an interactive couples massage. ⊠ *Viceroy Los Cabos,*

Paseo Malecón San José, Zona Hotelera ☎ *624/104–9999* ⊕ *viceroyhotelsandre-sorts.com/los-cabos* ✉ *Hydrotherapy: $125. Body treatments: from $120.*

Zen Spa at Hyatt Ziva

SPA | The concept at Hyatt Ziva's spa is to explore water, earth, and air. Lounge by the communal pool or duck into one of 15 treatment rooms for revitalizing massages, romantic packages, anti-aging facials, detoxifying body wraps, and deep-cleansing scrubs using local, natural ingredients. For those interested in a quick fix, manicures and pedicures are popular, and the on-site salon can help turn a bad-hair day into something grand. ⊠ *Hyatt Ziva Los Cabos, Paseo Malecón s/n, Lote 5, San José del Cabo* ☎ *624/163–7730* ⊕ *hyatt.com* ✉ *Massages: from $134. Facials: $144. Mani-Pedi: from $55.*

SURFING

You can rent a board right at the beach at Costa Azul in San José del Cabo, or at the Cabo Surf Hotel, and paddle right into the gentle, feathering waves at the Old Man's surf spot. If you're at the intermediate level or above, walk a short distance eastward to La Roca (The Rock) break. Big waves are best left to the experts up north, in Todos Santos.

Baja Wild

SURFING | Baja Wild offers daylong trips to surfing hot spots throughout the Cape region for beginners and experts. A fee of $150 per person includes transportation, equipment, and instruction for a half day at Costa Azul. Full-day surf tours on the Pacific cost $150 per person. ⊠ *Carretera Transpeninsular, Km 28, Plaza Costa Azul, San José del Cabo* ☎ *624/122–0107* ⊕ *bajawild.com* ✉ *From $150.*

★ **Costa Azul Surf Shop**

SURFING | For epic surfing tips, rentals, and lessons, head to Costa Azul Surf Shop. They have the best quiver in Los Cabos with more than 150 hand-shape boards from their popular Olea line. They also offer paddleboards, bodyboards, and snorkel gear. Private, two-hour lessons include transportation, the surfboard rental, a rash guard, and bottled water. All instructors are CPR certified and have 25 years of surfing experience. ⊠ *Carretera Transpeninsular, Km 28, San José del Cabo* ☎ *624/142–2771* ⊕ *costaazul-surfshop.com* ✉ *Rentals, $25 per day, $20 per day for 4 days or more; private lessons $150.*

WALKING TOURS

Land's End Tours

HIKING & WALKING | FAMILY | One of the best ways to experience Los Cabos in a single day is through Land's End photo city tour. The outing covers the top attractions of Cabo San Lucas, the Corridor, and San José del Cabo; photographs of your adventure are captured throughout the tour and sent to you within one week by email. Tour highlights include San José's historical center, a boat trip to the arch, a visit to a glass-blowing factory, tequila tasting, shopping, and snorkeling. The six-hour tour begins at 8:15, and the price includes entrance fees, a tour guide, lunch, transportation, and photographs. Tours are offered from Monday through Saturday. ⊠ *Carretera Transpeninsular, Km 5, 5 de Febrero, San José del Cabo* ☎ *624/154–3532* ⊕ *landsendtours.com* ✉ *$80.*

Chapter 6

LOS CABOS SIDE TRIPS

6

Updated by
Jenny Hart

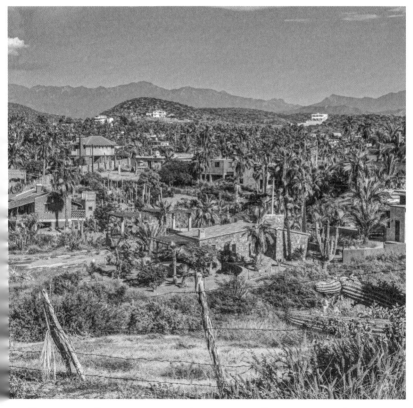

 Sights
★★★★☆

 Restaurants
★★★☆☆

 Hotels
★★★☆☆

 Shopping
★★★☆☆

 Nightlife
★★☆☆☆

WELCOME TO
LOS CABOS SIDE TRIPS

TOP REASONS TO GO

★ **Shopping in Todos Santos:** A hub for artists and craftspeople, Todos Santos is the region's trendiest and highest quality shopping destination.

★ **The Best of Urban Baja:** La Paz is your best bet for the urban pleasures of a charming, low-key Mexican city—and one with a grand seaside promenade, to boot.

★ **The Aquarium of the World:** Jacques Cousteau gave the Sea of Cortez its nickname, and nowhere is it more fitting than the East Cape's Parque Nacional Cabo Pulmo, a protected marine sanctuary teeming with life and one of the oldest coral reefs in North America.

★ **Low-Key Beaches:** If you find Cabo to be too expensive or crowded, consider La Paz or the East Cape's Los Barriles as superb, swimmable alternatives.

★ **A Whale of a Time:** The annual December-through-April migration of gray whales, humpback whales, and others is a guaranteed stunner.

Coming into Todos Santos from the south, Highway 19 parallels area beaches without necessarily hugging the coastline. Roads leading to the shore are in decent shape, but twist and turn at points.

To the north is La Paz, the focal point of which is the dense grid of streets in the city center, with most sights, lodgings, and restaurants either on the *malecón* (aka Paseo Álvaro Obregón) or a few blocks inland at most.

Finally, the East Cape curves over 70 miles northeast from the outskirts of San José del Cabo to the tranquil (if seasonally breezy) shores of Bahía las Palmas. Every mile you travel on the old East Cape Road is like traveling a little farther back in time toward the "Old Cabo": when the population was smaller, the beaches less crowded, and the amenities far simpler.

1 **Todos Santos.** Todos outgrew its surfing roots without abandoning them entirely, but you'll more likely come here for its growing number of galleries and craft shops. The arts scene has fueled a rise in gracious small inns and boutique hotels, making this popular Los Cabos–area day trip an overnight destination in its own right.

2 **La Paz.** Don't let La Paz's workaday hustle and bustle fool you. This seaside state capital is one of Mexico's loveliest small cities—you'll be sold after an evening stroll on the oceanfront *malecón*, ice cream cone in hand—and the launching point for Baja's best diving, fishing, and whale-watching excursions.

3 **East Cape.** This lesser-visited area is paradise for outdoor activity enthusiasts, from the interior mountains of the Sierra de la Laguna in the west to the azure waters of the Sea of Cortez in the east. The big-game fishing, scuba diving, and surfing may not be as famous here as in Cabo San Lucas, but they're every bit as good (if not better).

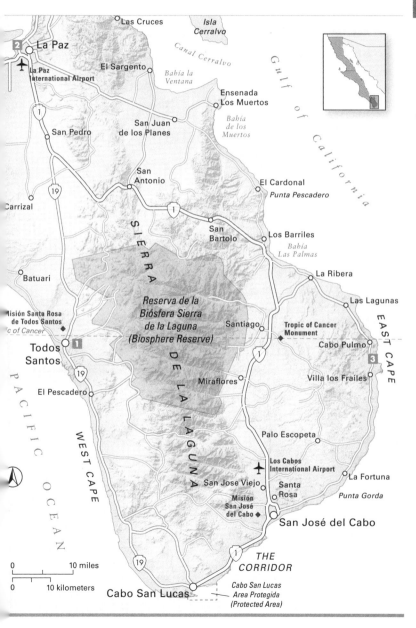

Las Cruces

Isla Cerralvo

2 La Paz

Canal Cerralvo

La Paz International Airport

El Sargento

Bahía la Ventana

Gulf

Ensenada Los Muertos

1

San Pedro

San Juan de los Planes

Bahía de los Muertos

of

California

San Antonio

El Cardonal

Punta Pescadero

19

Carrizal

1

San Bartolo

Los Barriles

Bahía Las Palmas

Batuari

S I E R R A

La Ribera

Las Lagunas

Misión Santa Rosa de Todos Santos

ic of Cancer

Reserva de la Biósfera Sierra de la Laguna (Biosphere Reserve)

Santiago

Tropic of Cancer Monument

E A S T

C A P E

Todos Santos

1

Cabo Pulmo

3

D E

19

Miraflores

Villa los Frailes

L A

El Pescadero

P A C I F I C

Palo Escopeta

L A G U N A

W E S T   C A P E

Los Cabos International Airport

La Fortuna

San Jose Viejo

Santa Rosa

Punta Gorda

Misión San José del Cabo

San José del Cabo

O C E A N

THE CORRIDOR

0   10 miles

0   10 kilometers

19

1

Cabo San Lucas Area Protegida (Protected Area)

Cabo San Lucas

Depending on the type of trip you're looking to have, we might suggest that you skip Los Cabos altogether, as the highlights of your visit to the far southern tip of the Baja peninsula could include two very un-Cabo-like destinations. One is an objectively small community, and the other—though actually the region's largest city—will always feel like a small town at heart. Their tranquil, reverent names—Todos Santos ("All Saints") and La Paz ("Peace")—are the first hint that you have left the glitz of Los Cabos behind, and that it's time to shift gears and enjoy the enchantment of Mexico.

The appeal of Todos Santos is becoming more well known, as a growing number of expats—North American and European alike—move to the area. There's a lot to love here: the surf on the Pacific, just a couple of miles west of town, is good; weather is always a bit cooler than in Los Cabos; and the lush, leisurely feel of this artsy colonial town (think a smaller version of central Mexico's San Miguel de Allende) is relatively undisturbed by the many tourists who venture up from Los Cabos for the day. Though Todos Santos has always been the quintessential day trip, it is now a destination in its own right. Break the typical pattern and spend at least one night here amid the palms, at one of the lovely boutique hotels.

La Paz plants itself firmly on the Sea of Cortez side of the Baja peninsula. A couple of hours north of Los Cabos, it remains slightly outside the Cabo orbit, yet has always attracted visitors (and an expanding expat population) who make La Paz their exclusive Baja destination. Of course, 250,000-plus Paceños view their city as being the center of the universe, thank you very much. (La Paz is the capital of the state of Baja California Sur and Los Cabos is in *their* orbit.) In addition to many urban trappings, La Paz offers a large number of options for aquatic adventure. This city on the water is all about what's in the water: sport-fishing and scuba diving are big here, and La Paz is a major launching point for whale-watching excursions.

The East Cape has always been "the other side" of Los Cabos... the side most tourists never see. Although mostly lacking the resorts and luxury amenities of municipality mates Cabo San Lucas and San José del Cabo, the East Cape is every bit their equal when it comes to world-class conditions for outdoor activities like fishing, diving, and surfing. Plus, its small towns and old-school hotels have a nostalgic appeal for those who fell in love with Southern Baja when it was a sleepier and decidedly more rustic place. Much of the East Cape still remains off the grid and reachable only by dirt roads, with the firm exception of Costa Palmas, a luxury development outside of the town of La Ribera. It's home to the spectacular **Four Seasons Resort Los Cabos at Costa Palmas** and the soon-to-open six-star **Amanvari**, suggesting that the East Cape may soon start catching up to "the Cabos" in terms of development and popularity.

Planning

Getting Here and Around

AIR

The vast majority of tourists arrive in Baja California Sur at either Los Cabos International Airport (SJD) in San José del Cabo or Manuel Márquez de León International Airport (LAP) in La Paz. Those with private jets, meanwhile, often land at Cabo San Lucas International Airport (CSL).

CONTACTS Manuel Márquez de León International Airport (La Paz International Airport). ⊠ *La Paz* ☎ *612/124–6307* ⊕ *www.aeropuertosgap.com.mx.*

BOAT
While cruise ships are a common sight in Cabo San Lucas Bay, you'll only see a few smaller, expedition-theme cruise ships come to La Paz. Yachts, however, are quite popular, with those belonging to the estates of billionaires Jeff Bezos and Steve Jobs often anchored in the Bay of La Paz. Sailors seeking the trip of a lifetime can bring their boats down from San Diego, easily finding a berth in local marinas. The Baja Ha-Ha Cruisers Rally (⊕ *www.baja-haha.com*) each November sees sailboats undertake this journey en masse.

Ferry service from La Paz to Topolobampo or Mazatlán is an excellent option for those who drove down the Baja California peninsula and want to continue their journey by car across mainland Mexico.

FERRY CONTACTS Baja Ferries. ⊠ *La Paz Pichilingue Terminal, La Paz* ☎ *800/337–7437* ⊕ *www.bajaferries.com.mx.*

BUS
Autobuses Aguilas is the primary bus tour operator for Los Cabos and La Paz. Service is available to and from Cabo San Lucas, San José del Cabo, El Pescadero, Todos Santos, La Paz, Miraflores, Santiago, Las Cuevas, and Los Barriles (all prices $20 or under one-way). Buses are air-conditioned with drop-down screens for Spanish language movies or Spanish-dubbed international releases.

Ecobaja Tours offers shuttle service to and from the Los Cabos International Airport in San José del Cabo to Todos Santos ($25), Los Barriles ($20), and La Paz ($40). All prices are one-way.

BUS CONTACTS Autobuses Aguila. ⊠ *Terminal Turística, Av. Álvaro Obregón 125, La Paz* ⊹ *Between Independencia and 5 de Mayo* ☎ *800/026–8931* ⊕ *autobusesaguila.com.* **Ecobaja Tours.** ⊠ *Terminal Turística, Av. Álvaro Obregón 125, La Paz* ⊹ *Between Independencia and 5 de Mayo* ☎ *612/123–0000* ⊕ *ecobajatours.com.*

CAR

Rental cars are the recommended option for those taking side trips to destinations like Todos Santos, La Paz, and the East Cape of Los Cabos. International companies like **Avis, Hertz, Budget,** and **Alamo,** among others, have offices here, and rentals can be arranged from all these companies directly upon arrival at Los Cabos International Airport. You can also reserve a car through a locally owned rental company like **Exacto Rent a Car** for lower prices and more personalized service.

A U.S. driver's license and credit card are all that are required for rentals. Visitors should not be scared off by Spanish language street signs as most are easy to understand. Traffic lights are identical and stop signs say *alto*, but have the same color and shape.

TAXI

Taxis and rideshares are readily available in La Paz. In Todos Santos, there are privately owned taxis that may or may not pass you on the street. Every taxi driver has a business card with their cell phone number; if you ride with one who seems reliable and trustworthy, collect their card to text them through the messaging app WhatsApp about future pickups, rather than chancing hailing one on the street. For a ride within town, you should not be charged more than $200 MXN. Drivers that ask for more than that (there are no meters) may be taking advantage of you. Always ask for the price before starting your journey. There are no taxis in the East Cape. Your options are to rent a car or hire a transfer service in advance.

Hotels

The towns outside of Cabo San Lucas, San José del Cabo, and their connecting corridor have not been historically known for their hotels, but that's changed in recent years. Todos Santos has numerous cute, boutique properties both in and outside of downtown; a mix of high-end and locally owned. La Paz, which previously only offered budget accommodations along its 3-mile malecón, is experiencing some glamorous remodels and new builds—although don't worry about it turning into a mini Cabo anytime soon (or ever), as the destination is committed to keeping all-inclusives out. The East Cape is still primarily known for old-school fishing resorts, but the luxury lodgings at Costa Palmas are bringing in a totally new clientele.

Restaurants

A rich variety of restaurants, including fine-dining establishments and internationally eateries, may be found in both Todos Santos and La Paz. The East Cape does not offer the same variety or overall quality, although Los Barriles and Costa Palmas both provide excellent options.

HOTEL AND RESTAURANT PRICES

⇨ *Hotel prices in the reviews are the lowest cost of a standard double room in high season. Restaurant prices in the reviews are the average cost of a main course at dinner, or if dinner is not served, at lunch.*

What It Costs in U.S. Dollars			
$	$$	$$$	$$$$
RESTAURANTS			
under $15	$15–$25	$26–$50	over $50
HOTELS			
under $250	$250–$350	$351–$500	over $500

⇨ *Restaurant and hotel reviews have been shortened. For full information, visit Fodors.com.*

Safety

Many visitors have preconceived notions about safety in Mexico. The Los Cabos and La Paz municipalities are both very safe, but travelers should exercise the same caution and alertness they would at home, particularly if venturing into neighborhoods off the beaten path. But, since none of the primary regional tourist attractions are located in such neighborhoods, this is rarely an issue. For emergencies, dial ☎ 911. If you need a medical center, try CEM La Paz (⊕ cemla-paz.com ☎ 612/124–0402).

More important is the caution against driving at night outside well-populated areas. This has nothing to do with *bandidos* (bandits), but rather the dangers of free-ranging livestock, and, in some areas, poorly tended roads.

Tours

Several Los Cabos tour operators offer day trips with round-trip transportation to each of these destinations; walking tours of Todos Santos, whale shark swims in La Paz, and scuba diving in the East Cape's Cabo Pulmo are among the most popular. That means if your side trip is premised around a single activity, it may not be necessary to rent a car.

Visitor Information

The Baja California Sur State Tourist Office is in La Paz, about a five-minute drive northeast of the malecón (seaside promenade), on the highway to Pichilingue near Playa El Coromuel. The office is open weekdays 8–3, and both office and website are excellent resources for information about La Paz and surrounding areas.

Todos Santos

73 km (44 miles) north of Cabo San Lucas, 81 km (49 miles) south of La Paz.

From the hodgepodge of signs and local businesses you see on the drive into Todos Santos, south on Highway 19, it appears that you're heading to the outskirts of a typical Baja town. But climb the hill to its old colonial center with its mission church and blocks of restored buildings, and the Todos Santos that is gaining rave reviews in tourism circles is revealed.

Todos Santos was designated one of the country's *pueblos mágicos* ("magical towns") in 2006, joining 120 other towns around Mexico chosen for their religious or cultural significance. Pueblos mágicos receive important financial support from the federal government for development of tourism and historical preservation. Architects and entrepreneurs have restored early-19th-century adobe-and-brick buildings around the main plaza of this former sugar town and have turned them into charming hotels. A good number of restaurateurs provide sophisticated, globally inspired food at hip eateries.

Todos Santos has always meant shopping, or at least since a number of Mexican and international artists first began relocating their galleries here three decades ago. Day-trippers will often head up here from Los Cabos to enjoy lunch and a day of browsing. But should you decide to base yourself here for a couple days or even a week, you'll leave feeling very satisfied indeed.

GETTING HERE AND AROUND

Highway 19, which connects Todos Santos south with Cabo San Lucas and north with La Paz, is an easy drive. Nonetheless, we recommend making the trip before dark, as the occasional cow or rock will block the road. Autobuses Águila provides comfortable coach service over a dozen times a day in both

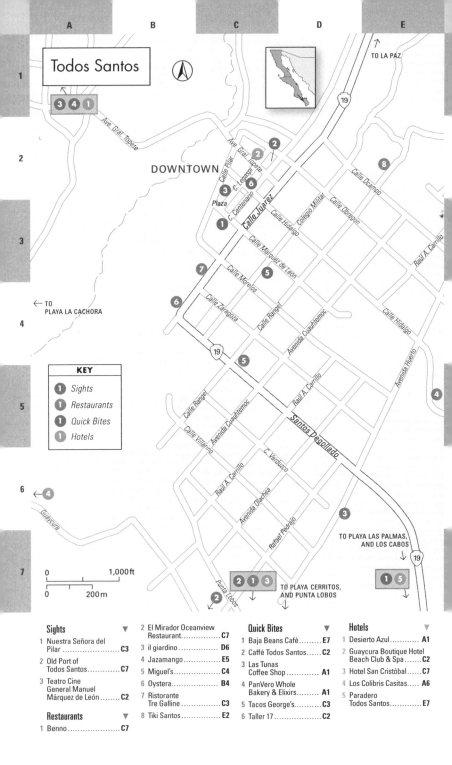

Todos Santos

TO LA PAZ

DOWNTOWN

← TO
PLAYA LA CACHORA

← TO
PLAYA LA CACHORA

Plaza

Calle Pilar
Ave. Gral. Topete
C. Centenario
C. Legaspi
Calle Juarez
Calle Hidalgo
Calle Márquez de Leon
Calle Morelos
Calle Zaragoza
Calle Rangel
Avenida Cuauhtemoc
Colegio Militar
Calle Obregon
Calle Ocampo
Raúl A. Carrillo
Calle Hidalgo
Avenida Tiuerto
Santos Degollado
Calle Rangel
Avenida Cuauhtemoc
Calle Villarino
Raúl A. Carrillo
Raúl A. Carrillo
C. Verduzco
Avenida Olachea
Rafael Pedrajo
Guaycura
Punta Lobos

Ave. Gral. Topete

TO PLAYA LAS PALMAS,
AND LOS CABOS

TO PLAYA CERRITOS,
AND PUNTA LOBOS

KEY

- **1** Sights
- **1** Restaurants
- **1** Quick Bites
- **1** Hotels

0		1,000 ft
0	200 m	

Sights ▼

1 Nuestra Señora del
Pilar **C3**
2 Old Port of
Todos Santos **C7**
3 Teatro Cine
General Manuel
Márquez de León **C2**

Restaurants ▼

1 Benno **C7**

2 El Mirador Oceanview
Restaurant **C7**
3 il giardino **D6**
4 Jazamango **E5**
5 Miguel's **C4**
6 Oystera **B4**
7 Ristorante
Tre Galline **C3**
8 Tiki Santos **E2**

Quick Bites ▼

1 Baja Beans Café **E7**
2 Caffé Todos Santos **C2**
3 Las Tunas
Coffee Shop **A1**
4 PanVero Whole
Bakery & Elixirs **A1**
5 Tacos George's **C3**
6 Taller 17 .... **C2**

Hotels ▼

1 Desierto Azul **A1**
2 Guaycura Boutique Hotel
Beach Club & Spa **C2**
3 Hotel San Cristóbal **C7**
4 Los Colibris Casitas **A6**
5 Paradero
Todos Santos **E7**

directions between Los Cabos (San José and San Lucas) and La Paz, with an intermediate stop in Todos Santos. Plan on an hour from La Paz or Cabo San Lucas and 90 minutes from San José del Cabo. Ecobaja Tours offers scheduled shuttle service (about $26 one-way) a few times a day between Todos Santos and Los Cabos Airport, 90 minutes away.

 Sights

The original colonial town center is itself a sight, with its lovely views, landmark mission church, and many small shops and galleries.

Old Port of Todos Santos

VIEWPOINT | Once a vital maritime hub, the Old Port of Todos Santos has been reduced to (literal) ruins, but remains an awe-inspiring viewpoint. Reachable only by a hiking trail or with an ATV, the striking vistas from the top of the trail are easily worth the sweat and dust you'll be covered in upon arrival. If you have it in you, you can take a steep 2½-mile trek down to a stunning, secluded beach to cool off. The trail, also called the Sugar Port, starts at Punta Lobos. ⊠ *Punta Lobos, Todos Santos.*

Nuestra Señora del Pilar

CHURCH | Todos Santos was the second-farthest south of Baja California's 30 mission churches, a system the Spanish instituted to convert (and subdue) the peninsula's indigenous peoples. Jesuit priests established an outpost here in 1723 as a *visita* (circuit branch) of the mission in La Paz, a day's journey away on horseback. The original church north of town was sacked and pillaged twice during its existence, before being relocated in 1825 to this site in the center of town. Additions in the past two centuries have resulted in a hodgepodge of architectural styles, but the overall effect is still pleasing, and the structure serves to this day as the community's bustling parish

church. ⊠ *Calle Márquez de León, Todos Santos* ✛ *Between Centenario and Legaspi* ☎ .

Teatro Cine General Manuel Márquez de León

NOTABLE BUILDING | The mouthful of a name denotes Todos Santos's 1944 movie theater, which was quite a grand movie palace back in the day for remote, small-town Mexico. A few cultural events take place here, including the annual Todos Santos Film Festival each March. ⊠ *Calle Legaspi s/n, Todos Santos.*

 Beaches

Las Palmas

BEACH | Todos Santos is an oasis, meaning fresh water naturally runs through the desert into the ocean. Greenery blooms alongside cracking stretches of hardened sand, with palm trees and cacti living as neighbors. Within the heart of the oasis sits Playa Las Palmas, one of the only swimmable beaches in Todos Santos. You need to walk through a corridor of lush plant life (and potentially an ankle-deep stream) to reach the ocean, which feels so surprisingly out of place, you'd think it was planted by a gardener. It's a quiet, beautiful place to spend some time, although beware of horse droppings and sand fleas. There are no amenities, so bring your own umbrellas and snacks. **Amenities:** none. **Best for:** swimming. ⊠ *Todos Santos.*

Punta Lobos

BEACH | The closest beach to downtown Todos Santos, Punta Lobos is where fishermen launch their boats in the early morning. It's fascinating to watch them go out, as well as return in the afternoon, boats barreling onto the sand at high speed. You may see the occasional swimmer, but it generally isn't advised due to strong currents. Strolling along the sand and enjoying the scenery, however, is highly recommended. Punta Lobos, named after the sea lions native to the area, is also the starting point of some of the town's most beloved hikes. **Amenities:** parking (free). **Best for:** sunrise; walking. ✉ *Todos Santos.*

Playa Los Cerritos

BEACH | This long, expansive beach on the Pacific Ocean, about 64 km (40 miles) north of Cabo San Lucas and on the way to the town of Todos Santos, is famous among surfers for its wonderful breaking waves in winter. Great for beginners, the waves here are consistent, accessible, and not overly powerful. Boards and lessons are available via multiple surf shops right on shore. This beach works best on northwest swells. Even if you don't ride the waves, you can watch them crash along the shore. The sandy beach is wide, flat, and ideal for wading and swimming close to shore. Swimming farther out is not recommended because of the strong currents.

There are a small but lively number of beach bars and restaurants, including **Barracuda Cantina,** which was featured on Netflix's *Taco Chronicles,* plus a couple of modest beachfront hotels. Several condo and hotel developments are in progress, with locals predicting that Cerritos will be the "next Médano" (the mega-popular beach in Cabo San Lucas) in a decade or so. You can still camp or stay in RVs near the beach, although there are no organized campsites or RV parks in the area. The beach is quite dog-friendly, and you'll no doubt cross paths with a few four-legged friends (and their owners) on any given day. It's also a nice place to get an affordable massage, with a number of massage beds set up right in the sand.

Access to the beach is marked on Highway 19 (which connects Cabo San Lucas and Todos Santos) by a sign for Playa Los Cerritos at Km 64 (13 km [8 miles] south of Todos Santos). The graded dirt road to the beach is 2½ km (1½ miles) from Highway 19. **Amenities:** food and drink; parking (free); showers (for restaurant patrons); toilets. **Best for:** surfing;

swimming; walking. ✉ *64 km (40 miles) north of Cabo San Lucas, 13 km (8 miles) south of Todos Santos, Todos Santos.*

 Restaurants

Todos Santos's dining selection echoes the town—stylish expat with traditional Mexican—and makes a nice outing during any Los Cabos–area stay. Restaurants here do a brisk business at lunch, less so at dinner. It's well worth the trip to drive up from Los Cabos or down from La Paz for a special meal. At an hour each way, that's easier to do before dark.

Benno

$$$ | MEXICAN FUSION | Located right at Playa Punta Lobos, this is a brilliant place to grab an elegant, beachside bite. Recently recognized by Michelin Guide, Benno serves a mix of Mexican and Mediterranean cuisine, with every dish crafted from local ingredients. **Known for:** charred salad; wines from Valle de Guadalupe and abroad; hearty breakfast. ⑤ *Average main: $27* ✉ *Hotel San Cristóbal, Carretera Federal #19, Km 54, Todos Santos* ⊹ *At Punta Lobos* ☎ *855/227–1535* ⊕ *www.bunkhousehotels.com.*

★ **El Mirador Oceanview Restaurant**

$$$ | MEXICAN | This cliffside restaurant offers the most spectacular view in Todos Santos—the excellent Mexican cuisine is an added bonus. **Known for:** lovely jazz music; stargazing after sunset; ticketed and private events. ⑤ *Average main: $30* ✉ *Calle Legaspi esq. Topete, Centro* ☎ *612/175–0800* ⊕ *guaycura.com/en/el-mirador-restaurant.*

il giardino

$$ | ITALIAN | Nestled on top of a small hill on the outskirts of town, this charming Italian restaurant by Chef Daniela Borghini overlooks pretty gardens (hence the name) and the ocean. The ambiance is pleasantly pleasing, and the pizzas (which are 33 cm, in between a size medium and large) and pasta dishes are a guaranteed hit. **Known for:** homemade

Festivals in Todos Santos

Todos Santos hosts various arts-related festivals throughout the year. It's a good idea to make reservations weeks in advance if you plan to be here at those times.

The **Tropic of Cancer Concert Series** (⊕ www.tropicofcancerfestival.mx) features live music spread across two back-to-back weekends in January, with an international lineup of performers appearing at venues throughout town. Proceeds benefit local children's charities.

The city goes all out for **Festival del Arte Todos Santos** (Todos Santos Art Festival;⊕ www.facebook.com/ Festivaldelartetodossantos), which celebrates Mexican dance, music, folklore, and culture for a week in early February each year. Local artists and several of the downtown galleries hold special events as well.

Several new Latin American films are shown during **Festival de Cine de Todos Santos** (Todos Santos Film Festival;⊕ www.todossantoscinefest.

org) in March. The 1940s-era Teatro Cine General Manuel Márquez de León serves as the main venue, with some films shown at other sites in Todos Santos, Pescadero, and La Paz.

ABC Art Baja (⊕ abcartbaja.com), the region's newest cultural festival, goes from early March to early May, with exhibitions across Tijuana, Ensenada, San José, Todos Santos, and La Paz. It encourages the development and promotion of the local art community and celebrates the region's culture and talent.

Summer harvest festivals are among the most traditional yearly events in Baja California Sur and offer a taste of regional culture and regional produce. In Todos Santos, mangoes are celebrated each year with a **Festival del Mango Todos Santos** in late July or early August (whenever the fruit ripens), highlighted by mango-flavored desserts, as well as live music, dancing, and the coronation of a festival queen.

pasta, including a gluten-free option; wood oven pizza; tips are cash-only. ⓈÌ *Average main: $20* ⊠ *C. Del Huerto, San Vicente, Todos Santos* ☎ *612/145–0237* ⊕ *www.facebook.com/IlGiardinoTodosSantos/* ⊗ *Closed Mon. No lunch.*

Jazamango

$$ | **MEXICAN FUSION** | Set next to a beautiful garden that provides many of the fruits, veggies, and herbs used in the kitchen, Jazamango is a feast for the eyes as well as the taste buds, and one of the most iconic restaurants in Todos Santos. It's helmed by well-known Mexican chef Javier Plascencia, known for his organic, sustainable approach to creating Baja-Mediterranean fusion dishes.

Known for: atmospheric garden setting; straight-from-the-earth ingredients; Baja craft-brewed beers. Ⓢ *Average main: $27* ⊠ *Calle Naranjos, Todos Santos* ⊹ *At Esquina Jardín, Plaza Principal, Fraccionamiento Las Huertas* ☎ *612/688–1501* ⊕ *jazamango.mx* ⊗ *Closed Tues.*

Miguel's

$ | **MEXICAN** | Deliciously prepared chiles rellenos—stuffed with cheese, beef, fish, and vegetables—are the attraction at Miguel's; the signature version is made with shrimp. Look for the sign out front claiming these are the main attraction, as well as the faded but framed *New York Times* article, which proclaims them the best in all of Baja. **Known for:**

friendly owner; hearty chiles rellenos; semi-outdoor dining. $ *Average main: $10* ⊠ *Degollado at Calle Rangel, Centro* ☎ *613/134–4149* 🚫 *No credit cards* 🕐 *Closed Mon.*

Oystera

$$$$ | SEAFOOD | If a restaurant could be an "It Girl," the queen bee of Todos Santos would be Oystera. The historic building that houses it—the town's oldest (former) sugar mill—is covered with lush, elegant ivy and the oysters here are some of the best you'll find in Baja. **Known for:** variety of oyster types from all throughout Baja; Michelin-recommended; nice shops that share the space. $ *Average main: $36* ⊠ *Calle Benito Juárez, Ignacio Zaragoza and Santos E, Todos Santos* ☎ *612/228–0621* ⊕ *oystera-ts.com.*

Ristorante Tre Galline

$$ | ITALIAN | Sitting on the intimate patio of this adorable restaurant feels like visiting a friend's home—should that friend happen to be the best Italian chef that you know. The fresh pasta is incredibly tasty, but the best part of your meal might be the straight-from-the-oven bread basket that gets served first. **Known for:** rich, delicious pasta sauce; Italian wines; nice for groups and events. $ *Average main: $18* ⊠ *C. Benito Juárez, Todos Santos* ☎ *612/234–4243* ⊕ *www.instagram.com/ tregallinets* 🕐 *Closed Mon.*

Tiki Santos

$$ | MEXICAN | A favorite spot among the dwindling community of local Mexican residents, Tiki Santos can be a little difficult to find (the location shown on Google Maps is not correct), but if you persevere, you'll be rewarded with generous portions of classic Mexican seafood dishes at moderate prices. The decor is as basic as they come—plastic chairs on a dirt sand floor—but that's part of the charm. **Known for:** tostadas; Zarandeado style (butterflied then grilled) fish; margaritas. $ *Average main: $13* ⊠ *Calle Rangel, Panteon Antiguo, Todos Santos* ☎ *612/168–0075* ⊕ *www.tikisantosbar.com.*

 # Coffee and Quick Bites

Baja Beans Café

$ | CAFÉ | This long-loved Pescadero roaster, known to produce some of the area's best gourmet coffee drinks using beans from the Sierra Norte mountains, has finally opened a location in downtown Todos Santos! The owners, committed to giving back to their community, have pledged to donate a significant portion of their profits from the new café to local charities. **Known for:** gourmet coffee; early morning hours; convenient location. $ *Average main: $5* ⊠ *Guaycura Hotel, Calle Legaspi esq. Topete, Todos Santos* ☎ *612/176–6620* ⊕ *bajabeans.com.*

Caffé Todos Santos

$$ | ECLECTIC | This cute and casual eatery was the first in Todos Santos to open with tourists intentionally in mind, back in 1993. The building is over a century old, and was a house in the late 1800s; the flooring is original from 1933. **Known for:** coffee and pastries; Italian lunches; fun decor. $ *Average main: $15* ⊠ *Calle Centenario 33, Todos Santos* ☎ *612/145–0300* 🕐 *Closed Tues.*

Las Tunas Coffee Shop

$ | BAKERY | Las Tunas is a residential neighborhood north of downtown that's almost exclusively filled with vacation homes, short-term rentals and inns, and construction sites building the two. Amid all of that, however, is a coffee shop and bakery with perhaps the best breakfast in all of Todos Santos. **Known for:** freshly baked bread; garden setting; nice for co-working. $ *Average main: $6* ⊠ *Las Playitas, Todos Santos* ☎ *612/238–1717* ⊕ *www.instagram.com/cabanaslastunas_coffeeshop* 🕐 *Closed Mon.*

PanVero Whole Bakery & Elixirs

$ | BAKERY | PanVero is an absolute godsend for travelers with dietary restrictions: every item on the menu is gluten-free, dairy-free, and plant-based—and at least half of the items are vegan, as well. Only natural and organic ingredients are used, so feel free to order a sweet treat without feeling guilty. **Known for:** house blend of nut milk; convenient to-go window; damiana love tonic. $ *Average main: $4* ⊠ *Las Playitas, Las Tunas, Todos Santos* ☎ *612/233–2789* ⊕ *www. panvero.com* ⊗ *No dinner.*

Tacos George's

$ | MEXICAN | Street eats aren't as ubiquitous in Todos Santos as they are in Cabo or La Paz, but if you're craving tacos and want something cheap, easy, and oh-so-good, go to George's. Choose between fish or shrimp; either will cost you just a few bucks cash (credit cards not excepted), with agua de jamaica (hibiscus water) as the available beverage. **Known for:** best tacos in town; casual, outdoor taco stand; family business. $ *Average main: $3* ⊠ *Heroico Colegio Militar 85, Centro* ☎ *612/102–8768* ⊕ *www. facebook.com/Tacosgeorgestsbcs* ⊟ *No credit cards* ⊗ *No dinner.*

Taller 17

$ | COFFEE | If you are a pastry lover… then heaven awaits. Every single one is a delicacy, although the sticky buns and scones have a particular fan following. **Known for:** gluten-free and dairy-free options; warm, friendly service; very limited seating. $ *Average main: $3* ⊠ *Centenario 17, Todos Santos* ☎ *612/145–2019* ⊕ *www.instagram.com/taller17todossantos* ⊗ *Closed Wed. No dinner.*

Hotels

Boutique hotels are the name of the game when it comes to lodging in Todos Santos, with a mix of luxury properties and locally owned gems.

Desierto Azul

$$$ | HOTEL | Husband and wife duo Fabrizio Cavallo and Nilú Feregrino have dedicated their lives to "conscious living," and Desierto Azul ("where the desert meets the ocean") is their brainchild. **Pros:** everything is organic and sustainable; staff is very charming

and kind; beautifully furnished rooms. **Cons:** far from downtown in Las Tunas; the grounds are quite small; can feel a bit isolated. $ *Rooms from: $300* ⊠ *Las Playitas, Las Tunas, Todos Santos* ☎ *612/233–2789* ⊕ *www.desiertoazulbaja.com* ⊅ *4 rooms* ⦿| *Free Breakfast.*

★ Guaycura Boutique Hotel Beach Club & Spa

$ | HOTEL | Located within a gorgeous 19th-century redbrick building in the heart of Todos Santos, Guaycura is a city hotel with resort-like amenities. **Pros:** spacious rooms with handcrafted furniture; ideal location in the center of town; transportation can be arranged between venues. **Cons:** some rooms can hear street noise; old-school Mexican decor doesn't suit all tastes; street parking only. $ *Rooms from: $144* ⊠ *Calle Legaspi esq. Topete, Todos Santos* ☎ *612/175–0800* ⊕ *guaycura.com* ⊅ *14 rooms* ⦿| *No Meals.*

Hotel San Cristóbal

$$$$ | HOTEL | The location of Todos Santos' most popular hotel is quite extraordinary as you'll immediately be mesmerized by the sights and sounds of crashing waves; you can audibly hear them from your room. **Pros:** the only beachfront hotel in town; excellent dining; fun, tasteful design. **Cons:** out of touch with the local community, which has caused some controversy; only accessible by a bumpy dirt road; fewer pool loungers than guests. $ *Rooms from: $495* ⊠ *Playa Punta Lobos, Carretera Federal #19, Todos Santos* ☎ *855/227–1535* ⊕ *www.bunkhousehotels.com* ⊅ *32 rooms* ⦿| *No Meals.*

Los Colibris Casitas

$$ | GUESTHOUSE | If you like your accommodations to feel like a warm embrace, you'll love being welcomed at this hillside property, which is completely covered in color between blooming, bird-filled gardens and original wall mosaics. **Pros:** rooms come equipped with a binder full of local recommendations; the owners are also professional tour guides; joyful comraderie among guests. **Cons:** uneven

Welcome to the Hotel California

If you walk down Calle Benito Juárez in Todos Santos, you will undoubtedly pass a cluster of tourists standing in front of **Hotel California** (⊕ *www. hotelcaliforniabaja.com/todos-santos. html*), an old-school inn that first opened in 1950. Depending on the integrity (and/or general knowledge) of their tour guide, you may catch wind of a tale of how the Eagles used to come surfing in Baja, and that this is the location that inspired the hit song.

But alas: while it's fun to imagine you're walking in the footsteps of rock royalty, there's no relation between the two. In fact, the Eagles sued the hotel in 2017, alleging that they were purposefully misleading guests into believing the association, and were profiting greatly off selling

trademarked "Hotel California" merch. The hotel is no longer allowed to play the band's music (which they had on repeat in the lobby) as a result.

Where *is* the "real" Hotel California, then? Some locals will insist it exists in the northern part of Mexico, but the Eagles' lead singer Don Henley has gone on the record saying it was completely fiction, and simply their interpretation of "the high life in Los Angeles."

Sometimes the truth hurts, but that doesn't make the actual Hotel California any less fun to visit! Enjoy a margarita at the bar, browse the souvenir shop, Emporio, or even spend the night: the hotel has 11 rooms and you can check out any time you like!

flooring within some rooms; no dining on-site besides breakfast; hot tub takes a long time to turn on. $ *Rooms from: $155* ⊠ *88 Calle Guaycura, La Poza* ☏ *619/446–6827 in U.S., 612/145–0189* ⊕ *www.loscolibris.com* ⇄ *11 casitas* ⫯⊙⫯ *No Meals.*

Paradero Todos Santos
$$$$ | **HOTEL** | No lodging in Todos Santos has a more spectacular location than Paradero, which is set within an organic farming community and offers panoramic vistas of desert, mountains, and the Pacific Ocean. **Pros:** every room has private, scenic outdoor space; Michelin-recommended restaurant; daily off-site activities and tours are included. **Cons:** very remote location; pretentious atmosphere; rooms lack basic amenities. $ *Rooms from: $600* ⊠ *La Mesa, Km 59, Carretera Todos Santos – Cabo San Lucas, Todos Santos* ☏ *800/614–7562 in U.S., 557/005–5094* ⊕ *www.paraderohotels.com* ⇄ *41 suites* ⫯⊙⫯ *No Meals.*

 Nightlife

As tourism grows in Todos Santos, so do its nightlife options. You'll never mistake this place for Los Cabos, however, and the town is quite fine with that state of affairs. Lingering over dinner remains a time-honored way to spend a Todos Santos evening.

The Dirty Rose
COCKTAIL BARS | This cocktail bar is the main "late night" option in Todos Santos, staying open until a whopping 11 pm. Visited primarily by the local expat community, owner and bartender James Katona is happy to chat up new faces as he slings his signature margaritas. Decorated with quirky artifacts that are mostly gifts from regulars, The Dirty Rose is located within the unmarked building with the thatched roof (speakeasy meets tiki bar, anyone?) across from Shut Up Frank's. ⊠ *Calle Degollado at Rangel, Todos Santos* ☏ *612/102–9354* ⊕ *www.*

instagram.com/thedirtyrosespeakeasy
⊘ Closed Sun.–Tues.

El Refugio Mezcaleria

BEER GARDENS | Like mezcal? Come here. Don't like mezcal? Come here anyway and your mind will be changed. El Refugio serves a constantly changing list of artisanal mezcals sourced directly from small, family producers from across five different states in Mexico. Try them in a cocktail, or better yet, order a flight—but don't forget to read the written descriptions of what each mezcal tastes like; crafted by co-owner Rachel Glueck, they are among the most unhinged segments of creative writing you'll find outside of a hipster poetry slam, and only become more amusing with each pour you consume. It's cash-only and not cheap, so make sure your wallet is packed with pesos. ✉ Heroico Colegio Militar at Alvaro Obrego, Todos Santos ✛ Behind Tecolote Bookstore ☎ 612/149–3482 ⊕ www.elrefugiobaja.com ⊘ Closed Sun. and Mon.

La Confianza Wine & Coffee Bar

WINE BAR | This trendy spot serves natural wine primarily from Mexican women-en-owned labels, plus coffee and dessert from Taller 17. ✉ Av. Legaspy, Todos Santos ⊕ www.instagram.com/laconfianza.ts ⊘ Closed Mon.–Wed.

La Morena

BARS | Live music and various two-for-one deals can be found at this happening spot, which on certain weekdays is among the only open bars in town. Don't expect a wild party, however: La Morena usually closes up shop around 9 pm. ✉ Av. Benito Juárez, Todos Santos ☎ 612/145–0789 ⊕ www.facebook.com/LaMorenaTodosSantos ⊘ Closed weekends.

Shut Up Frank's

SPORTS BARS | Take your pick from the sporting events shown on seven big-screen TVs at the consummate sports bar in Todos Santos. Enjoy the scrumptious burgers here, too. ✉ Degollado at Rangel, Todos Santos ✛ Across from Pemex station ☎ 612/145–0707 ⊕ www.facebook.com/ShutUpFranks ⊘ Closed Tues. and Wed.

Sky Lounge Bar

LOUNGES | Catch the sunset at this rooftop lounge while enjoying a "Margarita Guaycura," made with lemon, tequila, orange liqueur, and the local spirit, damiana. There's a pool, too, you can swim in or relax beside, should you visit during the day. ✉ Guaycura Hotel, Calle Legaspi esq. Topete, Todos Santos ☎ 612/175–0800 ⊕ guaycura.com/en/sky-lounge-bar/.

★ Todos Santos Brewing

BREWPUBS | Los Cabos' Baja Brewing Company tends to get all of the love when it comes to the local craft beer scene, but this brewery in Todos Santos has a wider variety with arguably better flavor—all 28 taps are made fresh on-site. Todos Santos Brewing is open seven days a week and regularly organizes fun entertainment like live music, trivia, and karaoke. ✉ Álvaro Obregón, between Militar and Rangel, Todos Santos ☎ 612/145–0789 ⊕ www.facebook.com/TodosSantosBrewing.

Violeta

WINE BAR | Wine and charcuterie are the orders at this simple but sophisticated spot, conveniently located right in the historic town square. ✉ Calle Centenario and Manuel Marquez de Leon, Todos Santos ⊕ violetavino.com ⊘ Closed Mon.–Wed.

Shopping

Artists from the American Southwest (and a few from Mexico) found a haven in Todos Santos some two decades ago and their galleries are among the town's most famous attractions. You'll see a mix of traditional and contemporary work, with a strong Baja emphasis in the art. There are several local boutiques selling a curated collection of clothing, jewelry, and fine crafts sourced from throughout Mexico.

The markets and galleries of Todos Santos make it a top shopping destination.

ART GALLERIES

Benito Ortega Vargas, Sculptor

ART GALLERY | Sculptor Benito Ortega's studio and gallery showcases evocative, often sea-inspired works in wood, bronze, stone, and other materials. ✉ *24 Centenario, at Obregón, Centro* ☎ *612/136–2760* ⊕ *www.benitoortega. mx* ☉ *Closed Sun.*

Ezra Katz Gallery

ART GALLERY | Ezra Katz is considered by many to be one of the most important and original artists ever to emerge from Baja California Sur. Born in the United States but raised in La Paz, Katz's evocative and inspired paintings depicting the local landscape have been on display in his latest Todos Santos gallery since 2015. ✉ *Calle Juárez at Topete, Todos Santos* ☉ *Closed Sun.*

★ Galería de Todos Santos

ART GALLERY | When Michael Cope opened this gallery 30 years ago alongside his wife, Pat, it was the first in Todos Santos to represent a group of artists from different mediums: painters, sculptors, and photographers. The rule was (and remains) simple: you could be from anywhere, but you had to live in Mexico. Today, Michael and his partner-in-paint Erick Ochoa (Pat has retired) showcase the work of 12 different artists, the majority of whom are Mexican. ✉ *Calle Topete, Centro* ✛ *Between Juárez and Centenario* ☎ *612/145–0500* ⊕ *www. galeriatodossantos.com.*

Jill Logan Galería

ART GALLERY | This house-turned-gallery features the work of four artists, including its namesake Jill Logan, a Southern Californian who has been in Todos Santos since 1998. Expect to find bold oil-on-canvas paintings and complexly layered multimedia pieces. ✉ *Calle Juárez at Morelos, Todos Santos* ☎ *612/145–0151* ⊕ *www.jilllogan.com.*

BOOKS

El Tecolote Bookstore

BOOKS | El Tecolote Bookstore is a top bookstore in the region for English-language reads. Stop here for Latin American literature, poetry, children's books, current fiction and nonfiction, and books on Baja. ✉ *Colegio Militar, Centro* ✛ *Between Hidalgo and Obregón* ☎ *662/359–4443* ⊕ *www.facebook.com/eltecolotebookshop.*

CLOTHING AND FOLK ART

Desert Fox Baja

CLOTHING | This sustainable shop sells a mix of original designs and cool vintage finds. ✉ *Calle Miguel y Hidalgo, Centro* ☎ *612/169–4489* ⊕ *www.instagram.com/desertfoxbaja.*

Étnica

CLOTHING | Cotton and linen clothing and wool and leather accessories are among the goods you can find here. Everything is crafted by Mexican artisans. ✉ *Bonifacio Topete, Centro* ☎ *612/143–7585* ⊕ *www.instagram.com/etnicatodossantos.*

Manos Mexicanas

CRAFTS | Manos Mexicanas is a treasure trove of fine Mexican crafts, jewelry, decorative objects, and work by local potter Rubén Gutiérrez. Owner Alejandra Brilanti has amassed an incredible collection of affordable pieces. You are not likely to leave empty-handed. ✉ *Manuel Márquez de León, Todos Santos* ✛ *Between Juárez and Centenario* ☎ ⊕ *facebook.com/ManosMexicanasTS* ⊘ *Closed Sun.*

Nomad Chic

TEXTILES | The romance of travel influences Nomad Chic's stock of apparel, accessories, and furnishings. Curated by designer Linda Hamilton, the collections are inspired by Mexico (naturally), along with Greece, Peru, Spain, Turkey, and beyond. ✉ *Juárez at Hidalgo, Centro* ☎ *415/381–9087* ⊕ *www.nomadchic.mx.*

Tierra Madre

SPECIALTY STORE | Tierra Madre ("Mother Earth") is one part store, one part outlet for unique experiences—both of which are focused exclusively on Mexico's traditions. Whether you're purchasing handwoven apparel or attending a cacao ceremony, you'll walk away enriched from

having experienced and supported a special part of the country's ancient culture. ✉ *Bonifacio Topete, Centro* ☎ ⊕ *www.instagram.com/tierramadre.store.*

★ ZÓCALO

CLOTHING | This ethical and sustainable boutique sells a curated selection of Mexican-made clothing, jewelry, homewares and more. It's a shop that genuinely cares about giving back: beyond providing a space for 150-plus talented local artisans to showcase their products, portions of every sale are donated to a children's charity, recycling center, and dog rescue, all in Todos Santos. ✉ *Benito Juarez and Topete, Todos Santos* ⊕ *shopzocalo.com.*

JEWELRY AND ACCESSORIES

Bésame Mucho Bazaar

ACCESSORIES | Bésame Mucho is as much a tourist attraction as a shop, as the patio outside is the most photographed in Todos Santos: just try *not* posing in front of the colorful Aztec Calendar or on the romantic kiss bench. Inside, the boutique sells a wildly wonderful variety of glittery goods: everything from clothing to accessories to home decor. Owner Rouss Del Toro's tastes may be more eclectic than most, but the people who love her merch will *love* it. ✉ *Av. Legaspy 15, Centro* ☎ *612/145–0539* ⊕ *www.instagram.com/besamemuchobazaar.*

Brilanti Fine Art

JEWELRY & WATCHES | Brilanti Fine Art is a showcase for the stunning jewelry and design works of famed Taxco silversmith Ana Brilanti, in addition to a number of other contemporary jewelry artists whose work shares the same dramatic aesthetic. Be sure to look at the silver tea services and other functional pieces. You'll also find selected stone carvings and bronzes from local artists. Extended members of the (clearly gifted) family have gone to open a total of five distinct jewelry shops to sell their work, all on Centenario. ✉ *Centenario, Centro* ✛ *Near Calle Topete* ☎ *612/148–6023* ⊕ *brilanti.com.*

MARKETS

Cielito Lindo

SOUVENIRS | Originally started as a way to support local craftsmen during the pandemic, this permanent craft fair in the parking lot of Hotel California has become the premiere spot to buy handcrafted souvenirs. You can find all of the typical goods, like jewelry, T-shirts, and glass ornaments, but quirky, creative items, too. Take, for example, maker Adrián Bailón Garcia, who sells swords he fastens out of swordfish and marlin bones. There are whispers that the present owner of Hotel California is looking to retake the land, so the physical site may change, but fear not! There's no way the local community will let this gem disappear. ⊠ *C. Marquez de Leon esq., Todos Santos* ⊕ *instagram.com/cielitolindomarket.*

 Activities

SPAS

El Faro Beach Club & Spa

SWIMMING | If you're staying in town but craving some beach time, snag a day pass to El Faro. It's home to an infinity pool and swim-up bar, a refreshing seafood grill, a spa that offers a specialty "seaside massage," and plenty of places to set up and relax, whether by the pool or on the sand. During winter, you can easily spot whales breaching, just off the shore. ⊠ *Camino al Faro 1, Todos Santos* ☎ *612/175–0800* ⊕ *guaycura.com/en/el-faro-beach-club* ⊡ *$30.*

SURFING

Todos Santos can be great surfing destination for beginners to experts. Los Cerritos, located south of Todos Santos on Highway 19, offers gentle waves for beginners during the summer and more challenging breaks for advanced surfers during the northwest swell from December to March. San Pedrito, also south of town, has great surfing for experienced surfers during the winter swells, with a number of popular, low-key, surf-oriented motels along the beach. In summer, the surf is generally pretty mellow along this stretch, so locals and surfers who demand greater challenge head to the Corridor or East Cape for more satisfying breaks.

Todos Santos Surf Shop

SURFING | Swing by Todos Santos Surf Shop for board rentals, to arrange a lesson, buy gear, or get that ding in your board repaired. Other activities are also available, including day trips to Magdalena Bay during whale-watching season, and to La Paz to swim with sea lions and whale sharks. ⊠ *Calle Hidalgo, Todos Santos* ⊕ *Between Colégio Militar and Rangel* ☎ *612/145–1114* ⊕ *explorabaja.com/todossurfshop.*

TOURS

Omega Tours

FOUR-WHEELING | Many of the "regular" roads in Todos Santos are difficult enough to drive on without four-wheel drive, but making it to the mountain top? Forget about it. That's where an ATV tour comes in! You can choose between two routes with Omega Tours; the more popular one will take you along the coast from La Poza (the lagoon) to Playa Las Palmas, with stops at Punta Lobos and the Old Port in between. Request a guide who is a motocross rider for an extra adventurous ride. ⊠ *H. Colegio Militar y Santos Degollado, Todos Santos* ☎ *612/136–2372* ⊕ *omegatours.mx* ⊡ *From $200.*

★ Todos Santos Eco Adventures

EDUCATIONAL PROGRAMS | This beloved local tour company offers a wide breadth of experiences to help you get to know Todos Santos on an intimate level. Get in tune with nature on a Pacific bluffs cliff walk (from $90), which takes you on a guided journey from Punta Lobos to Las Palmas, or to the fauna living in La Poza on a birdwatching walk ($65). Around town, expert guides will teach you everything there is to know about what makes a good fish taco (and feed you several of their favorites) on a taco crawl ($75) and personally escort you to the best galleries, shops, and restaurants on an art and shopping tour ($75). TOSEA prioritizes the social and economic benefits for the local community; they are the first and only Mexican tour operator to be a member of the Global Sustainable Tourism Council. ✉ *Guaycura 88, Todos Santos* ✛ *West on Calle Olachea, follow signs toward La Poza* ☎ *612/145–0189, 619/446–6827 in U.S.* ⊕ *www.tosea.net.*

La Paz

81 km (49 miles) north of Todos Santos, 178 km (107 miles) north of San José del Cabo (via Hwy. 1), 154 km (92 miles) north of Cabo San Lucas (via Hwy. 19).

Prosperous La Paz may be the capital of the state of Baja California Sur and home to nearly 300,000 residents, but it still feels like a small town. You'll quickly get the impression that everybody knows each other, and given how welcoming *Paceños* can be, that may include you by the end of your visit. Many will say that La Paz is the last true Mexican town in Baja Sur—meaning that while tourism plays an incredibly important role and folks from around the world happily call it home, local culture will always come first.

With any amount of growth, there is change. La Paz is doing its best to navigate this as seamlessly as possible. Visitors to the city were previously relegated to staying at dated and dingy (though wonderfully located) accommodations, but there is now a selection of upscale boutique properties to choose from, with more to come: for example, **Hotel Perla,** the oldest hotel in Baja California Sur, is undergoing a transformative renovation to keep up with the times and attract new guests.

High-end resort developments, complete with hotels, golf courses, marinas, and vacation homes, are arising. The most prominent is the newly minted and refreshed **Puerta Cortés** (previously called CostaBaja under past ownership), which has finally found its footing after a decades-long dream to bring something different and special to La Paz. It's been a welcome addition, being outside of the Zona Central and thus not disrupting its flow. Locals swear that the sushi restaurant in its Marina Village, Odayaka Sushi Bar, is the best in town. Less well received is Paraiso del Mar, which was built—despite strong opposition and controversy—on El Mogote, the desert peninsula directly across the bay from the malecón. Some feel its an eyesore when gazing out at the ocean, and there are serious concerns about the resort's affect on La Paz's environment and natural resources.

If you were counting on finding an all-inclusive deal here, stick to Los Cabos. La Paz is committed to keeping this type of accommodation out; in one sense, to differentiate themselves from Cabo and attract a different type of tourist, and in another, to keep the tourism dollars it earns better circulating within and supporting the local community.

GETTING HERE AND AROUND
Aeropuerto General Manuel Márquez de León (LAP) is 11 km (7 miles) northwest of La Paz. At the time of publication, there are no direct flights from the United States. All three of Mexico's airlines (Aeromexico, Viva Aerobus, and Volaris) connect La Paz to other airports throughout the country.

Flying into the Aeropuerto Internacional de Los Cabos, three hours away in San José del Cabo, offers a far better selection of fares and itineraries. Ecobaja Tours operates shuttles six times daily between Los Cabos Airport and La Paz for just under $40 one-way. A private transfer is likely to run you $200 or more. In La Paz, both taxis and Uber are readily available. A ride within town costs under $10; a trip to Pichilingue may cost around

The Steinbeck Connection

For an account of the Baja of years past, few works beat John Steinbeck's *The Log from the Sea of Cortez*, published in 1951. It recounts a six-week voyage he took in 1940 with marine biologist Ed Ricketts for the purpose of cataloging new aquatic species on the gulf side of Baja California. (*Phialoba steinbecki*, a previously unknown species of sea anemone discovered during the excursion, was later named for the author.)

Steinbeck lamented the inevitable tourism growth bound to arrive on the peninsula. The author was mistaken on one key point however: he was certain the megaboom would come to La Paz and not to then-sleepy Cabo San Lucas.

$20. The main bus terminal is on the malecón, at the corner of Independencia. From here, you can catch hourly bus service to Todos Santos ($10) and Los Cabos ($20).

Baja Ferries connects La Paz with the mainland state of Sinaloa with daily ferries to two different ports. You can buy tickets for ferries at La Paz Pichilingue terminal or via www.bajaferries.com.mx. The ferries carry passengers with and without vehicles. If you're taking a car to the mainland, you must obtain a vehicle permit before boarding. Ferry officials will ask to see your Mexican auto insurance papers and tourist card, which are obtained when crossing the U.S. border into Baja. Ferries to Topolobampo take eight hours and cost $100/person and $300/car. Ferries to Mazatlán take 14 hours and cost $100/person and just shy of $350/car.

◉ Sights

Catedral de Nuestra Señora de la Paz

CHURCH | The downtown church, Catedral de Nuestra Señora de la Paz, is a simple, unassuming building near the site of La Paz's first mission, which no longer exists. Built in 1861, it's one of La Paz's oldest buildings, and so no changes can be made, even for restoration. It was built with volcanic stone, the primary available material at the time; inside you can find a modest gilded altar but beautiful stained-glass windows. ⊠ *Revolución de 1910, Centro* ✛ *Between 5 de Mayo and Independencia.*

★ Isla Espíritu Santo

NATIONAL PARK | Ask anyone living in La Paz for their favorite place or top recommendation and they're bound to reply with a passionate sigh, "La Isla." It's no wonder, as Espíritu Santo, an uninhabited island about an hour's boat ride into the ocean, is unbelievably special. It's a UNESCO World Natural Heritage Site as well as a national park, and a number of tour operators will take you out for the day to snorkel or scuba dive at Los Islotes, a bustling sea lion colony, kayak across the still waters, or relax on a completely vacant beach. With a few, you can even camp overnight. ⊠ *La Paz.*

Jardín Velasco

PLAZA/SQUARE | This small but sweet town square sits between the cathedral and the former government palace, which now houses El Museo de Arte de Baja California Sur (MUABCS). Admission to the museum is free, so stop in to see a collection of work by local and national artists. Concerts are held in the garden's gazebo and locals gather here for art fairs and farmers markets. ⊠ *Bordered by Av. Independencia, Calles 5 de Mayo, Revolución de 1910, and Madero, La Paz.*

Malecón La Paz

PROMENADE | This seaside promenade is La Paz's seawall, tourist zone, and social center all rolled into one. It runs for 5 km (3 miles) along Paseo Álvaro Obregón and has a broad palm-lined walkway, statues of whale sharks, dolphins, sharks, and other local denizens of the deep, as well as several park areas in the directly adjacent sand. You can swim here, but the beaches outside town are of significantly better quality. The center point is Malecón Plaza, which features a white gazebo and small concrete square where musicians sometimes appear on weekend evenings. Paceños are fond of strolling the malecón at sunset when the heat of the day finally begins to subside. ⊠ *Paseo Álvaro Obregón, La Paz.*

Museo de la Ballena y Ciencias del Mar

MUSEUM VILLAGE | **FAMILY** | Commonly referred to by English speakers as The Whale Museum, this popular malecón-adjacent attraction actually celebrates myriad forms of marine life, from dolphins and sharks to sea lions and endangered sea turtles. The enormous whale skeletons, built from bones sourced from specimens that washed up on nearby shores, are undoubtedly the most spectacular items on display, however. Sperm, humpback, and other whale re-creations hang suspended from the high ceilings, with brains and other organs preserved in accompanying exhibits. Guided tours provide a wonderful introduction to the region's aquatic abundance, and are available in several languages, including English. The gift shop next door, meanwhile, offers souvenir T-shirts and other cetacean-theme memorabilia. ⊠ *Antonio Navarro 855, Centro* ☎ *612/348–5238* ⊕ *www.museodelaballena.org* ☎ *$4* ⊙ *Closed Sun.; closes at 2 pm.*

Museo Regional de Antropología y Historia de Baja California Sur

MUSEUM VILLAGE | **FAMILY** | La Paz's culture and heritage are well represented at the Museo de Antropología, which has re-creations of indigenous Comondu and Las Palmas villages, photos of cave paintings found in Baja, and copies of Cortéz's writings on first sighting La Paz. All exhibit descriptions are labeled in both English and Spanish. If you're a true Baja aficionado and want to delve into the region's history, this museum is a must; otherwise, a quick visit is all you need. ⊠ *Calle Altamirano at Calle 5 de Mayo, Centro* ☎ *612/125–6424* ⊕ *culturabcs. gob.mx* ☎ *$3.*

Serpentario de La Paz

ZOO | **FAMILY** | Better that you encounter all the creatures that slip and slither here in the safety of Mexico's largest serpentarium than out in the wilds of Baja. More than 100 species are on display in indoor and outdoor exhibits, including turtles, pythons, rattlesnakes, and a rather large iguana. A majority are rescued from precarious situations in the wild (like being abandoned at birth or seriously injured) and are either rehabilitated and released, or if not possible, continuously cared for. Labeling is entirely in Spanish, but the staff offers guided tours in English with advance notice. A gift shop sells reptile-theme souvenirs. ⊠ *Calle Brecha California, Centro* ⊹ *Between Nueva Reforma and Guaycura* ☎ *612/122–5611, 612/104–0584 Whats App* ☎ *$8* ⊙ *Closed Mon.–Wed.*

🏖 Beaches

The beaches of La Paz are often ranked the best in Mexico. The most convenient one to visit (though a fraction as alluring as the rest) is right off the malecón. The water is swimmable and the palapa-dotted sand makes for a pleasant place to sit and relax. The second closest is Playa El Coromuel. Though a bit too far to walk, it is reachable by bike, and quite built up with facilities. Notably, El Coromuel is wheelchair accessible.

Sights ▼

1 Catedral de Nuestra
Señora de la Paz.................... **F4**
2 Isla Espíritu Santo **H1**
3 Jardín Velasco **F4**
4 Malecón La Paz..................... **F3**
5 Museo de la Ballena y
Ciencias del Mar.................... **E6**
6 Museo Regional
de Antropología y Historia
de Baja California Sur............. **G4**
7 Serpentario de La Paz............ **A7**

Restaurants ▼

1 Azotea.............................. **F3**
2 Baja Club Restaurante **E3**
3 Biznaga Baja Bistro **E3**
4 Casamarte Oyster Bar & Grill **E3**
5 Hambrusia........................... **F3**
6 NEMI **F3**

Quick Bites ▼

1 DoceCuarenta
Coffee Roasters.................... **F3**
2 Giulietta e Romeo
Heladería Italiana.................. **E4**
3 Mariscos El Tigre **I6**
4 Taco Fish La Paz **F6**

Hotels ▼

1 Baja Club Hotel **E3**
2 Camp Cecil de la Isla............. **H1**
3 Hotel Indigo La Paz
Puerta Cortés **H1**
4 República Pagana **F3**

For the beaches beyond (each one gets prettier the further north you go), you'll need proper transportation. A rental car or taxi does the trick, but there's a semi-hourly public bus you can take called the Playa Bus about $3 each way. It leaves from the bus terminal on the malecón and stops at each of the beaches along the coast. It is easy to spot (it's bright blue with "Playa Bus" and waves painted on the side), so long as you keep track of the pick up schedule.

Playa Balandra

BEACH | A rocky point shelters a clear, warm bay at Playa Balandra, 21 km (13 miles) north of La Paz. Several small coves and pristine beaches appear and disappear with the tides, but the water is calm and shallow enough that you can wade between them. This is Mexico's most famous beach, so the most popular way to visit is with a boat tour, whose guide typically provides beach chairs, snorkeling gear, and lunch. If you go independently, there are some restrictions, as Balandra was named an ecological conservation site by UNESCO. There is an entrance fee of about $3 per person, and you can stay for up to a maximum of four hours during either a morning (8–noon) or afternoon (1–5) time slot. A maximum of 450 people are allowed to enter during each time slot, so if you're traveling during peak season (or even on a weekend), you may want to arrive and line up early to guarantee admission. You will be made to leave once your time slot closes, regardless of when you arrived. The most iconic site at Balandra is "El Hongo," a rock formation that looks like a mushroom. It's a photo op, for sure, but climbing on it is forbidden. There's also a 30-minute hike from the parking lot up to a panoramic viewpoint overlooking the bay. When walking in the shallow waters, you're advised to shuffle your feet, kicking up sand to disturb any potentially sleeping sting rays. Sand flies can be a nuisance on the beach, particularly between July and October. **Amenities:**

Sunrise, Sunset

La Paz sits on the east coast of the Baja peninsula, but a convoluted curvature of the shoreline here positions the city to look out west over the Sea of Cortez. That means that you can enjoy beautiful sun *sets* over the water here at the end of the day. In fact, La Paz known as the City of 365 Sunsets, with each one seeming more breathtaking than the last. Your camera roll will be filled by the time you depart!

parking (fee). **Best for:** snorkeling; swimming. ⊠ *La Paz* ✛ *21 km (13 miles) north of La Paz.*

Playa Caimancito

BEACH | Situated 5 km (3 miles) north of La Paz, half of Caimancito "belongs" to the locals (though anyone is welcome), with sun-shading palapas and some government signage. It's a good beach for families with young children, as the calm, shallow waters feel more like a large natural pool than ocean. The second half houses El Caimancito Restaurant & Beach Club, which is owned by the boutique hotel, Orchid House Baja. There are very cute day beds and wooden swings, plus a DJ and fan to keep cool in the heat. A $500 MXN ($25) consumption minimum is required for nonguests of the hotel. **Amenities:** food and drink; parking (free). **Best for:** partiers; swimming. ⊠ *La Paz* ✛ *5 km (3 miles) north of La Paz.*

Playa El Tecolote

BEACH | On a calm, sunny day, Playa El Tecolote could pass for being in the Caribbean. It's extremely gorgeous, and extremely fun, with the total vibe of a true Mexican beach. Restaurants and bars serve all sorts of seafood, though some will try to charge you a minimum spend ($400 MXN [$20])or flat rate($100

MXN [$5]) to dine on the sand versus inside their open-air establishment. Vendors rent out beach chairs, umbrellas, and kayaks, and will give banana boat rides. To the right of the restaurants is where the locals station up, often setting up tailgates from the backs of their cars and/or under large awnings. Camping is permitted (no hookups), and you'll see vans and RVs parked right on the sand, facing the beautiful surf. To the left is a hidden, quiet beach, accessible only by hiking or by boat, called El Tecolotito. Visit during the summer (May through November) for the best conditions. From January through March, it can be windy and the waves rough. **Amenities:** food and drink; parking (free); toilets; water sports. **Best for:** partiers; swimming; walking. ⊠ *Carretera La Paz–El Tecolote, La Paz* ⊕ *25 km (15 miles) north of La Paz.*

Playa Pichilingue

BEACH | Playa Pichilingue is a good backup beach for when El Tecolote and Balandra are too crowded. The water is pretty, and a local BYOB beach club, A Plein Soleil, will rent you cushioned chaise loungers for $150 MXN ($8) for the day. Points could be docked for the nearby ferry terminal, number of fishing boats, and sound of traffic, but those are rather surface-level complaints. The clear, shallow ocean water is great to sit—or even lay down—in and watch tiny fish swim by. There are a couple of restaurants to patron for lunch and drinks. **Amenities:** food and drink; parking (free); toilets. **Best for:** swimming. ⊠ *La Paz* ⊕ *16 km (10 miles) north of La Paz.*

🍴 Restaurants

Azotea

$$ | CONTEMPORARY | Though the architecture looks a little strange from the street, this five-story rooftop restaurant is sexy as hell. Bring your bathing suit, because select counter seating comes with a private plunge pool, along with a cheeky-chic, golden framed button that

instructs you to "Press for Champagne." With expansive ocean views, this is a great spot to take a date or meet up with friends. **Known for:** fantastical design; robust food and drink menus; adults-only. $ *Average main: $13* ⊠ *República Pagana, Belisario Domínguez 387, La Paz* ☎ *612/103–2952* ⊕ *www.instagram.com/ azotea_hrp.*

Baja Club Restaurante

$$ | MEDITERRANEAN | At a restaurant known colloquially as "La Pergola" due to its lovely location under one in Baja Club's garden, executive chef Panagiotis Vounos prepares Mediterranean cuisine inspired by his native Greece with a touch of French flair (it's where he received his training and worked before moving to La Paz). When it comes to beverages, however, that's all Mexico: the wine is sourced exclusively from Valle de Guadalupe, and Baja Club was the first establishment to officially collaborate with GUAYCURA Damiana Liqueur to create hyperlocal craft cocktail recipes. **Known for:** 14-hour cooked lamb; damiana spritz cocktail; outgoing, attentive chef. $ *Average main: $17* ⊠ *Baja Club Hotel, Paseo Álvaro Obregón 265, La Paz* ☎ *612/122–5176* ⊕ *bajaclubhotel.com/ baja-club-restaurant.*

Biznaga Baja Bistro

$$ | MEDITERRANEAN | New-kid-on-the-block Biznaga is one of La Paz's trendiest restaurants, and a top spot for young, cool locals to gather. Its splashy design and solid mixology is garnering even more praise than its bites, but you won't leave disappointed or hungry if you order a selection of starters and tacos for the table. **Known for:** craft cocktails; beautiful bar; hip clientele. $ *Average main: $18* ⊠ *C. Francisco I. Madero 1125, La Paz* ☎ *612/150–3021* ⊕ *www.instagram.com/ biznagabistro.*

★ Casamarte Oyster Bar & Grill

$$ | SEAFOOD | Dining at Casamarte offers the quintessential La Paz experience: truly nothing can beat slurping back raw

oysters and chocolate clams while people watching on the malecón at sunset. Though the menu is pretty diverse, the seafood (and the raw bar, especially) is what you come for. **Known for:** exceptional location; indoor (with a/c) and outdoor (with views) seating; quality service. ⑤ *Average main: $15* ⊠ *Paseo Álvaro Obregón at 16 de Septiembre, La Paz* ☎ *612/155–6929* ⊕ *www.facebook.com/casamartemx.*

Hambrusia

$$ | MEXICAN | Chef Lalo Pino is one of the most interesting characters you'll meet in La Paz, and his food reflects that. Perhaps because both his menu of craft tacos and the concept of Hambrusia (which is slang for hungry, like "munchies") were inspired by growing up on the peninsula before there were supermarkets and accessible ingredients from the mainland. **Known for:** grilled cheese bacon quesadilla; local craft beer; punk rock wall art. ⑤ *Average main: $13* ⊠ *Paseo Álvaro Obregón at Constitución, La Paz* ☎ *612/202–4853* ⊕ *www.hambrusia.com.*

★ NEMI

$$$$ | MEXICAN | The tasting menu at NEMI, whose name means "give life" in the Indigenous Mexican language, Nahuatl, is beyond exquisite. Choose five- or nine courses, plus an optional (but recommended) wine pairing, and prepare to be blown away by the modern Mexican cuisine that is created by chef Alejandro Villagomez and his team. **Known for:** ever-changing menu; award-winning cuisine; private catering available for 2–400 people. ⑤ *Average main: $65* ⊠ *Francisco I. Madero 565, La Paz* ☎ *612/159–5502* ⊕ *www.nemirestaurante.com* ⊘ *Closed Sun. No lunch.*

🅒 Coffee and Quick Bites

★ DoceCuarenta Coffee Roasters

$ | CAFÉ | This fabulous coffee roaster has three locations in La Paz, plus locations in Todos Santos and Cabo San Lucas. Named simply after the physical location of their first café (#1240), the brand is now synonymous with fresh coffee, great pastries, cute merch, and a welcoming atmosphere. **Known for:** three different types of coffee beans; charming selection of local souvenirs; serves beer and wine in the evening. ⑤ *Average main: $5* ⊠ *C. Francisco I. Madero 1240, La Paz* ☎ *612/178–0067* ⊕ *www.instagram.com/docecuarentacafe.*

Giulietta e Romeo Heladería Italiana

$ | ICE CREAM | Nothing beats walking down the malecón with an ice cream in hand… or in this case, Italian gelato. Choose among 28 artisan flavors at Giulietta e Romeo. **Known for:** vegan, keto, low carb, and lactose-free options; open daily until 10:30 pm; delivery available. ⑤ *Average main: $3* ⊠ *Agustin Arriola M. 25, La Paz* ☎ *612/131–7307* ⊕ *facebook. com/GiuliettaeRomeoLaPaz.*

Mariscos El Tigre

$ | SEAFOOD | Want to go where the locals eat lunch? El Tigre is a bit out of the way, in a residential neighborhood (take an Uber rather than walk), but it has the some of the absolute freshest seafood in town. **Known for:** freshly shucked clams; seafood sourced directly from fishermen; cash-only. ⑤ *Average main: $3* ⊠ *Francisco Javier Mina 1229, La Paz* ☎ *612/238–0017* ⊕ *www.facebook.com/mariscoseltigrelapazbcs* ▭ *No credit cards* ⊘ *Closed Tues. No dinner.*

Taco Fish La Paz

$ | MEXICAN | Fish tacos for breakfast? It may take getting used to, but that's how things are done in La Paz. **Known for:** battered fish tacos; marlin and shrimp empanadas; stingray machaca. ⑤ *Average main: $3* ⊠ *Paseo Álvaro Obregón #710, La Paz* ☎ *612/198–1194* ⊕ *www. tacofishlapazbcs.com* ⊘ *Closed Mon. No dinner.*

🛏 Hotels

Baja Club Hotel

$$$ | HOTEL | Since its opening in 2021, Baja Club has been considered *the* hotel to stay at in La Paz; the first of now several high-end boutique properties to make themselves home in the capital city. **Pros:** privileged location on the malecón; exclusive feel; great views from balconies and rooftop. **Cons:** awkward room layout; small rooms with no desk and limited closet space; pool area is not very comfortable. *Rooms from: $200* ✉ *Paseo Álvaro Obregón 265, La Paz* ☎ *612/122–5176* ⊕ *bajaclubhotel.com* ⤳ *32 rooms* ¶◎¶ *Free Breakfast.*

Camp Cecil de la Isla

$$$$ | PERMANENT CAMP | Complete with furnished canvas tents, this glamping experience on Isla Espíritu Santo has had to take the glam down a notch thanks to new (though hopefully temporary) government legislation that forbids any permanent island encampments; this new need to break down and rebuild twice weekly has resulted in a simpler overall setup, but guests are hardly "roughing it." Every tent at Camp Cecil comes with a real (and comfortable) bed, and a quite sophisticated, environmentally friendly bathroom set up so guests may comfortably shower and do their business while leaving no trace. **Pros:** well-maintained camp and professional, friendly crew; restaurant-quality dining; activities, gear, and meals are all included. **Cons:** no Wi-Fi or cell reception; tents aren't soundproof (bring earplugs to sleep); occasionally disrupted by day-trippers. *Rooms from: $395* ✉ *Isla Espíritu Santo, La Paz* ☎ *619/446–6827 in U.S., 612/145–0189* ⊕ *tosea.net/the-camp-cecil-de-la-isla* ⤳ *8 tents* ¶◎¶ *All-Inclusive.*

Hotel Indigo La Paz Puerta Cortés

$$ | HOTEL | A small, stylish hotel with beach resort amenities, boutique chain Hotel Indigo's new property within the sprawling Puerta Cortés development complex gives travelers the best of both worlds. **Pros:** access to private beach club; more rooms and availability than other hotels in town; striking views from the lobby. **Cons:** far from the malecón; some resort amenities are for members-only; unreliable transportation within the resort. *Rooms from: $200* ✉ *Puerta Cortés Resort, Carretera Pichilingue, Km 7.5, La Paz* ☎ *612/123–6000* ⊕ *indigolapaz.com* ⤳ *115 rooms.*

República Pagana

$$$ | HOTEL | This strictly adults-only boutique arts hotel is one block back from the malecón, but the views from the towering (for the area) fifth floor rooftop cannot be beat. **Pros:** spacious rooms with fabulous design; on-site art installations; priority rooftop reservations. **Cons:** uneven flooring in lobby; poorly lit hallways; hard-to-reach front desk. *Rooms from: $325* ✉ *Belisario Domínguez 387, La Paz* ☎ *612/103–2952* ⊕ *www.instagram.com/republicapagana* ⤳ *12 rooms* ¶◎¶ *No Meals.*

🎡 Nightlife

BARS AND DANCE CLUBS

Cotorritos

DANCE CLUB | Open later than any other venue in La Paz, this is the place to wind up if you have one more dance left in you before calling it a night. Tacos are sold for under a buck-fifty, should you need some sobering up, too. ✉ *Esquerro 10, La Paz* ☎ *612/228–7050* ⊕ *facebook.com/CotorritosLaPaz.*

Elbuen Bar

COCKTAIL BARS | Owner Os Navarro is always coming up with original recipes and inventive twists on classic cocktails from behind "the good" bar. There's limited seating here, so try to come early (or prepare to hover) to claim a spot. ✉ *Constitución 207, La Paz* ☎ *612/133–0923* ⊕ *instagram.com/elbuen_bar* ☉ *Closed Tues.*

Did You Know?

Just north of La Paz, Playa Balandra has small coves and pristine beaches that appear and disappear with the tides. The shallow, clear water is ideal for snorkeling.

El Parnazo

BARS | Liter-size bottles of beer (called *caguamas* throughout Mexico, but in Baja specifically, you can also say *ballena*, which means "whale") line the shelf behind this classic bar, part of which has been converted into an epic stage for live music. Every night of the week from 10 pm until 1 am a band performs either rock n' roll or *banda*, traditional Mexican music with brass instruments. ⊠ *Calle 16 de Septiembre 15, La Paz* ☎ *612/129–7272* ⊕ *facebook.com/ElParnazoBar.*

Mezcalería La Miserable

COCKTAIL BARS | "Mezcal for everything bad… and also for everything good" is one of La Miserable's punchy catch phrases. You can order 1 oz. or 2 oz. pours of nearly every varietal under the sun, all from artisan distilleries from different states of Mexico. The house cocktails mix an espadín with fresh fruit juices, and both domestic and craft beers are available, too. Open until 2 am six nights a week, this is one of the most reliable late-night haunts in La Paz. ⊠ *Calle Belisario Dominguez 274, La Paz* ✛ *Between 5 de Mayo and Constitución* ☎ *612/129–7037* ⊕ *www.instagram.com/lamiserablemezcaleria* ⦵ *Closed Sun.*

612 Rooftop

LOUNGES | Seis Uno Dos (La Paz's area code) is a nice rooftop lounge overlooking the malecón. Come here for sunset cocktails or to dance the night away to an upbeat DJ set. ⊠ *Paseo Álvaro Obregón 2130, La Paz* ☎ *612/139–0642* ⊕ *instagram.com/612rooftop* ⦵ *Closed Mon.*

🛍 Shopping

ART AND SOUVENIRS

★ Casa del Artesano Sudcaliforniano

CRAFTS | This is the place in La Paz to buy goods and souvenirs handmade by local artisans. Some of the most culturally relevant items include pearl jewelry, bottles of damiana, and picture frames made from dried cholla cactus wood, but there are plenty of bookmarks, magnets, and coffee mugs, as well. The prices are very affordable, so be sure to leave room in your suitcase for some great finds! ⊠ *Paseo Álvaro Obregón at Nicolás Bravo, La Paz* ☎ *612/169–6350* ⊕ *facebook.com/casadelartesanosudcaliforniano.*

Taller Connus Art and Press

STATIONERY | Local artist Karla Antuna designs compelling ink prints of Baja-theme flora and fauna, like cactus, octopus, whales, and donkeys. ⊠ *Manuel Pineda 215, La Paz* ☎ *612/122–1749* ⊕ *instagram.com/taller_connus_art_and_press.*

CLOTHING

Baja Chic Boutique

CLOTHING | Cute clothing, accessories, and more can be found at this brand new waterfront boutique. ⊠ *Paseo Álvaro Obregón 820, La Paz* ⊕ *instagram.com/bajachicboutique.*

MAJA Sportswear

SPORTING GOODS | If you need protection from the sun and surf (sunscreen should be avoided when swimming near coral reefs), MAJA has you covered. They sell UPF, water-resistant clothing for men and women, some in sweet, locally inspired designs, like the pattern of a whale shark's skin. You can get high-quality swim trunks, caps, sunglasses, towels, and more here, too. ⊠ *Paseo Álvaro Obregón 1086, La Paz* ☎ *612/106–8325* ⊕ *majasportswear.com.*

JEWELRY

The Velvet Box

JEWELRY & WATCHES | Perhaps the most iconic gift you could buy for yourself or another while in La Paz is a beautiful pearl. You would be in good company, as Queen Elizabeth II had one found in these very waters on her crown. The Velvet Box designs and creates lovely pieces (perhaps just a tad more modest than the monarch's!) for you to try on and take home. ⊠ *Paseo Álvaro Obregón*

1775, La Paz ☎ *612/153–8631* ⊕ *insta-gram.com/thevelvetboxbcs.*

 Activities

BOATING AND FISHING
Baja Molinito Experience
FISHING | There are many places to fish in and near La Paz, but Baja Molinito Experience opts to take anglers about an hour south to Bahía de los Sueños, one of the most prolific big game–fishing spots in the world. Their "Fishing Day Tour" includes a seven-hour charter for up to four people, bait and equipment included. An upgrade to "Fish & Cook Tour" adds on RT transportation from La Paz, onboard refreshments, and your catch of the day prepared fresh back at their restaurant on the malecón. ⊠ *Carr Escénica, La Paz* ☎ *612/234–1503* ⊕ *ba-jamolinito.com* ✉ *$400 for Fishing Day Tour; $665 for Fish & Cook Tour.*

We Boat Baja
BOATING | Spend a gorgeous day cruising the bay, spotting and snorkeling with marine life, and relaxing on the beach, all with an impeccably kept Regal Boat as your base. We Boat Baja's tours are customizable, but a common itinerary includes snorkeling with sea lions at the Lobera San Rafaelito then indulging in a gourmet lunch (your guide will set up a table, chairs, and shade) on Playa Balandra. The boats come equipped with refreshments, towels, and snorkel gear. ⊠ *Topete 3040, La Paz* ☎ *612/127–2245* ⊕ *instagram.com/weboatbaja* ✉ *$600 for up to 5 people.*

GOLF
El Cortés Golf Club
GOLF | The only Gary Player Signature course in Mexico, certain celebrities have been known to helicopter in for the day just to play a few holes. All but one have panoramic views of the Sea of Cortez, and hole 14 (called The Cortés Challenge) is one of the country's longest par 5. Though there's a comfort station serving

drinks and light bites, save room for a proper breakfast at the stunning Cardón Restaurant after, which sits on the high-est point of La Paz Bay. ⊠ *Puerta Cortés Resort, Km 7.5, Carretera a Pichilingue, La Paz* ☎ *612/175–0122* ⊕ *elcortesgolf. com* ✉ *Greens fee: $270. Twilight: $210. 9 holes: $170.* 🏌 *18 holes, 6,991 yards (black tees), par 72* 🕒 *Closed Mon.*

KAYAKING
The calm waters off La Paz are perfect for kayaking, and you can take multiday trips along the coast to Loreto or out to the nearby islands.

SCUBA DIVING AND SNORKELING
Popular diving and snorkeling spots include the coral banks off Isla Espíritu Santo, the sea-lion colony off Isla Partida, and the seamount 14 km (9 miles) farther north (best for serious divers).

Cortez Club
SCUBA DIVING | The Cortez Club is a full-scale water-sports center with equipment rental and scuba, snorkeling, kayaking, and sportfishing tours, as well as the complete slate of PADI instructional courses. ⊠ *Hotel La Concha, Carretera a Pichilingue Esquina, Km 5, La Paz* ⊹ *Between downtown and Pichilingue* ☎ *612/121–6120, 877/408–6769 in U.S.* ⊕ *www.cortezclub.com* ✉ *2-tank dives from $165.*

TOUR OPERATORS
On Board Baja
ADVENTURE TOURS | One of the few nonaquatic activities to try in La Paz is sandboarding. A fairly easy though adventurous activity for all-ages, you "surf" down the side of a sand dune on a greased up snowboard. On Board Baja will show you the ropes at El Mogote, starting first at a smaller dune until your confidence builds for a higher peak. Gear and snacks are included, and your guide will take GoPro footage of you shredding up a storm. ⊠ *Gral Manuel Márquez de León #2415, La Paz* ☎ *612/183–5278* ⊕ *www.onboardbaja.com* ✉ *$60.*

A diver gets up close and personal with a sea lion in the waters of the Sea of Cortez.

WHALE-WATCHING

La Paz is a good entry point for whale-watching expeditions to **Bahía Magdalena,** 266 km (165 miles) northwest of La Paz on the Pacific coast. Note, however, that such trips entail about six hours of travel from La Paz and back for two to three hours on the water. Only a few tour companies offer this as a day-long excursion because of the time and distance constraints.

Many devoted whale-watchers opt to stay overnight in Puerto San Carlos, the small town by the bay. Most La Paz hotels can make arrangements for excursions, or you can head out on your own by renting a car or taking a public bus from La Paz to San Carlos, and then hire a boat captain to take you into the bay. The air and water are cold during whale season from December to April, so you'll need to bring a warm windbreaker and gloves. Captains are not allowed to "chase" whales, but that doesn't keep the whale mamas and their babies from approaching your *panga* (skiff) so closely you can reach out and touch them.

An easier expedition is a whale-watching trip in the Sea of Cortez from La Paz, which involves boarding a boat in La Paz and motoring around until whales are spotted. They most likely won't come as close to the boats and you won't see the mothers and newborn calves at play, but it's still fabulous watching the whales breeching and spouting nearby.

Baja Expeditions

RAFTING | Seasonal four-day, three-night gray whale–watching excursions are offered for $2,995 per person, double occupancy. Tours are typically scheduled in February and March, and include flights, meals, an expert natural guide, and comfortable glamping conditions at Laguna San Ignacio. ⊠ *Calle Sonora 585, La Paz* ✛ *Between Topete and Abasolo* ☎ *612/125–3828, 800/843–6967 in U.S.* ⊕ *www.bajaexpeditions.com.*

East Cape

At its northernmost point, Los Barriles, it is 78 km (49 miles via Hwy. 1) from San José del Cabo and 106 km (65 miles) from La Paz.

First-time visitors may think Los Cabos is only Cabo San Lucas, San José del Cabo, and their connecting 20-mile tourist corridor, but that's not true at all. Yes, those two towns are the genesis of the name Los Cabos (The Capes), but the Los Cabos municipality as a whole comprises nearly 1,500 square miles, including more than a dozen smaller towns and at least one microregion full of natural treasures: the East Cape. Known as "the other side" of Los Cabos, the off-the-grid area is home to rustic fishing resorts, great surfing and diving in Cabo Pulmo National Park, pristine beaches with no vendors, and spectacular views that make it well worth a trip.

The East Cape proper begins at the outskirts of San José del Cabo and then traces the coast for nearly 70 miles, all the way to Los Barriles. Los Barriles is the largest East Cape coastal community (with more than 1,000 residents, many of whom are retired expats), and the only one that is not in the Los Cabos municipality but in La Paz.

The East Cape also includes small inland towns like Miraflores and Santiago, easily accessed from the Carretera Transpeninsular (Federal Highway 1). The highway provides the safest and quickest means to reach most East Cape communities; either directly in the case of Buena Vista and Los Barriles, or via the turnoff at La Ribera that loops back to San José del Cabo along the largely dirt Camino Cabo Este, or East Cape Road. The latter is the only way to reach tucked-away communities like Cabo Pulmo, whose national park includes a marine sanctuary with one of the oldest living coral reefs in North America.

With the exception of the Four Seasons Resort Los Cabos at Costa Palmas (in La Ribera), luxury is in short supply along the East Cape. Rather, this off-the-grid region provides a snapshot of what Cabo San Lucas and San José del Cabo were like 50 years ago, before they were developed into international tourist destinations. In other words, it's the last chance to see "Old Cabo."

GETTING HERE AND AROUND

Buses do travel to the East Cape, despite its off-the-radar status. Autobuses Aguila leaves every morning and afternoon from Plaza Golden Palace in Cabo San Lucas, picking up passengers in San José del Cabo before continuing on through Miraflores, Santiago, La Ribera, and Los Barriles on the way to La Paz. Tickets for all these destinations are around $10 from Cabo San Lucas. But buses are a less-than-ideal mode of transportation for East Cape travel, since these small towns largely lack central shopping, dining, and resort areas within walking distance of bus stops. Los Barriles is the lone exception, since everything visitors could want (hotels, restaurants, beach, activities) is on or within easy walking distance of Calle 20 de Noviembre, the town's main drag. Every other destination requires a car.

Cars are the best way to travel the East Cape. Rentals are available throughout Cabo San Lucas and San José del Cabo, including at the airport and on-site at some upscale resorts. The airport toll road from Cabo San Lucas to the airport in San José del Cabo dramatically reduces the travel time to reach the East Cape by means of the Carretera Transpeninsular (Federal Highway 1), and at a reasonable cost (about $6). Miraflores can be reached in about one hour by this route; Los Barriles in just under two hours.

Coastal road Camino Cabo Este, accessible from Highway 1 at La Ribera, is also widely used. It remains almost completely dirt, with slow speed limits

(20 to 25 mph) in most of the 45-mile route between Cabo Pulmo and San José del Cabo. Driving this dirt road should never be attempted without a four-wheel-drive vehicle, and not at all during or in the days immediately after a rainstorm. Visitors should also avoid driving at night, on all roads, due to the possibility of hazardous encounters with the region's free-ranging *chinampo* cattle.

While some are advocating for the Camino Cabo Este to be completely paved, there's opposition from locals who enjoy living in a remote, less accessible destination. They worry about the risk of too much development. So while it may happen one day, it's unlikely to be anytime soon. An alternative does exist, however, in that many local dive companies offer round-trip transportation for Cabo Pulmo scuba trips, and a few adventure providers, like High Tide Los Cabos, offer jeep tours of the region.

 Sights

Aguas Termales Santa Rita

HOT SPRING | It might not be an obvious bet to seek out natural hot springs in a warm weather destination, but the Aguas Termales Santa Rita are truly special. This divinely sculpted Jacuzzi is an enchanting place to soak and relax, and there's a refreshing, cool-water river bend just a few steps away, ideal for moving back and forth between the two. The smell of sulfur is strong, but you get used to it, and it does wonders for your skin and any body aches. Assuming you bring your own provisions, there are areas to sit and eat (complete with picnic tables and basic grills) and even overnight campsites. It's a long drive down a dirt road to get here, but it adds to the charm and adventure of the experience. You will not have cell reception, so downloading Maps in advance is a must. You'll need cash to pay the entry fee, collected presumably by the family who lives on the land.

Note: there are two hot springs compounds right next to each other, with separate entrances and fees. The first, Los Encinos, is not as nice as Santa Rita, but could be ideal for families with young children as the water is more shallow and space more confined, making it easier to supervise your brood. Everyone else should continue driving just another hundred yards more to reach Santa Rita. ⚓ *2.3 km (1½ miles) west of San Jorge* ✉ *$8*.

Cascada La Ciénega

WATERFALL | A (usually) dry riverbed called an *arroyo* runs through the center of Los Barriles, and it is a wild landscape to rip through on an ATV. About 20 km (12½ miles) in is a waterfall whose size changes by the month; sometimes its pool is only deep enough for a splash, but it's still miraculous to see freshwater rapidly gushing out of rocks in the middle of an otherwise barren desert. ✉ *Los Barriles*.

Cascada Sol de Mayo

WATERFALL | If you've heard whispers of a waterfall, it was likely this: Cascada Sol del Mayo, located at the base of a canyon within the Rancho Ecológico Sol de Mayo, just outside of the town of Santiago. It's a bit of a journey to reach, but it's a fun adventure for active travelers. First, head down a long dirt road from the **Mirador Santiago de Yola**, a small observation platform overlooking Santiago's lagoons and palm groves; you'll likely lose cell reception, but it's hard to get lost (download the route on Google Maps ahead of time if you'd like the reassurance). Once you reach the ranch, you'll need to pay an entrance fee, and it's a short but steep hike down into the canyon. You'll be rewarded halfway with a view of the twinkling green swimming hole and dainty but powerful cascade. The crystal clear, freshwater pool is incredibly refreshing (especially after that descent on a warm day) and has pockets

Continued on page 186

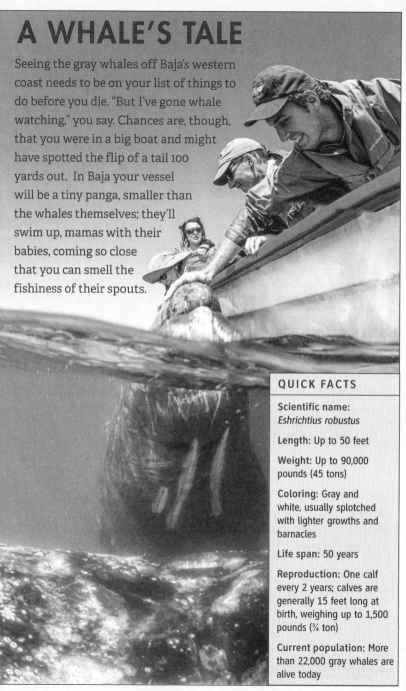

A WHALE'S TALE

Seeing the gray whales off Baja's western coast needs to be on your list of things to do before you die. "But I've gone whale watching," you say. Chances are, though, that you were in a big boat and might have spotted the flip of a tail 100 yards out. In Baja your vessel will be a tiny panga, smaller than the whales themselves; they'll swim up, mamas with their babies, coming so close that you can smell the fishiness of their spouts.

QUICK FACTS

Scientific name:
Eshrichtius robustus

Length: Up to 50 feet

Weight: Up to 90,000 pounds (45 tons)

Coloring: Gray and white, usually splotched with lighter growths and barnacles

Life span: 50 years

Reproduction: One calf every 2 years; calves are generally 15 feet long at birth, weighing up to 1,500 pounds (¾ ton)

Current population: More than 22,000 gray whales are alive today

Grey whales in the San Ignacio Lagoon.

WHEN TO GO

Gray whales and tourists both head south to Baja around December, staying put through to April to shake off the chill of winter. So the beaches, hotels, restaurants, and bars during whale-watching season will be bustling. Book your room two to three months ahead to ensure a place to stay. The intense experience that awaits you at Magdalena Bay, San Ignacio, or Scammion's Lagoon is worth traveling in high season.

THE GRAY WHALE:
Migrating Leviathan

Yearly, gray whales endure the longest migration of any mammal on earth—some trave 5,000 miles one way between their feeding grounds in Alaska's frigid Bering Sea and their mating/birthing lagoons in sunny Baja California. The whales are bottom-feeders, unique among cetaceans, and stir up sediment on the sea floor, then use their baleen—long, stiff plates covered with hair-like fibers inside their mouths—to filter out the sediment and trap small marine creatures such as crustaceanlike Gammarid amphipods.

DID YOU KNOW?

Gray whales' easygoing demeanor and predilection for near-shore regions makes for frequent, friendly human/whale interactions.

Grey whale encounters in the San Ignacio Lagoon.

WHALE ADVENTURES

Calafia Whales (*www.tourballenas.com*) offers the most convenient gray whale adventure option to those already enjoying their Los Cabos vacations. Round trip-transportation whisks guests from resort to airport to Magdalena Bay and back in a single-day (in time for dinner even), with at least three hours in between devoted to up-close encounters with gray whales.

Whale Watch Cabo (*whalewatchcabo. com*) gets clients to Magdalena Bay a little slower, but the six-hour van ride (both ways) is worth it for six hours of dedicated whale encounters over the course of the two-day adventure, as well as the incredible scenery en route. One night in a hotel and all meals are included, as are the photos taken by your expert guide.

WHALE NURSERIES: THE BEST SPOTS FOR VIEWING

If you want an up-close encounter, head to one of these three protected spots where the whales gather to mate or give birth; the lagoons are like training wheels to prep the youngsters for the open ocean.

Laguna Ojo de Liebre (Scammon's Lagoon). Near Guerrero Negro, this lagoon is an L-shaped cut out of Baja's landmass, protected to the west by the jut of a peninsula.

Laguna San Ignacio. To reach the San Ignacio Lagoon, farther south than Scammon's, base yourself in the charming town of San Ignacio, 35 miles away. This lagoon is the smallest of the three, and along with Scammon's, has been designated a UNESCO World Heritage site.

Bahía de Magdalena. This stretch of ocean, the farthest south, is kept calm by small, low-lying islands (really just humps of sand) that take the brunt of the ocean's waves. Very few people overnight in nearby San Carlos; most day-trip in from La Paz or Loreto.

WHAT TO EXPECT

The experience at the three lagoons is pretty standard: tours push off in the mornings, in pangas (tiny, low-lying skiffs) that seat about eight. Wear a water-resistant windbreaker—it will be a little chilly, and you're bound to be splashed once or twice.

The captain will drive around slowly, cutting the motor if he nears a whale (they'll never chase whales). Often the whales will approach you, sometimes showing off their babies. They'll gently nudge the boat, at times sinking completely under it and then raising it up a bit to get a good, long scratch.

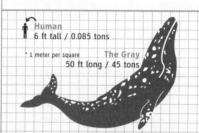

Human
6 ft tall / 0.085 tons

1 meter per square   The Gray
50 ft long / 45 tons

Breaching grey whale at Guerrero Negro.

East Cape in One Day

If you do just one thing in the East Cape, make it snorkeling or diving in **Cabo Pulmo National Park**. This protected marine sanctuary is like an undersea fantasia, with the highest concentration of sea life found anywhere in the Sea of Cortez, from unforgettable tornado-like columns of big eye jacks to dolphins, giant sea turtles, moray eels, manta and mobula rays, and several species of sharks.

Cabo San Lucas–based companies like **Cabo Adventures** (⊕ www.cabo-adventures.com) can provide round-trip transportation to Cabo Pulmo. Driving is part of the fun, though, and allows more freedom to explore on your own schedule. To get there, take either the coast road (primarily dirt) 45 miles from San José del Cabo or the inland Highway 1, about 65 miles.

Local guides from Cabo Pulmo dive centers will show you the eight fingers of offshore coral reef and prime sites

to see incredible marine life. Afterward, relive your undersea adventures with tacos and beer at **Tacos and Beer**, of course. This little comfort food restaurant offers gorgeous beachfront views and laid-back, local atmosphere.

Between drive time and dive time, this will take up the majority of the day. Remember, driving at night is *never* recommended in this rural area due to the conditions of the road and the dangers of collisions with free-ranging livestock. If there are a few hours of free time left, however, head 30 miles up the road to Buena Vista and spring for the day pass ($30) at **Buena Vista Oceanfront & Hot Springs Resort** (⊕ www.buenavistaresort.mx). The roomy hot tub is said to get its hot water from underground thermal hot springs, the pool and beach views are beautiful, generations of family recipes are featured at the beachfront **El Navegante**, and kids will love the Ping-Pong tables.

both deep (nice for jumping) and shallow (nice for standing or floating). ⊠ *Rancho Ecológico Sol de Mayo, Santiago* ☎ *612/219–5409* ⊕ *www.facebook.com/RanchoEcologicoSolDeMayo* 🎫 *$10* ☞ *No pets allowed.*

★ **Parque Nacional Cabo Pulmo**
NATIONAL PARK | At this 27 3/4-square-mile national park, a 20,000-year-old coral reef has been legally protected since 1995 and is home to more than 2,000 different kinds of marine invertebrates—as well as more than 800 species of marine life, from mantas and giant sea turtles to dolphins and sea lions, and most famously, bull sharks, who divers can get face-to-face with year-round. The park comprises both land and sea, and is renowned among diving aficionados for its eight fingers of hard

coral reef, plus its immense abundance of colorful tropical fish. The best months to visit are August, September, and October, when visibility is highest. The park isn't difficult to access. Head southwest from La Ribera and it's just 8 km (5 miles) from the end of the paved road; it's bordered by Playa Las Barracas in the north and Bahía Los Frailes to the south. It can also be reached by the dirt road running along the coast from San José del Cabo. It'll take you two hours or more this way, but the coast along this route is unmatched. (Though, if it's raining, stick to the paved route.) Dive centers line Cabo Pulmo's main street, leading to the beach, all of whom offer dive trips and snorkeling tours, full gear rentals, and more. ⊠ *Camino Cabo Este, Cabo Pulmo* 🎫 *$10.*

Did You Know?

The East Cape is best known for Parque Nacional Cabo Pulmo, a pristine park covering land, sea, and a vibrant coral reef.

188

Trópico de Cáncer

MONUMENT | A globe-shape monument marks the spot where the Tropic of Cancer line (the northernmost circle of latitude at which the sun can be seen directly overhead on the summer solstice) crosses Baja California Sur. The line separates Earth's temperate zone and the tropics. Of course, Baja is Baja, and you won't detect any difference in climate no matter which side of the line you are on. The geographical milepost is easily seen from the highway, but it's worth getting out of the car to pop into the shops surrounding it, which offer arts and crafts from local communities. There are restrooms available (but bring your own toilet paper) and a nice ice-cream shop next door. Also, here is a beautiful shrine to the Virgin of Guadalupe, where Catholics will visit to light candles and pray. It is a stop on a local pilgrimage that takes place each year on the *Dia de la Virgen* (December 12) and ends in nearby Miraflores. ⊠ *Federal Hwy. 1, Km 81, Santiago* ✛ *Between Miraflores and Santiago.*

Beaches

Nine Palms

BEACH | There are more than nine palms here, but who's counting? People who brave the dirt road to this off-the-beaten-track beach are here to surf the rippable right-hand point break. It's about an hour drive northeast from San José del Cabo, along with two other great surf spots, Shipwrecks and Punta Perfecta, which are clustered around La Fortuna and Boca de la Vinorama. The best time to surf is during the summer months, when southwesterly swells provide optimal conditions. But for those seeking only sun, sand, and breathtakingly beautiful views, Nine Palms is a year-round pleasure. **Amenities:** none. **Best for:** surfing; swimming; walking. ⊠ *Camino Cabo Este, La Fortuna.*

Playa La Ribera

BEACH | White sand lines this quiet public beach in La Ribera, a sleepy town just north of Cabo Pulmo National Park. The beach feels almost untouched, with calm water that's great for sportfishing, kayaking, paddleboarding, swimming, and snorkeling. Costa Palmas is just down the beach. **Amenities:** toilets. **Best for:** solitude; snorkeling; swimming. ⊠ *Camino Cabo Este, Km 13.5, La Ribera.*

Playa Los Barriles

BEACH | Playa Los Barriles runs the entire length of town, curving gently toward Bahía de las Palmas. Amazingly, it is almost completely free of people, except from November to March, when wind-sports companies offer rentals during the gusty season and it becomes a jumping-off point for activities including kiteboarding, kitesurfing, windsurfing, and foilboarding. Those seeking sun and sea views recline on chaise lounges at beachfront resorts, and those seeking a congenial atmosphere hang out at restaurants or beach bars set just off the main shoreline. You can drive your ATV or truck onto the beach, and many locals do. Beware of jellyfish in the water. **Amenities:** none. **Best for:** walking; swimming; fishing; wind sports. ⊠ *Los Barriles.*

Restaurants

El Navegante

$$$ | MEXICAN | The dinner menu is forever changing at this family-owned and-run restaurant, and that's a good thing. Whether you order soup and salad, steak or fresh catch of the day prepared any way you like it, this is a one-of-a-kind dining experience with amazing sea views. **Known for:** fresh catch of the day; ever-changing menu; gorgeous ocean-view patio dining. $ *Average main: $25* ⊠ *Buena Vista Oceanfront & Hot Springs Resort, Calle Bonito* ☎ *624/142–0099* ⊕ *hotelbuenavista.com.*

LIMÓN

$ | **SEAFOOD** | Located in the middle of a lemon grove garden, you won't soon forget this alfresco dining experience. Menu items that highlight the peninsula's fresh seafood and produce like bluefin tuna steaks or pork ribs are expertly cooked over an open flame grill. **Known for:** bluefin tuna dishes—tartare, crudo, cheeks, or steaks; fairy light–adorned bushes and trees surround restaurant; fireside seating area. $ *Average main: MP565* ⊠ *Four Seasons Resort Los Cabos at Costa Palmas, Calle Eureka, La Ribera* ☎ *624/980–1054* ⊕ *www.fourseasons.com/loscabos* ⊗ *No lunch.*

Mozza

$ | **ITALIAN** | An outpost of Los Angeles' Michelin-starred Osteria Mozza, Mozza Baja blends the best parts of LA and Italy with the cool, casual spirit of the East Cape. The menu features wood-fired pizzas, pasta dishes, and excellent antipasta options. **Known for:** wood-fired pizza; co-owned by celebrity chef Nancy Silverton; marinafront dining. $ *Average main: MP4344* ⊠ *Costa Palmas Marina Village, La Ribera* ☎ *624/171–3469* ⊕ *www.mozzabaja.com* ⊗ *Closed Mon. No lunch Tues.*

Restaurant & Bar La Playa

$ | **MEXICAN FUSION** | La Playa is one of the nicest places to have fresh seafood or beverage in Los Barriles. It's a little pricey, but everything tastes incredibly fresh, and you can't beat the location or beach access. **Known for:** beachfront dining; mango cocktails; live music. $ *Average main: MP45* ⊠ *Barracuda Blvd., Los Barriles* ⊹ *Off Calle 20 de Noviembre* ☎ *612/131–9336* ⊕ *www.facebook.com/Restaurantandbarlaplaya* ⊗ *No dinner Sun.*

Taqueria El Viejo

$ | **BASQUE** | If you're going to eat at one place in Los Barriles, this family-owned Mexican taqueria should be it. This casual spot quickly becomes every diners favorite eatery serving up delicious

breakfast and lunch options at reasonable prices—don't miss the taco bar. **Known for:** authentic Mexican food; best breakfast in Los Barriles; ample taco toppings. $ *Average main: MP200* ⊠ *C. 20 Noviembre 141, Los Barriles* ⊟ *No credit cards* ⊗ *No dinner.*

Zai Sushi

$ | **SUSHI** | Zai may be one of just a few restaurants in the La Fortuna area, but that doesn't mean you should go only as a default. It is the most buzzed about restaurant in the East Cape, with plenty of diners making the drive up from San José just for a taste of their sushi, which is said to be the best in Los Cabos. **Known for:** vegan options; beautiful presentation of dishes; overlooks the ocean and plenty of surfers. $ *Average main: MP555* ⊠ *Camino Cabo Este, La Fortuna* ☎ *624/191–3645* ⊕ *www.facebook.com/zaisushi* ⊗ *Closed Mon. and Tues.*

☕ Coffee and Quick Bites

Dodo's Sandos

$ | **SANDWICHES** | Sandwiches are a surprisingly uncommon treat in Mexico, prompting local couple Nicole and Robert Ellingwood to meet the need with their gourmet food truck. Located in the Buenos Aires Food Park along with a few other businesses-on-wheels, you can enjoy your "sando" in their shaded yard (stocked with fun yard games for kids young and old) or easily take it to-go. **Known for:** sandwich of the day option comes with chips and a soda; the cubano or bacon burgers; breakfast menu. $ *Average main: MP250* ⊠ *Buenos Aires Food Park, Carretera al Cardonal, Los Barriles* ☎ *612/291–1840* ⊕ *www.instagram.com/dodos.sandos* ⊗ *Closed weekends. No dinner.*

Maxico MX

$ | **BUFFET** | Maxico is the main spot in town for coffee and coworking. The menu features healthy options like avocado toast, omelets, wraps, and smoothies, as

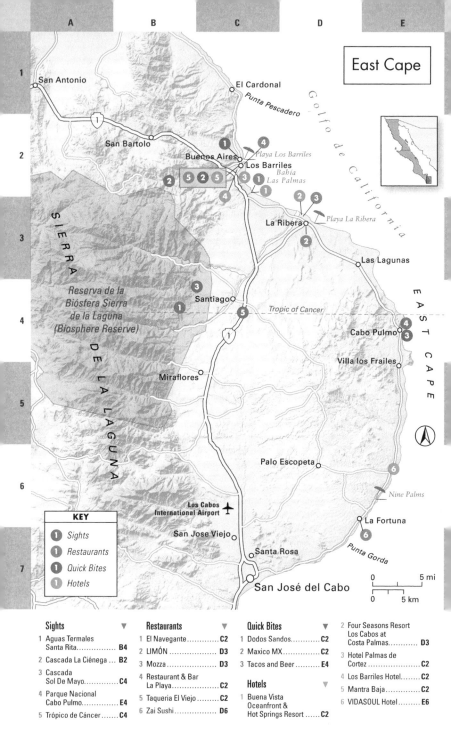

East Cape

A · B · C · D · E

1 San Antonio
El Cardonal
Punta Pescadero

Golfo de California

2 San Bartolo
Buenos Aires
Los Barriles
Playa Los Barriles
Bahía
Las Palmas
La Ribera
Playa La Ribera
Las Lagunas

3 Reserva de la
Biósfera Sierra
de la Laguna
(Biosphere Reserve)
Santiago
Tropic of Cancer
Cabo Pulmo
Villa los Frailes

SIERRA DE LA LAGUNA

EAST CAPE

4 Miraflores

5 Palo Escopeta
Nine Palms

6 Los Cabos
International Airport
San Jose Viejo
Santa Rosa
La Fortuna
Punta Gorda

7 San José del Cabo

0 — 5 mi
0 — 5 km

KEY
1 Sights
1 Restaurants
1 Quick Bites
1 Hotels

Sights ▼
1 Aguas Termales
Santa Rita............... **B4**
2 Cascada La Ciénega ... **B2**
3 Cascada
Sol De Mayo............. **C4**
4 Parque Nacional
Cabo Pulmo............. **E4**
5 Trópico de Cáncer **C4**

Restaurants ▼
1 El Navegante............. **C2**
2 LIMÓN **D3**
3 Mozza.................... **D3**
4 Restaurant & Bar
La Playa................. **C2**
5 Taqueria El Viejo **C2**
6 Zaï Sushi................. **D6**

Quick Bites ▼
1 Dodos Sandos............ **C2**
2 Maxico MX............... **C2**
3 Tacos and Beer **E4**

Hotels ▼
1 Buena Vista
Oceanfront &
Hot Springs Resort **C2**
2 Four Seasons Resort
Los Cabos at
Costa Palmas............ **D3**
3 Hotel Palmas de
Cortez **C2**
4 Los Barriles Hotel........ **C2**
5 Mantra Baja.............. **C2**
6 VIDASOUL Hotel......... **E6**

well as numerous vegetarian and vegan options. **Known for:** healthy meal options; low-fat smoothies; cute decor. $ *Average main:* MP150 ⊠ *Main St., Los Barriles* ☏ *624/132–4268* ⊕ *www.facebook.com/maxicofb.*

Tacos and Beer

$ | MEXICAN | In need of refreshments after a magical day diving or snorkeling in Cabo Pulmo National Park? Stop by Tacos and Beer, and soak up the *muy tranquilo* vibes while you eat delicious seafood tacos and admire views so paradisiacal they look like the set of a Corona commerical. **Known for:** Baja-style fish tacos; locally brewed beer; gorgeous views of Playa Cabo Pulmo and Sea of Cortez. $ *Average main:* $5 ⊠ *Camino Cabo Este, Cabo Pulmo* ☏ *624/191–3081* ⊟ *No credit cards.*

Hotels

Buena Vista Oceanfront & Hot Springs Resort

| RESORT | FAMILY | Underground hot springs are the secret ingredient at this benchmark fishing getaway in Buena Vista; for proof, check out the amazing hot tub. **Pros:** amazing fishing; beautiful beach; enormous swimming pool. **Cons:** no refrigerators; only two rooms have TVs; dated decor in some rooms. $ *Rooms from:* $110 ⊠ *Calle Bonito, Buena Vista* ☏ *624/142–0099* ⊕ *www.buenavistaresort.mx* ⤴ *60 rooms* ⦿| *No Meals.*

★ Four Seasons Resort Los Cabos at Costa Palmas

$$$ | RESORT | More than 2 miles of pristine beach and breathtaking Baja flora surround this five-star resort, where rooms all have spectacular sea views, access to ample amenities, and the personalized luxury only Four Seasons can deliver. **Pros:** chic, contemporary interiors; top-rate spa, on-site dining, and golf course; balconies or plunge pools in every room. **Cons:** expensive;

remote location; far from Cabo San Lucas and San José del Cabo. $ *Rooms from:* $1,350 ⊠ *Calle Eureka, La Ribera* ☏ *624/980–1009* ⊕ *www.fourseasons.com/loscabos* ⤴ *141 rooms* ⦿| *No Meals.*

Hotel Palmas de Cortez

$ | HOTEL | Tried-and-true Palmas de Cortez remains the primary option in Los Barriles for travelers seeking central and comfortable beachfront accommodations. **Pros:** most amenities in town; multibed rooms can fit large families or groups; on-site fishing charters. **Cons:** lack of local competition affects hospitality; online booking isn't available; pricey by Los Barriles standards. $ *Rooms from:* $120 ⊠ *Calle 20 de Noviembre 2, Los Barriles* ☏ *818/224–4744, 877/777–8862 in U.S.* ⊕ *vanwormerresorts.com* ⤴ *74 rooms* ⦿| *No Meals.*

Los Barriles Hotel

$ | HOTEL | If you're looking for a reliable and comfortable place to spend the night, this old-school hotel certainly does the trick. **Pros:** budget-friendly rates; lively swimming pool; complimentary coffee in the morning. **Cons:** often fully booked; decor is dated; no beach or ocean views. $ *Rooms from:* $85 ⊠ *Apartado, Postal 50, Los Barriles* ☏ *624/141–0024* ⊕ *los-barrileshotel.com* ⤴ *20 rooms* ⦿| *No Meals.*

Mantra Baja

$ | HOTEL | The town's first boutique property, Mantra is a welcome fresh face to an otherwise dated Los Barriles. Owner Gunnar Williamson is building the property himself from the ground up, and not a single detail has been overlooked including the design and comfort of the spacious studio-style villas and the provided amenities, like a stocked kitchenette and full set of beach gear. Expansion plans include more rooms and the installation of a pool and spa. **Pros:** extreme comfort and style; friendly owner can act as a local concierge; each villa has a private rooftop terrace with

BBQ dining area. **Cons:** only two villas (for now); likely ongoing construction as the build continues; current view is of an empty lot. ⑤ *Rooms from: $110* ☎ *624/320–5362 Whats App, 940/252–4553 in U.S.* ⊕ *www.mantrabaja.com* ⤳ *2 units* ⦿ *No Meals.*

★ VIDASOUL Hotel
$$ | **HOTEL** | Local art and modern architecture, plus beautiful Sea of Cortez and beach views make this solar-powered, eco-friendly lodging one of the top East Cape accommodations. **Pros:** trendy decor; swimmable beach; warm and welcoming staff. **Cons:** only accessible via the old dirt East Cape Road; more than an hour drive from San José del Cabo; remote from shopping and nightlife areas. ⑤ *Rooms from: $170* ✉ *Camino Cabo Este 1000, Boca de la Vinorama* ☎ *624/154–6966* ⊕ *www.vidasoul.com* ⤳ *16 rooms* ⦿ *No Meals.*

Nightlife

Cactus Restaurant
BARS | This is a townie hangout joint, but then again, that's everywhere in the East Cape. Cactus is one of your best bets in the entire region for nightlife; it can get a little sloppy as it gets late, but you are guaranteed to befriend a friendly expat or 10 on any given visit. There's karaoke every Saturday, though a bigger crowd usually congregates on an outdoor patio with a billiards table. ✉ *Mercado La Costa, Los Barriles* ✛ *Next to Chapitos* ☎ *624/117–9754.*

Crossroads Restaurant
LIVE MUSIC | On most days, this restaurant at the boutique solar-powered VIDASOUL Hotel is a quiet place to enjoy a drink or meal overlooking gorgeous beachfront views of the Sea of Cortez. But on Friday and Saturday night in-season (November through May), live bands play, and it becomes the best of the scant nightlife options between Los Barriles and San José del Cabo. Locals and visitors alike

party down, East Cape style, and the restaurant closes when the last guest goes to bed. ✉ *Camino Cabo Este 1000, Boca de la Vinorama* ☎ *624/154–6966, 626/840–0485 in U.S.* ⊕ *www.vidasoul.com.*

Smokey's Curing Company & Cantina
SPORTS BARS | This sports-bar style cantina is the de facto after-work meeting place in Los Barriles for cocktails and cervezas, or whenever there's a big game on TV. For visitors, the main attraction is the barbecue straight from curing in the on-site smokehouse. Highlights include the pulled pork and the char-grilled chicken breast slathered in Maker's Mark and barbecue sauce. ✉ *Calle 20 de Noviembre 113, Los Barriles* ☎ *624/141–0294* ⊕ *www.facebook.com/bajasmokeys.*

SweetPea's Tiki Bar & Grill
BARS | This warm, unpretentious spot has all-day drink deals and tasty Hawaiian-inspired food. There's often live music, drawing in the same faces night after night. Credit cards aren't accepted, but you can pay with either pesos or dollars, or even PayPal and Venmo. ✉ *Calle 20 de Noviembre, Costa Brava, Los Barriles* ⊕ *www.facebook.com/sweetpeastikibar*

Activities

The East Cape is a world-class playground for a wide variety of outdoor sports, from fishing, diving and surfing to camping, hiking, climbing, and more.

Fishing has long been the major tourist attraction in small towns like Los Barriles and Buena Vista, where the larger resorts either maintain their own fishing fleets or have relationships with local charter boats to refer guests looking to get their hooks into marlin, tuna, dorado, wahoo, roosterfish, and more.

Scuba diving has increasingly become more popular since the offshore coral reef at Cabo Pulmo became protected as part of a larger national park in 1995. The effect of this protected status has been remarkable, and Cabo Pulmo now boasts the highest density of marine life of any area in the Sea of Cortez, an abundance that includes sharks, dolphins, giant sea turtles, mobula rays, and hundreds of colorful tropical fish species.

Some East Cape attractions are more seasonal. For example, each winter when strong El Norte winds blow down the Sea of Cortez, small towns like Los Barriles and La Ventana become windsports meccas. Not only do windsurfers flock here, but also kiteboarders, kitesurfers, foilboarders, and others seeking to take advantage of the ideal 18- to 24-knot winds. If winter means wind, summer means surf off some of the East Cape's pristine beaches thanks to often ideal southwesterly swells.

Inland town Santiago, meanwhile, is the jumping-off point for those who love hiking, camping, and climbing. ATVs are particularly popular in Los Barriles, where expats tool around town on them, but rentals are readily available throughout the region.

GOLF
Costa Palmas Golf Club
GOLF | Tee time access at this gorgeous Robert Trent Jones Jr.–designed course is exclusive to Costa Palmas guests and homeowners. Traffic is light on this 7,221-yard layout, which features spectacular scenery on all 18 holes, including breathtaking backdrops from the nearby Sierra de la Laguna mountain range, and a finish next to the yacht-filled marina. Five sets of tee boxes are on hand for players of various skill levels, as well as two on-site comfort stations/cafés that can be enjoyed by all. Twilight greens fees take effect after 2 pm. ⊠ Costa Palmas East Cape, Calle Eureka-Buenavista, La Ribera ☎ 624/980–0591 ⊕ costapalmas.com/experience/golf-club ⌘ 18 holes, 7,221 yards, par 72 ☞ $300 greens fee for Four Seasons guests; $200 twilight.

SNORKELING AND SCUBA DIVING
Cabo Pulmo Dive Center
SCUBA DIVING | Cabo Pulmo Dive Center provides some of the more exceptional dives in the area and has everything you need, including multiday certification classes. This five-star PADI-certified outfit is a local family-run shop. It's right on the beach and offers full diving services, as well as cheap rooms at the adjoining solar-powered Cabo Pulmo Beach Resort from $100 per night. ⊠ Camino Cabo Este, Cabo Pulmo ☎ 624/212–0097 ⊕ www.cabopulmo.com ⌘ 2-tank dives: $150. Equipment rentals: $33/day. Snorkeling tours: $80.

Cabo Pulmo Sport Center
DIVING & SNORKELING | Visit four diverse and different snorkeling sites at Cabo Pulmo National Park with a certified guide. A mask, fins, water, and snacks are included. ⊠ Camino Cabo Este, Cabo Pulmo ✛ Acceso Principal a la Playa (Main Beach Access) ☎ 624/157–9795 ⊕ www.cabopulmosportcenter.com ⌘ $70.

SPA
Oasis Spa at Four Seasons Resort Los Cabos
SPA | Romantic experiences are a specialty at Oasis Spa, where two of the eight on-site treatment rooms are set aside solely for couples. But other massages are expertly applied, too, including the signature 90-minute version which incorporates hot stones and indigenous herbs. The spa's wet area, which include a sauna, steam room, hydrotherapy whirlpools, and individual cold pools, are available to all guests with or without booking a treatment. Those who want to maintain their workout regimen on vacation will find a state-of-the-art fitness center with Sea of Cortez views, as well as tennis and basketball courts and an Olympics-style lap pool. ⊠ Four Seasons Resort Los Cabos at Costa Palmas, Calle Eureka, La Ribera ⊕ www.fourseasons.com/loscabos/spa.

SPORTFISHING

Just north of Cabo Pulmo (where you are not allowed to fish), there are a number of excellent spots to try your luck at hooking a marlin, tuna, giant sea bass, or snapper. Many hotels in Los Barriles or Buena Vista were built with charter fishing in mind, and it's easy to book a fishing trip through them. If you contact a fisherman directly, however, you're bound to get better prices; Anzuelo Sport Fishing Fleet in Los Barriles is a popular one.

Hotel Palmas de Cortez

FISHING | Hotel Palmas de Cortez is the gold standard for charter fishing in Los Barriles, offering four sizes of fishing vessels, ranging from a superpanga (a 25-foot boat that can accommodate three anglers for $415 per day) to a superdeluxe cruiser (35- or 36-foot boat for six anglers starting at $900), all of which leave from the beachfront dock. Lower rates are available to those who opt for lodging and fishing packages, and a weigh-in station is on hand for the several big tournaments based at the hotel each year, including the East Cape Dorado Shootout in July and the East Cape Gold Cup Wahoo Jackpot in August. ⊠ *Calle 20 de Noviembre 2, Los Barriles* ☎ *624/141–0044, 877/777–8862 in U.S.* ⊕ *vanwormerresorts.com* ☞ *From $415.*

TOURS

CanDoo ATV Rentals

FOUR-WHEELING | A visit to Los Barriles is synonymous with driving an ATV. It's the preferred and primary mode of transportation and you'll see them everywhere you go: on the street, on the beach, on the arroyo. It can get expensive, so decide if you want one just to explore for an afternoon (prices from $120 for four hours) or to serve in lieu of a rental car ($575 for seven days). CanDoo has

a variety of options, seating between one- and six people, and is known to get brand new models every year. ⊠ *Camino al Cardonal s/n esq. Datil., Los Barriles* ☎ *624/142–8945* ⊕ *candoorentals.com.*

WIND SPORTS

Exotikite Kiteboarding

WATER SPORTS | Meet the kiteboarding king of Los Barriles. Like most wind-sports specialists in Los Barriles, Exotikite is only open during the windy season (November to April), offering rentals and intensive, professionally guided lesson packages, with "La Playa" studio accommodations available next door. Surfing and foilboarding lessons are also offered, as are SUP rentals. ⊠ *Accesso a la Playa, Los Barriles* ☎ *624/165–2612, 541/380–0948 in U.S.* ⊕ *www.exotikite. com.*

Vela Baja

WINDSURFING | Vela Baja is open every day during the East Cape wind-sports season (mid-November to mid-March), arranging guided tours for windsurfing, kiteboarding, mountain biking, free diving, and stand-up paddleboarding. Windsurfing is their specialty, with rentals available by the hour ($35), half-day ($60), or day ($80). Lessons start at $90. ⊠ *Hotel Play del Sol, Calle 20 de Noviembre Unica, Los Barriles* ☎ *624/150–4146* ⊕ *velabaja. com.*

Chapter 7

BAJA CALIFORNIA

Updated by
Marlise Kast-Myers

7

 Sights
★★★☆☆

 Restaurants
★★★★★

 Hotels
★★★★☆

 Shopping
★★★☆☆

 Nightlife
★★★☆☆

WELCOME TO BAJA CALIFORNIA

TOP REASONS TO GO

★ **Scenic Driving:** Driving along the Pacific coast south of Tijuana on the Carretera Transpeninsular (Highway 1) is half the fun of traveling to Baja's historic missions and remote beaches.

★ **Wine Tasting:** The Valle de Guadalupe, near Ensenada, is a gorgeous valley blanketed with sprawling vineyards and boutique hotels ranging from eco-lofts to country inns.

★ **Whale-Watching:** Gray whales swim to Baja California every winter to mate and calve in three lagoons on the peninsula's western coast.

★ **Shopping for Handicrafts:** In Ensenada, stores are filled with unique souvenirs in addition to the usual sunglasses and sombreros.

★ **Beach Towns:** Soak up the sun and party on Rosarito Beach, just across the border from California, or indulge in fried lobster by the sea in Puerto Nuevo.

Flanked by the Pacific Ocean to the west and the Sea of Cortez to the east, Baja California comprises the northern half of the Baja peninsula. The majority of the narrow state is accessible by the Carretera Transpeninsular (Highway 1), but it's easy to feel as if you've gone far off the grid when 100 miles of barren land stands between you and the nearest town or gas station. Embrace the feeling; Baja is really Mexico's Wild West and has stark desert landscapes, secluded coves, and striking mountains to prove it.

1 Rosarito. Just 16 km (10 miles) south of the U.S. border are Rosarito's beautiful wide beaches, fronted by a less-than-beautiful town full of touristy bars targeting college students looking for a weekend of partying. Further south is the village of Puerto Nuevo where fried lobster brings in the crowds.

2 Ensenada. A seaport town sandwiched by beaches, Ensenada is home to some of the best fish tacos and margaritas Mexico has to offer.

3 Valle de Guadalupe. Explore the Ruta de Vino dotted with award-winning wineries, farm-to-table restaurants, and boutique hotels with unpretentious hosts.

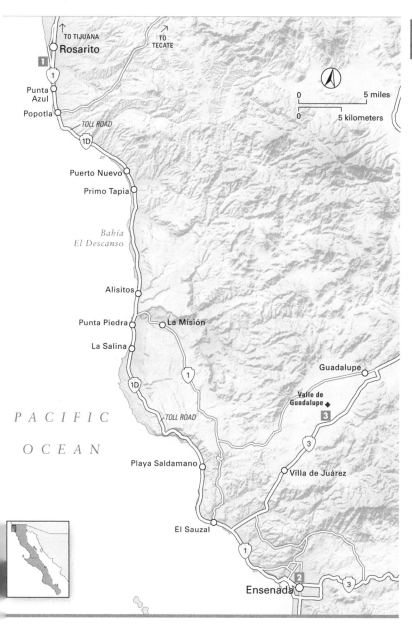

The northern Baja peninsula known as Baja California, may be far from La Paz and Los Cabos in Baja California Sur, but it's no less dreamlike: its beaches have fine brown sand, water that's refreshing but not too cold, sunshine, and some of the West Coast's top waves. The beach towns themselves are not as inspiring or as well known, but they offer incredible vistas and a growing number of beachside experiences en route to Baja's biggest draws: the port town of Ensenada and the vineyards of the Valle de Guadalupe.

Baja California's proximity to Southern California makes it a popular weekend road trip destination. Rosarito, just 30 minutes away from the U.S. border, is a nightlife hot spot for rowdy American spring breakers, as are several towns along the Carretera Transpeninsular (Highway 1). The party crowd can interrupt the serenity that these towns offer midweek before the masses arrive, its wide and long beaches often full of ATVs and horses trotting in the sand. But the longer you stay, the more you'll find that partying is just a small part of the picture. The true riches of Rosarito are found in the authentic Mexican experience, in interactions with the genuine locals, in the courtyard shops and eateries, and in the punchy waves near the pier or further along the coast at Km 38 and Las Gaviotas.

Twenty minutes south is Puerto Nuevo, a small fishing village in Rosarito whose famous fried lobster put it on the map in 1956. These days it's best to stop in for lunch en route to other destinations; be prepared for the reality that many vendors and parking attendants in town may approach to ask you to shop, park, or take a look at a menu. Still, if lobster is on the mind, it's a must-visit stop in Rosarito.

The jewel of Baja's beachside towns is Ensenada, a charming fishermen's enclave with the feel of a small village, complete with beachside trinket stores and fish taco stands (the town's beaches, conversely, are not a big draw). Along this part of the peninsula, towns are close together, and the essentials (gas, food, lodging) are never far. Ensenada's main "downtown" drag along Calle

Primera is worth checking out, though not for everyone. You'll get a repeat of Rosarito's party scene alongside its souvenir shops, tattoo parlors, and motels, but there are a smattering of boutiques, food carts, and restaurants well worth pausing for.

Thirty minutes inland, Valle de Guadalupe is Baja California's pièce de résistance, showcasing Mexico's finest wines and trendiest places to stay. Along the Ruta del Vino are endless vineyards, olive groves, orange orchards, and architectural masterpieces at hip B&Bs. From country inns and luxurious haciendas to container hotels and glamping tents, there's no shortage of lodging—or wine tastings—in this region. Capitalizing on the fertile land are talented young chefs serving refreshing, experimental takes on regional cuisine, their farm-to-table restaurants operating right in the middle of dreamy ranches.

Planning

Getting Here and Around

The main artery of the Baja peninsula is a road of legend: Carretera Transpeninsular (Highway 1) winds down from Tijuana to Los Cabos through deserts and coastal bluffs, past fertile estuaries, and through bleak towns that eke out a few crops from the dry soil. A faster alternative to the coastal road is Highway 1D connecting Tijuana to Ensenada. Three toll booths in Tijuana, Rosarito Beach, and Ensenada charge MXN $50 to pass.

If you're driving into Baja California from San Diego during peak hours, you might try heading 35 km (19 miles) east to the much less congested border crossing at Tecate. From there, Highway 3 takes you south through the Valle de Guadalupe to Ensenada.

Highway 3 continues southeast from Ensenada over the San Martír Pass, where it meets Highway 5. From here you can head north to Mexicali or south to San Felipe, where the road ends. In northern Baja, Highway 2 hugs the border from Mexicali to Tijuana. Although the hairpin turns make for beautiful overlooks during the day, the road east of Tecate is best avoided at night.

If you're driving in from the United States, purchase Mexican insurance (required) from any of the brokers near the border. It's also possible to rent a car in Tijuana or Mexicali from any of the major chains. Pack plenty of water and make sure your tires are in good shape: although the major highways are well-maintained, a number of smaller roads are unpaved.

There are few international flights into Tijuana, Baja California's only major airport. Aeroméxico flies to Los Cabos, to La Paz on the Baja Peninsula, and to several cities in mainland Mexico. Alaska Airlines, Spirit, Southwest, United, Delta, and American all fly into Los Cabos. American Airlines operates flights from Phoenix to Tijuana.

It's also possible to park in the secured lot in San Diego at the Cross Border Xpress (CBX). This pedestrian bridge connects the Tijuana International Airport with its terminal in San Diego.

Restaurants

With a modern history not much older than the Carretera Transpeninsular, most Baja California towns have appropriated their local cuisine from the cultures of mainland Mexico. In many regions, the best lunches and dinners are had at curbside taco stands, where fried fish is served atop tortillas—with shredded cabbage and salsa to add at your discretion. Exceptional restaurants are available in Ensenada and Valle de Guadalupe where award-winning chefs offer farm-to-table experiences. You can also try something more familiar, such as BajaMed cuisine (fusion of Mexican and Mediterranean) or Caesar salad, both of which were invented in this region. When restaurants are limited, opt for the local hot spot, which is always a better option than paying premium for half-baked takes on "international cuisine."

Hotels

Expect private bathrooms, daily housekeeping service, Wi-Fi, a secure parking lot, and clean quarters in all but the most basic of establishments. Many hotels offer breakfast for an extra fee, and swimming pools are prevalent. Luxury is never far in Baja California; almost every touristed locale has at least one "Resort & Spa" that tacks on Jacuzzis, massages, and dollar signs to the above basics (especially along the coast near Ensenada). Be aware that only camping (no hotels) is available in some of Baja smaller towns, including those on Highway 1 between Ensenada and San Quintín, and those on Highway 3 between Ensenada and San Felipe.

What It Costs in U.S. Dollars			
$	$$	$$$	$$$$
RESTAURANTS			
under $15	$15–$25	$25–$35	over $35
HOTELS			
under $150	$150–$250	$251–$300	over $300

⇨ *Restaurant and hotel reviews have been shortened. For full information, visit Fodors.com.*

When to Go

Like the American Southwest, Baja California's weather is conducive to year-round travel, though "peak season" will have a different meaning for beachgoers and marine-life enthusiasts. The deserts can be sweltering between May and October, and parts of the Pacific coast are chilly between November and February. Whale-watching season on the Pacific runs roughly from December to late March, and although fishing is possible all year-round, local experts consider the summer months the best time to hook a big one.

In Valle de Guadalupe, the vines are fully matured in June and July, but April to May or October to November are best to avoid the scorching heat.

If you happen to be in Ensenada in March, don't miss the Ensenada Beer Fest. As Mexico's largest craft beer festival, the event brings together 130 breweries, 30 restaurants, and live music over the course of two days. Dates fluctuate year-to-year, so visit *www.ensenadabeerfest.com* for more info.

Rosarito

29 km (18 miles) south of Tijuana.

Southern Californians use Rosarito (population 126,000) as a weekend getaway, and during school vacations, especially spring break, the crowd becomes one big party. Off-season, the area is more *tranquilo.* The beach here, which stretches from the power plant at the north end of town to about 8 km (5 miles) south, is long with beautiful sand and sunsets, but it's less romantic for the party scene that booms every few minutes.

Just across the border from the United States, Rosarito's beaches are popular with the spring break crowd.

If staying the night, head out to the beach near the pier in front of Rosarito Beach Hotel, or head an hour inland for wine tasting in Valle de Guadalupe.

On the southern end of Rosarito, the lobster village of Puerto Nuevo is worth a visit where you can find about 20 restaurants serving grilled or fried lobster. Artisans' markets and stands throughout the village sell serapes (colorful, striped blanket shawl), paintings, ponchos, sombreros, T-shirts, and sour tamarind candy.

GETTING HERE AND AROUND

Rosarito is off Highway 1 about 30 minutes south of the border. Follow the exit road directly into town. Twelve miles (19 km) from the main center is the lobster village of Puerto Nuevo beside the Carretera Transpeninsular (Highway 1). When you pull off the highway and enter the town, it's best to park and explore by foot in this five-block hamlet.

CAR RENTAL Alamo. ⊠ *Blvd. Cuauhtemoc 1705, Zona Río* ☎ *664/686–4040, 800/849–8001* ⊕ *www.alamo.com.mx.*

 Sights

Puerto Nuevo

TOWN | In 1956 local Susana Diaz Plascencia first created the fried lobster recipe that put Puerto Nuevo on the map. Today more than a dozen restaurants are packed into this little five-block village that's 19 km (12 miles) south of Rosarito. Nearly all of the restaurants offer the same menu, but the quality varies drastically; some establishments cook up live lobsters, while others swap in frozen critters. Though the fried version is the Puerto Nuevo classic, some restaurants also offer steamed or grilled lobsters.

The town itself is dated, with waitstaff standing curbside to pressure tourists in passing cars to stop in for the day's catch. Watch your step along steep and uneven sidewalks where gaping holes can easily ruin a vacation. Still it's the best spot along the coast to try fresh lobster at a fair price. Expect a tableside serenade of mariachi music. If you want to explore a bit, souvenir stands throughout the village sell serapes, ponchos, sour tamarind candy, and other similar items. ✉ *Coastal Rd., Carretera Libre a Ensenada, at Km 44, Puerto Nuevo.*

 Beaches

Rosarito Beach

BEACH | Directly behind Rosarito Beach Hotel is your best bet for a true Baja beach experience. Fine sand, a wide strand, palapa umbrellas, and rolling waves near the pier make this a top choice south of the border. As Rosarito's most popular beach, it's also the hub for water sports and beach activities, meaning sunbathing might be interrupted by ATVs, horses, and partiers. Plenty of bars and restaurants are scattered nearby in downtown, and decent waves can be found between Rosarito and La Fonda at Km 59; the best breaks are around Km 38 approaching Puerto Nuevo. Point breaks and beach breaks abound the farther south you go, and you'll be treated to stunning coastlines where no-name breaks might beckon you toward the water. Park in a secured, paid lot (there's one at Rosarito Beach Hotel); and never leave valuables in your vehicle. Equipment rental, food, and restrooms can be found at Rosarito Beach Hotel. **Amenities:** food and drink; parking (fee); toilets; water sports. **Best for:** partiers; surfing; walking. ✉ *Blvd. Benito Juárez 31, Playas de Rosarito.*

 Restaurants

Colectivo Surf Tasting Room

$$ | **SEAFOOD** | If you need fuel after a day at the beach, walk across the street at Km 41 to this two-story blue collective where you'll find everything from poke bowls to craft beer. A tribute to surfing and all-things-local, Colectivo Surf serves produce from local farmers, fish from *pangueros* (fisherman) along Baja's coast, organic wine from Valle de Guadalupe,

and small batch beers from their own brewery. **Known for:** live music Friday–Sunday in summer; crispy fish tacos; artisanal beers on tap. ⑤ *Average main: $15* ✉ *Carretera libre Tijuana Rosarito–Ensenada, Km 41, Playas de Rosarito* ✚ *5 min south of Rosarito* ☎ *661/125–4144* ⊕ *www.colectivosurf.com.*

El Nido Steakhouse

$$$ | **STEAK HOUSE** | A dark, wood-paneled restaurant with leather booths, Mexican antiques, and a large central fireplace, this is one of Rosarito's oldest eateries, and the best in town for atmosphere. Diners unimpressed with newer, fancier places come here for grilled venison, lamb, and quail from the owner's farm in the Baja wine country. **Known for:** tortillas made table-side; strong margaritas; venison with quail eggs. ⑤ *Average main: $30* ✉ *Benito Juárez 67, Rosarito* ☎ *661/612–1430* ⊕ *www.elnidorosarito. net.*

La Casa de la Langosta

$$$ | **SEAFOOD** | **FAMILY** | Seafood soup and grilled fish are options at the "House of Lobster," but clearly the lobster, fried Puerto-Nuevo style, is the star. This is one of the best spots in town to try the deep-fried recipe created by Susana Diaz Plascencia in 1956; otherwise, try their fresh lobster steamed or stewed with seafood and salsa inside a traditional molcajete stone. **Known for:** fresh marlin soup; large portions; lobster prepared five different ways. ⑤ *Average main: $30* ✉ *Av. Renteria 3, Km 44, Puerto Nuevo* ☎ *661/614–1072* ⊕ *www.instagram.com/casalangosta.*

★ Mi Casa Supper Club

$$$ | **INTERNATIONAL** | What began as an underground supper club is now among the leading restaurants in Rosarito. Inspired by the founders' international travels, the decor reflects their love for Morocco and Bali while the regularly changing menu celebrates the Mediterranean and Mexico in dishes that incorporate local fish, such as yellowfin tuna with almond mojo. **Known for:** red velvet churros with dark chocolate; Sunday brunch and live music; seven-course tasting menu. $ *Average main: $31* ✉ *Estero 54, San Antonio Del Mar, Rosarito* ✛ *10 km (6 miles) north of Rosarito* ☎ *664/609–3459* ⊕ *micasasupperclub. wixsite.com/menu* ⊘ *Closed Mon.–Wed. No lunch Thurs. and Fri.*

Susanna's

$$ | **ECLECTIC** | In addition to the fresh Southern California cuisine, many come to this restaurant to connect with the charming owner Susanna who moved to Rosarito years ago to open a furniture shop. Her love for fine food prevailed, thus turning her store into a restaurant that makes people feel right at home. **Known for:** fresh California cuisine; homemade breads; sweet dressings and glazes. $ *Average main: $20* ✉ *Blvd. Benito Juárez 4356, Publo Plaza, Playas de Rosarito* ☎ *661/613–1187* ⊕ *www. susannasinrosarito.com* ⊘ *Closed Tues.*

Hotels

Rosarito Beach Hotel & Spa

$$ | **HOTEL** | Charm and location have the slight edge over comfort at this landmark hotel built in 1924. **Pros:** close to the beach; antique charm; good Sunday brunch. **Cons:** older furnishings; overpriced; slow elevator. $ *Rooms from: $199* ✉ *Blvd. Benito Juárez 31, Centro, Rosarito* ✛ *In front of Rosarito Beach Pier* ☎ *661/612–0144, 800/343–8582* ⊕ *www. rosaritobeachhotel.com* ⥮ *495 rooms* ⦿⊘ *No Meals* ☞ *Fast-track pass for border crossing often available for $35.*

Nightlife

Papas & Beer

BARS | Papas & Beer, one of the most popular bars in Baja California, draws a young, energetic spring-break crowd for drinking and dancing on the beach. The $5 beers and mechanical bull make for an entertaining combination. ✉ *Coronado 400, Playas de Rosarito* ✛ *On beach off Blvd. Benito Juárez* ☎ *661/612–0444* ⊕ *www.papasandbeer.com.*

Ensenada

65 km (40 miles) south of Puerto Nuevo.

The Yumano people were the original inhabitants of what is now Ensenada; the Spanish arrived in 1542 to the seaport that Sebastián Vizcaíno named Ensenada-Bahía de Todos Santos (All Saints' Bay) in 1602. Since then the town has drawn a steady stream of explorers and developers. After playing home to ranchers and gold miners, the harbor gradually grew into a major port for shipping agricultural goods, and today Baja's third-largest city (population 523,000) is one of Mexico's largest sea and fishing ports in addition to a popular weekend destination for Southern Californians.

There are no beaches in Ensenada proper other than a man-made cove at Hotel Coral, but sandy stretches north and south of town are satisfactory for swimming, sunning, surfing, and camping. Estero Beach is long and clean, with mild waves; the Estero Beach Resort takes up much of the oceanfront, but the beach is public. Although not safe for swimming, the beaches at several of the restaurants along the Carretera Transpeninsular (Highway 1) are a nice place to enjoy a cocktail with a view. Surfers populate the strands off Highway 1 north and south of Ensenada, particularly San Miguel, Tres Marías, and Salsipuedes, while scuba divers prefer Punta Banda, by La Bufadora. Lifeguards are rare, so be cautious.

Both the waterfront and the main downtown street, Calle Primera, are pleasant places to stroll. If you're driving, be sure to take the Centro exit from the highway, since it bypasses the commercial port area.

GETTING HERE AND AROUND

If you're flying into Tijuana, from Aeropuerto Alberado Rodriguez (TIJ) you can find buses that also serve Rosarito and Ensenada. Or you can hop on a bus at Tijuana Camionera de la Línea station, just inside the border, with service to Rosarito and Ensenada along with city buses to downtown. To head south from Tijuana by car, follow the signs for Ensenada Cuota, the toll road Carretera 1D along the coast. Tollbooths accept U.S. and Mexican currency; there are three tolls of about $2.50–$4 each between Tijuana and Ensenada. Restrooms are available near toll stations. Ensenada is an hour south of Tijuana on this road. The alternative free road—Carretera Transpeninsular Highway 1, or Ensenada Libre—is curvy and not as well maintained. (Entry to it is on a side street in a congested area of downtown Tijuana.)

Highway 1 continues south of Ensenada to Guerrero Negro, at the border between Baja California and Baja Sur, and on to Baja's southernmost resorts; there are no tolls past Ensenada. Highway 1 is fairly well maintained and signposted.

Although there are several rental car companies in Tijuana, Alamo is one of the few that includes insurance and tax in the quoted rate, rather than tacking on hidden fees at arrival. Drivers must carry mandatory third-party liability, an expense that is not covered by U.S. insurance policies or by credit card companies.

If driving your own vehicle across the San Ysidro border, ask your hotel if they offer a Fast Track Pass, which helps eliminate the long border wait on the return. If you hold a SENTRI pass , there is a designated fast lane at the San Ysidro entrance but not at the Tecate Port of Entry. Otherwise, on weekends expect to wait around three hours at San Ysidro and one hour at Tecate. Border wait times are available at ⊕ bwt.cbp.gov.

Taxis are a reliable means of getting around Ensenada, and you can flag them down on the street.

VISITOR INFORMATION Emergencies. ⊠ *Ensenada* ☎ *911.* **Ensenada Tourist Information Office.** ⊠ *Blvd. Costero 546, Zona Playitas* ✛ *Just south of cruise ship terminal* ☎ *646/624–2020* ⊕ *www.bajacalifornia.travel.* **Green Angels.** ⊠ *Ensenada* ☎ *078.*

Sights

Avenida López Mateos (*Calle Primera*)

STREET | Avenida López Mateos, commonly known as Calle Primera, is the center of Ensenada's traditional tourist zone and shopping district. Hotels, shops, restaurants, and bars line the avenue for eight blocks, from its beginning at the foot of the Chapultepec Hills to the dry channel of the Arroyo de Ensenada. The avenue also has sidewalk cafés, art galleries, and most of the town's souvenir stores, where you can find pottery, glassware, silver, and other Mexican crafts. ⊠ *Av. López Mateos, Ensenada.*

La Bufadora

NATURE SIGHT | Legend has it that La Bufadora, an impressive tidal blowhole (la bufadora means the buffalo snort) in the coastal cliffs at Punta Banda, was created by a whale or sea serpent trapped in an undersea cave. The road to La Bufadora along Punta Banda—an isolated, mountainous point that juts into the sea—is lined with olive, craft, and tamale stands; the drive gives you a sampling of Baja's wilderness. If you're in need of some cooling off, turn off the highway at the sign for La Jolla Beach Camp. The camp charges a small admission fee for day use of the beachside facilities, but it's a great place to do a few "laps" of lazy freestyle or breaststroke at La Jolla Beach. At La Bufadora, expect a small fee to park, and then a half-mile walk past T-shirt hawkers and souvenir stands to the water hole itself. A public bus runs from the downtown Ensenada station to Maneadero, from which you can catch a minibus labeled Punta Banda that goes to La Bufadora. Guided tours from Ensenada to La Bufadora will run you about $40. ⊠ *Carretera 23, Punta Banda* ⊕ *31 km (19 miles) south of Ensenada.*

La Cava de Marcelo

FARM/RANCH | FAMILY | For many, a visit to Baja Norte must include an afternoon drive to the cheese caves of Marcelo in Ojos Negros, just 45 minutes outside Ensenada. With Swiss-Italian roots, owner Marcelo Castro Chacon is now the fourth generation to carry on the *queso* tradition since it first began in 1911. A visit to the farm includes a tour of the milking facilities and a tasting of seven cheeses and their signature Ramonetti red wine. Milder selections seasoned with basil, black pepper, and rosemary are more popular with locals than their sharper cheeses, aged up to 2½ years, loved by out-of-towners. As Mexico's only cheese cave (and the first in Latin America), this beloved factory produces 450 pounds of cheese per day. Milking takes place at 5 pm daily and the small on-site shop sells the remarkable marmalade and wine that accompany your cheese tasting. Those with time and an appetite can dine under the shade of a peppertree for a lunch menu integrating Marcelo's cheeses and organic fruits and vegetables from his farm (expect flies in summer). The cactus salad and portobello mushrooms with melted cheese make the ideal starters to the regional trout served with roasted garlic. The fig mousse alone is worth a visit. Be aware that cell service is limited and the road here is winding. ⊠ *Rancho La Campana, Carretera Ensenada–San Felipe, Km 43, 48 km (30 miles) east of Ensenada, Ojos Negros* ⊕ *Off Hwy. 3, follow signs to La Cava de Queso* ☎ *646/117–0293* 🖂 *$20 tour and tasting* 🕑 *Closed Mon.–Wed.*

Las Bodegas de Santo Tomás
(*Cava Miramar*)

WINERY | Baja's oldest wine producers gives tours and tastings at its downtown Ensenada winery and bottling plant. Santo Tomás's best wines are the Alisio Chardonnay, the Cabernet, and the Tempranillo; avoid the overpriced Único. The winery also operates the enormous wineshop, a brick building across the avenue. The Santo Tomás Vineyards can be found on the eastern side of Highway 1 about 50 km (31 miles) south of Ensenada in Santo Tomás Valley, fairly near the ruins of the Misión Santo Tomás de Aquino, which was founded by Dominican priests in 1791. They have a third facility, Cava San Antonio de las Minas, at the entrance to Valle de Guadalupe at Km 94.7. ⊠ *Av. Miramar 666, Centro* ☎ *646/178–3333* ⊕ *www.facebook.com/BodegasdeSantoTomas1888* 🖂 *4 tastings $15.*

Mercado de Mariscos (*Mercado Negro*)

MARKET | At the northernmost point of Boulevard Costero, the main street along the waterfront, is an indoor-outdoor fish market where row after row of counters display piles of shrimp, tuna, dorado, and other fish caught off Baja's coasts. Outside, stands sell grilled or smoked fish, seafood cocktails, and fish tacos. You can pick up a few souvenirs, eat well for very little money, and take some great photographs. If your stomach is delicate, try the fish tacos at the cleaner, quieter Plaza de Mariscos in the shadow of the giant beige Plaza de Marina that blocks the view of the traditional fish market from the street. ⊠ *At boardwalk pier, Boulevard Costero, Ensenada.*

Beaches

Playa La Misión

BEACH | Halfway between Rosarito and Ensenada, this wide strand of sand is a great place to escape the masses. Palapa umbrellas line the sand making it feel more private than other beaches (local families arrive on Sunday), but you'll still

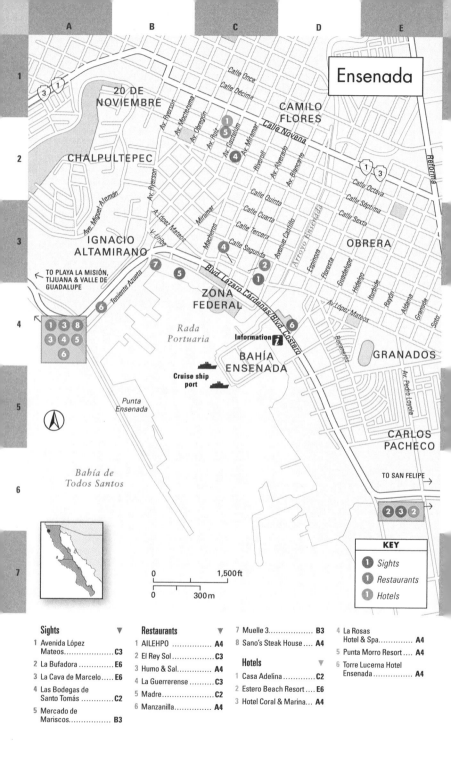

Ensenada

1,500ft
0 — 300m

TO PLAYA LA MISIÓN,
TIJUANA & VALLE DE
GUADALUPE

20 DE
NOVIEMBRE

CHALPULTEPEC

IGNACIO
ALTAMIRANO

ZONA
FEDERAL

Rada
Portuaria

Information

BAHÍA
ENSENADA

Cruise ship
port

Punta
Ensenada

Bahía de
Todos Santos

CAMILO
FLORES

OBRERA

GRANADOS

CARLOS
PACHECO

TO SAN FELIPE →

Blvd. Lázaro Cárdenas/Blvd Costera

KEY

1 Sights
1 Restaurants
1 Hotels

find everything from food and drinks to restrooms and parking. The dark, soft sand is perfect for long walks, but a few rocky sections mean you'll want to bring water shoes or snorkel gear if you venture into the water. Like Rosarito, you can gallop on the beach here, and horse rides will cost you about half the price you'll find elsewhere. Take all your personal belongings with you since car break-ins (especially closest to the bridge) are a problem. **Amenities:** parking; food and drink; toilets. **Best for:** walking; sunsets ⊠ *Federal Hwy. 1, La Misión ✛ Halfway between Rosarito and Ensenada, at Km 31.*

🍽 Restaurants

AILEHPO (*Ophelia*)

$$$ | **ECLECTIC** | Despite the rebrand—a restaurant on the other side of the world forced them to change their name (it's Ophelia backward)—you'll find this garden escape is still a favorite among the Ensenada foodie crowd. Here a blending of European, American, and Asian cuisines and a handful of dependable flavors and ingredients—fresh fish, tomatoes, chilies, and cilantro—mix with unexpected ingredients like shiitake mushrooms, pork, and ginger glazes. **Known for:** portobello tacos and shrimp ceviche; Zen vibe in garden patio; fresh yellowfin tuna. ⑤ *Average main: $35* ⊠ *Carretera Tijuana–Ensenada, Km 103, Ensenada* ☎ *646/175–8365* ⊕ *ailehpo.mx* ۞ *Closed Mon.*

El Rey Sol

$$$ | **FRENCH** | From its chateaubriand *bouquetière* to the savory chicken cooked in prune sauce, this classy French restaurant has been family-owned since 1947. Louis XIV–style furnishings and an attentive staff make it both comfortable and elegant. **Known for:** French pastries; table-side Caesar salad; first-rate service. ⑤ *Average main: $35* ⊠ *Av. López Mateos 1000, Centro* ☎ *646/178–1733* ⊕ *www.elreysol.com.*

Humo & Sal

$$ | **SEAFOOD** | A trendy offspring of neighboring Sano's Steakhouse, "Smoke and Salt" focuses on local seafood with a twist; guests of the casual hot spot can also order from the more formal steak house next door. The bar shakes up tequila and mezcal from small-batch labels and all their wines come from Mexico. **Known for:** fresh oysters; tamarind-mezcal margarita; blue-corn tortillas piled with shrimp and scallops. ⑤ *Average main: $22* ⊠ *Zona Playitas, Carretera Tijuana–Ensenada, Km 108, Zona Playitas* ☎ *646/174–4061* ⊕ *humoysal-baja.negocio.site.*

La Guerrerense

$ | **SEAFOOD** | This food-cart stall off Ensenada's bustling Calle Primera is *the* place where locals get a solid helping of the region's seafood. Established in 1960, La Guerrerense has been featured on international shows like Anthony Bourdain's *No Reservations.* **Known for:** world's best tostadas; fresh ceviche with mango; homemade salsas. ⑤ *Average main: $10* ⊠ *Calle Primera at Alvarado, Ensenada* ☎ *646/206–0445* ⊕ *www.laguerrerense.com* ۞ *Closed Mon. No dinner.*

★ Madre

$$$ | **MEXICAN FUSION** | Tucked away on a quiet street, this Ensenada restaurant is located in an 80-year-old house whose cozy dining room gives a glimpse of the home-turned-restaurant with local artwork and adobe archways piled high with books. Chef Miguel Bahena and Carolina Verdugo have created an innovative Baja fresh menu showcasing oysters with chili butter, squid ink risotto, confit duck with guava mole, and bay scallops with barley. **Known for:** guava galette with mint ice cream; five- and seven-course tasting menus and Sunday brunch; charming respite from downtown Ensenada. ⑤ *Average main: $30* ⊠ *Calle Octava #444, Centro* ☎ *646/183–7588* ⊕ *www.facebook.com/cocinamadreens* ۞ *Closed Mon. No lunch Tues.*

Manzanilla

$$$ | **ECLECTIC** | Two of the most exciting chef-owners in Baja, Benito Molina and Solange Muris, have taken a truly modern approach to Mexican cuisine at Manzanilla, integrating the freshest catches from the local waters—oysters, mussels, abalone, and clams, for instance—and using ingredients like ginger, smoked chilies, fresh herbs, and *huitlacoche* (corn truffle). The ahi with ginger raspberry vinaigrette melts in your mouth, and the white clam with Gorgonzola is delicious. **Known for:** fresh Baja seafood and steak; local beer and wines; grilled quail with wild mushrooms. ⑤ *Average main: $25* ✉ *Recinto Portuario, Teniente Azueta 139, Centro* ☎ *646/175–7073* ⊕ *www.rmanzanilla.com* ⊘ *Closed Mon. and Tues.*

★ Muelle 3

$ | **SEAFOOD** | This marina-front restaurant is a hole in the wall that will blow your mind, starting with the six-course menu. The small patio gives a front-row seat to the boardwalk action where locals stroll, sailboats bob, and seagulls squawk at the day's catch. **Known for:** cozy atmosphere; great prices; fresh-as-can-be house ceviche. ⑤ *Average main: $12* ✉ *Marina Boardwalk, Teniente Azueta 187-B, Centro* ☎ *646/174–0318* ⊕ *www.instagram.com/muelle3ens* ⊘ *Closed Sun. and Mon.*

Sano's Steak House

$$$ | **STEAK HOUSE** | This elegant restaurant, with its white linens, open trusses, and soft candlelight is the best steak house in Baja California. Prepared on mesquite wood, the steak is divine and tender, almost as if it's been marinated in butter (though the chef swears salt and a little love are the secret). **Known for:** aged rib eye; dishes cooked to perfection; old-school steak house vibe. ⑤ *Average main: $35* ✉ *Carretera Tijuana–Ensenada, Km 108, Ensenada* ✢ *Just after Playitas Club del Mar, heading south to Ensenada* ☎ *646/174–4061.*

 Hotels

★ Casa Adelina

$ | **B&B/INN** | As Ensenada's only boutique hotel, this historic home (circa 1887) also happens to be Baja's oldest, with five English-style rooms named after the original owner's favorite flowers—Daisy, Lily, Gardenia, Rose, and Jasmine. **Pros:** attached bistro with stellar service; historic property in great location; outstanding rates and gated parking. **Cons:** often booked; steep staircase to rooms; sound carries between rooms. ⑤ *Rooms from: $133* ✉ *428 Calle Octava between Ruíz and Gastélum, Centro* ☎ *646/151–3355* ⊕ *www.casaadelina.mx* ⇌ *5 rooms* ⒪ *Free Breakfast.*

Estero Beach Resort

$$ | **RESORT** | **FAMILY** | Families love this long-standing resort on Ensenada's top beach, especially because of its private location and endless activities like horseback riding, tennis, volleyball, kayaking, and Jet Skiing. **Pros:** wonderful breakfasts; right on the beach; good for families. **Cons:** rooms by parking lot aren't great; boat launch fee; food somewhat pricey. ⑤ *Rooms from: $200* ✉ *Carretera Tijuana–Ensenada, intersection of Lazaro Cardenas and Lupita Novelo, Estero Beach* ✢ *10 km (6 miles) south of Ensenada* ☎ *646/176–6235, 646/176–6225* ⊕ *www.hotelesterobeach.com* ⇌ *96 rooms* ⒪ *No Meals.*

Hotel Coral & Marina

$$$$ | **RESORT** | **FAMILY** | In addition to its own marina and artificial beach, this all-suites resort has indoor-outdoor pools, a spa, tennis courts, a water-sports center, and a sports bar overlooking the bay. **Pros:** midweek discounts; spacious rooms; outstanding Sunday brunch and daily buffet. **Cons:** pool can get noisy with kids; patchy Wi-Fi; slow elevator. ⑤ *Rooms from: $322* ✉ *Carretera Tijuana–Ensenada, Km 103, Zona Playitas* ☎ *646/175–0000, 800/862–9020 in U.S.*

⊕ www.hotelcoral.com ⟳ 147 suites
❑ No Meals.

Las Rosas Hotel & Spa

$$ | **RESORT** | This intimate hotel north of Ensenada has rooms facing the ocean, but it's the infinity pool spilling into the sea that will take your breath away. **Pros:** laid-back and relaxing; great ocean views; attentive staff. **Cons:** dated rooms; rocky beach; some street noise; weak Wi-Fi signal in rooms. ⓢ Rooms from: $220 ⊠ Carretera Tijuana–Ensenada, Km 105.5, Zona Playitas ⊹ Just north of Ensenada 🕾 646/174–4310, 646/174–4360 ⊕ www. lasrosas.com ⟳ 48 rooms ❑ No Meals.

Punta Morro Resort

$$ | **RESORT** | In one of Ensenada's most beautiful settings, this 27-room hotel has charm and tranquillity to spare with spacious rooms that have balconies facing the ocean. **Pros:** best oceanfront view rooms in Ensenada; great restaurant; personalized service. **Cons:** no bathtubs; uncomfortable couches in rooms; rocky beach not suitable for swimming. ⓢ Rooms from: $229 ⊠ Carretera Tijuana–Ensenada, Km 106, Zona Playitas 🕾 646/178–3507 ⊕ www.hotelpuntamorro.com ⟳ 27 rooms ❑ No Meals.

★ Torre Lucerna Hotel Ensenada

$$$$ | **HOTEL** | The most upscale hotel in Ensenada has a swanky "Mad Men" vibe, right down to the golden pillars, art deco terrace, and paintings of pin-up girls adorning the lobby and suites. **Pros:** spa, pool, and rooftop restaurant on-site; reasonable rates; underground secured parking. **Cons:** street-facing rooms have traffic noise; loud piano in the lobby; no direct beach access. ⓢ Rooms from: $380 ⊠ Carretera Tijuana–Ensenada, Km 108, Zona Playitas 🕾 646/222–2400 ⊕ www.lucernahoteles.com ⟳ 146 rooms ❑ No Meals.

Nightlife

When Valle de Guadalupe shuts down for the night, Ensenada is just getting started. The corner of Avenida Ruiz and Avenida López Mateos (Calle Primera) has the most action, with loud music and cheap beers in a cantina setting. For something a bit more refined, there are a few hip microbreweries near the coast.

Agua Mala

BREWPUBS | Don't be fooled by the name "bad water." This artisanal brewery pours a mean oatmeal stout and imperial IPA. Nearly a dozen handcrafted beers are served in the container bar where menu items like fish tacos and artisanal pizzas pair well with just about everything on tap. ⊠ Carretera Tijuana–Ensenada, Km 104, Ensenada 🕾 646/174–6068 ⊕ www. aguamala.com.mx.

Cerveceria Transpeninsular

BREWPUBS | This two-story brewery is a game changer for Ensenada, luring locals and travelers alike for craft beers in a warehouse-like setting. They have live music, jam sessions, open-mike night, and NFL Sunday. Check their Facebook page for upcoming events and specials. ⊠ Carretera Tijuana 107 and 240, Zona Playitas 🕾 646/175–2620 ⊕ www. cerveceriatranspeninsular.com.

Hussong's Cantina

BARS | Hussong's Cantina has been an Ensenada landmark since 1892, and has changed little since then. Ask anyone here and they'll tell you that this is where the margarita was invented by bartender Don Carlos Orozco in October 1941; however, this is just one of several local establishments that state that claim to fame. Regardless, come by Saturday when you can get two margaritas for the price of one, or two-for-one beers every Tuesday and Thursday. A security guard stands by the front door to handle the often-rowdy crowd. The floor is covered with sawdust, and the noise is usually deafening, pierced by mariachi and ranchera musicians and the whoops and hollers of the pie-eyed. ⊠ *Av. Ruíz 113, Centro* ☎ *646/178–3210* ⊕ *www.cantina-hussongs.com/inicio.html* ⊗ *Closed Mon.*

Papas & Beer

BARS | The massive Papas & Beer attracts a rowdy college crowd. There are daily specials on shots and cocktails, as well as regular drinking contests. Live music takes place on weekends. ⊠ *Av. Ruíz 105, Centro* ☎ *646/178–8826* ⊕ *www. papasandbeer.com.*

Wendlandt Cervecería

BARS | For a casual yet refined bar scene, this chic spot is a favorite of Ensenada's many vintners, chefs, and brewers. Showcasing local beers from the region, as well as wines from nearby Valle del Guadalupe, the friendly owners have literally mastered the craft with their own cervezas that landed them the titles of Mexico's best beer in 2015 and 2019. Beer tastings in their brew pub are available by reservation only. If you're hungry, Wendlandt serves elevated bar food using local ingredients. The nondescript bar is simply marked by their logo and an antique door. ⊠ *Blvd. Costero 248, Centro* ☎ *646/178–2938* ⊕ *www. facebook.com/WendlandtCerveceria* ⊗ *Closed Mon.*

 Shopping

Most of the tourist shops hold court along Avenida López Mateos (Calle Primera) beside the hotels and restaurants. There are several two-story shopping arcades, some with empty spaces for rent. Dozens of curio shops line the street, all selling similar selections of pottery, serapes, and tackier trinkets and T-shirts.

Adobe

SOUVENIRS | This modern shopping court is a one-stop shop for all your gift needs, with six vendors selling vanilla, clothing, pottery, jewelry, accessories, and souvenirs from the region. ⊠ *Av. López Mateos 490, Centro* ⊗ *Closed Mon.*

Bazar Casa Ramirez

LOCAL GOODS | Bazar Casa Ramirez sells high-quality Talavera pottery and other ceramics, paintings by local artists, jewelry from Taxco, wooden carvings, and papier-mâché figurines. Everything here is made in Mexico. Be sure to check out the displays upstairs. ⊠ *Av. López Mateos 498, Centro* ☎ *646/178–8209* ⊕ *www. facebook.com/bcasaramirez.*

Casanegra

SOUVENIRS | This indie boutique specializing in streetwear is the place to go for "cool souvenirs made in Mexico," as owner Juliett puts it. You'll find hats, shirts, jewelry, and vinyl records, plus apothecary products. The shop doubles as a café, meaning you can power up, shop, and hit Ensenada full steam ahead. ⊠ *Quintas Papagayo Hotel, Carretera Tijuana–Ensenada, Km 108, Zona Playitas* ☎ *646/117–2772* ⊕ *www.shopcasanegra. com* ⊗ *Closed Wed.*

 Activities

SPORTFISHING

The best angling takes place from April through October, with bottom fishing the best in winter. Charter vessels and party boats are available from several outfitters along the boardwalk and off the sportfishing pier. Mexican fishing licenses for the day ($13) are available from charter companies.

Sergio's Sportfishing

FISHING | One of the best sportfishing companies in Ensenada, Sergio's Sportfishing has year-round private charter or open party boats. Whale-watching tours are available from December 15 to April 15. ⊠ *Sportfishing Pier, Blvd. Lázaro Cárdenas 6, Centro* ☎ *646/178–2185, 619/399–7224 in U.S.* ⊕ *www.sergios-fishing.com* ✆ *Fishing $80 per person or a group boat, including the $13 cost of a license; whale-watching $40 per person.*

WATER SPORTS

Estero Beach and Punta Banda (en route to La Bufadora, south of Ensenada) are both good kayaking areas, although facilities are limited. A small selection of water-sports equipment is available at the Estero Beach Resort.

WHALE-WATCHING

Boats leave the Ensenada sportfishing pier for whale-watching trips from late December through March. The gray whales migrating from the north to bays and lagoons in southern Baja pass through Todos Santos Bay, often close to shore. Binoculars and cameras with telephoto capabilities come in handy. The trips last about four hours. Vessels are available from several outfitters at the sportfishing pier. Expect to pay about $40 for a three-hour tour.

Valle de Guadalupe

80 km (50 miles) southeast of Rosarito.

The Valle de Guadalupe, 15 minutes northeast of Ensenada on Carretera 3, is filled with vineyards, wineries, and rambling hacienda-style estates. Although Mexican wines are still relatively unknown in the United States, the industry is exploding in Mexico, and the Valle de Guadalupe is responsible for some 90% of the country's production. In 2004 there were 35 wineries in production, and today there are more than 200, including Bodegas de Santo Tomas, the oldest winery in Baja California.

Along with this splurge of growth comes award-winning chefs setting up "farm-to-fork" restaurants where nearly everything on their menu is harvested right outside their door. Designers, architects, and hoteliers are getting in on the action with dreamy properties ranging from villas and ranches to haciendas and eco-lofts. Lavender fields and bougainvillea add a splash of color to hillsides framing alfresco eateries with menus that will put most culinary destinations to shame. It's the patchwork of vineyards producing impressive blends that keep visitors coming back for more.

With a region that combines the right heat, soil, and a thin morning fog, some truly world-class boutique wineries have developed in the Valle de Guadalupe, most in the past decade. Many of these are open to the public; some require appointments. Several tour companies, including Bajarama Tours (☎ *646/178–3252*), leave from Ensenada on tours that include visits to wineries, a historical overview, transportation, and lunch. Better yet, visit the wineries yourself by car, as they all cluster in a relatively small area.

It seems that it's not only Mexican wine that's being discovered, but the potential of Guadalupe as a "wine destination," along with the mixed blessings that accompany such discovery.

Consequences of its growth include major development pre-Covid, which today has left some properties half-constructed and abandoned. In dry season, wineries tap into private reservoirs to keep the harvest alive during water shortages. Despite these challenges, Valle de Guadalupe is a sustainable destination, with practices of ecological architecture, energy efficiency, organic and biodynamic techniques, and waste reduction.

WHEN TO GO

The ideal time to visit Valle de Guadalupe's wine country is April to May or October to November to avoid the scorching heat. The vines fully mature in June and July. The annual Grape Harvest Festival (Fiestas de la Vendimia) runs from the end of July to the first two weeks of August. This celebration brings in thousands of wine lovers who commemorate the harvest with wine tastings, cultural blessings, live music, and elaborate paella feasts. Be sure to make hotel reservations well in advance.

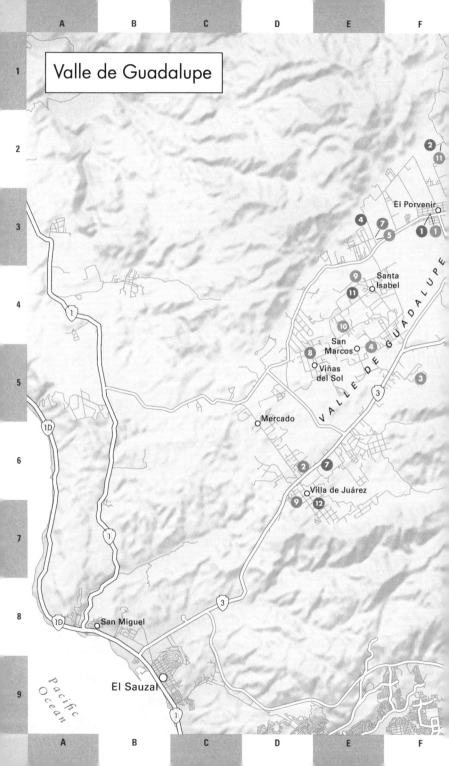

Valle de Guadalupe

El Porvenir

Santa
Isabel

San
Marcos

Viñas
del Sol

V A L L E   D E   G U A D A L U P E

Mercado

Villa de Juárez

San Miguel

El Sauzal

Pacific
Ocean

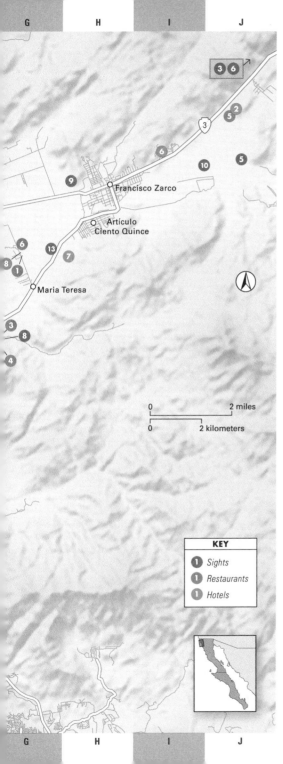

Baja California VALLE DE GUADALUPE

7

Sights ▼

Restaurants ▼

Hotels ▼

Francisco Zarco

Artículo
Ciento Quince

Maria Teresa

KEY

1 Sights
1 Restaurants
1 Hotels

0   2 miles
0   2 kilometers

GETTING HERE AND AROUND

If you're not on a tour, a private car (or hired taxi) is essential for touring the wine country. Main roads through the valley are paved. Once you branch off toward vineyards, you'll likely be on dirt roads, although progress is being made to smooth out roads to the larger wineries. The turnoffs for the major wineries are well marked; if you're looking for a smaller destination, you may end up doing a few loops or asking a friendly bystander. The general area is not too spread out, but you'll need to drive from one winery to the other. Watch out for hidden stop signs at nearly every street crossing. You can arrange a half- or full-day tour with many of the taxi drivers in Ensenada, and some drivers in Tecate may also be willing to take you. Expect to pay from $150 for a full day of transportation.

ESSENTIALS

Banks are few and far between in this area, so get cash before arriving. Nearly every business accepts credit cards and U.S. dollars. There are two gas stations in town: one at the entrance to the valley near Ensenada, and the second where Highway 3 meets Highway 1.

◉ Sights

Adobe Guadalupe

WINERY | Adobe Guadalupe makes an array of fascinating old-world-style blends named after angels. Don't miss the Rafael, which is a blockbuster blend; the Serafiel, Gabriel, and Miguel are also excellent. Gaining wide notice is the Jardín Romántico—100% Chardonnay—and, of course, the powerful tequila and mezcal. Tastings are offered daily 10–5 and include four reds, one white, and one rosé for $27 (free to hotel guests). Shipping is available. Be sure to visit the wine store and tapas food truck on your way out. ☒ Off Carretera Tecate–Ensenada,

Valle de Guadalupe ✛ Turn at sign and drive 6 km (4 miles) ☎ 646/155–2094 ⊕ www.adobeguadalupe.com ☒ From $27 ⚲ Reservations essential.

★ Baron Balché

WINERY | Despite up-and-coming wineries fighting for the spotlight, this premier producer is still considered the Rolls-Royce of Valle de Guadalupe's wineries. During the pandemic, the grounds were expanded to include a market, café, and restaurant. The wine tours are next level, unveiling an entire underground labyrinth of barrel hallways and tasting rooms where you can sample some of the most intense, bold wines in the valley. The majority of their wines live three years in the barrel, and four years in the bottle before hitting the shelf. Logos on the premium line are based on Mayan numbers, with outstanding selections like the Balché UNO, a Grenache with hints of raspberry and caramel. The Balché CERO 100% Nebbiolo is the king of their wines, having aged four years in the barrel. Even their younger wines are exceptional, which is understandable with old vines and French barrels behind the story, but expect to pay a hefty price to try them. Tastings for top selections will cost you about $60, but considering you are sampling $200 bottles of wine, it just might be worth it. Be sure to end your wine tour here, otherwise the rest of your tastings might pale in comparison. ☒ Ej. El Porvenir, Valle de Guadalupe ☎ 646/155–2141 ⊕ www.baronbalche.com ☒ Tastings from $18.

Casa de Piedra

WINERY | The brainchild of Hugo D'Acosta, Casa de Piedra is part of an impressive portfolio that includes Paralelo, Aborigen, and La Borde Vieille, known for its Mexican and French blends. Try Casa de Piedra's flagship wine Contraste or their sparkling wines. The space is interesting and modern, designed by the winemaker's architect brother. Visits are

Adobe Guadalupe Winery and Inn was one of the first vineyards in the region and names its wines after angels.

by reservation only. ✉ *Carretera Tecate–Ensenada, Km 93.5, San Antonio de las Minas* ☎ *646/155–5267, 646/278–6898* ⊕ *www.vinoscasadepiedra.com* ✉ *Tastings from $50* ⊗ *Closed Tues. and Wed.*

El Cielo

WINERY | Considered a giant among the region's vineyards, this winery produces 30,000 cases of wine, has its own concert venue, private villas, and the popular restaurant Latitude 32. Most stop by to sample the fine blends named after constellations in honor of the owner's love for astronomy. Behind the barrel is winemaker Jesus Rivera, responsible for much of the success of neighboring wineries where he previously consulted. For an elegant Chardonnay, try Capricornius, or for an Italian grape blend of Nebbiolo and Sangiovese, the Perseus aged 24 months in French oak barrels is also wonderful. The Orion is one of their most popular reds. Over 75 percent of their wines are certified organic, with eco-friendly practices at the root of their production (solar power, water wells, and aqua reserves). For the jewel of El Cielo, go big with their reserved collection, Estrellas (stars) that have been preserved up to 20 years. Be sure to book the "Blend Your Own Wine Experience" that includes a tour, tasting, and wine-lab workshop where a certified sommelier will teach you how to create your own wine. ✉ *Parcela 118, Km 7.5, Valle de Guadalupe* ☎ *646/155–2220* ⊕ *www. vinoselcielo.com* ✉ *Tastings and tours from $22.*

L.A. Cetto

WINERY | L.A. Cetto is a giant that produces 50% of the wines that come out of Valle de Guadalupe, making it the closest thing to a California wine country experience south of the border. When tasting or buying, avoid the more affordable wines, and go straight for the premiums. Having earned over 950 international awards for their 40 labels, they are well

Continued on page 219

VIVA VINO

About an hour and a half south of San Diego, just inland from Ensenada, lies a region that's everything Ensenada is not. The 14-mile-long Valle de Guadalupe is charming, serene, and urbane, and—you might find this hard to believe if you're a wine buff—is a robust producer of quality vino.

There's no watered-down tequila here. Red grapes grown include Cabernet Sauvignon, Merlot, Tempranillo, and Syrah, while whites include Chardonnay, Sauvignon Blanc, and Viognier. Drive down and spend a day at the vineyards and wineries that line la Ruta del Vino, the road that stretches across the valley, or better yet, base yourself here. The inns and restaurants in the Valle de Guadalupe welcome guests with refined material comforts, which complement the region's natural desert-mountain beauty and lovely libations.

(top) Adobe Guadalupe, (bottom left) Grapes from the Guadalupe Valley, Ensenada, (bottom right) Adobe Guadalupe

WINERY-HOPPING

Some wineries along la Ruta del Vino are sizeable enterprises, while others are boutique affairs. Here are a few choice picks.

THE FULL-BODIED EXPERIENCE

Serious oenophiles should visit the midsize **Monte Xanic**, which is a serious contender for Mexico's finest winery. Tastings are by appointment; don't miss the Gran Ricardo, a high-end Bordeaux-style blend. **L. A. Cetto** is bigger than Monte Xanic, but it offers a well-orchestrated experience with tastings. Free tours are offered daily every half-hour from 10–5. Look for celebrity winemaker Camillo Magoni's wonderful Nebbiolo. A spectacular terrazza overlooks Cetto's own bullring and a sweeping expanse of wine country.

Size Isn't Everything

Tiny, cozy **Casa de Piedra** is the legendary Hugo D'Acosta's winery. Tours and tastings of D'Acosta's high-end wines are by reservation only. Call ahead to visit the even smaller, but equally impressive, **Vinisterra**, where eccentric Swiss winemaker Christoph Gärtner turns out a small-production line of showstoppers called Macouzet, plus one of the only wines in the world made from mission grapes; these grapes come from vines descended from those planted by the Spanish in the 1500s for ceremonial services.

BACK TO THE BEGINNING

The imbibing of fermented fruit dates from the Stone Age (or Neolithic period; 8,500–4,000 BC), but the production of wine in the Americas is comparatively adolescent. Mexico actually has the New World's oldest wine industry, dating from 1574, when conquistadors and priests set off north from Zacatecas in search of gold; when none turned up, they decided to grow grapes instead. In 1597, they founded the Hacienda de San Lorenzo, the first winery in the Americas, in the modern-day state of Coahuila. By the late 1600s, Mexican wine production was so prolific, the Spaniards shut it down so it wouldn't compete with Spanish wine—sending Mexico's wine industry into a three-century hibernation. Now, most Mexican wine producers have moved to the thriving Valle de Guadalupe (a cooler, more favorable climate for vineyards).

L.A. Cetto Petite Sirah, Valle de Guadalupe

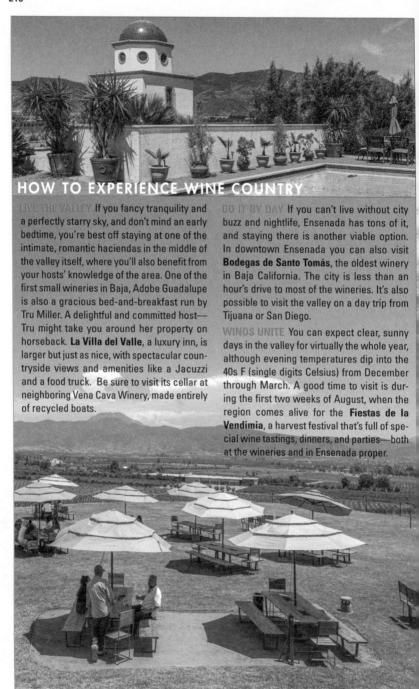

HOW TO EXPERIENCE WINE COUNTRY

LIVE THE VALLEY If you fancy tranquility and a perfectly starry sky, and don't mind an early bedtime, you're best off staying at one of the intimate, romantic haciendas in the middle of the valley itself, where you'll also benefit from your hosts' knowledge of the area. One of the first small wineries in Baja, Adobe Guadalupe is also a gracious bed-and-breakfast run by Tru Miller. A delightful and committed host—Tru might take you around her property on horseback. **La Villa del Valle**, a luxury inn, is larger but just as nice, with spectacular countryside views and amenities like a Jacuzzi and a food truck. Be sure to visit its cellar at neighboring Vena Cava Winery, made entirely of recycled boats.

DO IT BY DAY If you can't live without city buzz and nightlife, Ensenada has tons of it, and staying there is another viable option. In downtown Ensenada you can also visit **Bodegas de Santo Tomás**, the oldest winery in Baja California. The city is less than an hour's drive to most of the wineries. It's also possible to visit the valley on a day trip from Tijuana or San Diego.

WINOS UNITE You can expect clear, sunny days in the valley for virtually the whole year, although evening temperatures dip into the 40s F (single digits Celsius) from December through March. A good time to visit is during the first two weeks of August, when the region comes alive for the **Fiestas de la Vendimia**, a harvest festival that's full of special wine tastings, dinners, and parties—both at the wineries and in Ensenada proper.

(pictured top and bottom) Adobe Guadalupe

known for their lovely Nebbiolo and Chardonnay, and their nicely balanced Don Luis Concordia. Don't miss the Peninsula Espaldera, a Sangiovese-Aglianico blend with aromas of black fruit and toffee. Tours take place daily 10–5 on the half hour. ⊠ *Carretera Tecate–Ensenada, Km 73.5, Valle de Guadalupe* ☎ *646/155–2179, 646/197–5498* ⊕ *www.lacetto.mx.*

La Lomita

WINERY | Owned by Fernando Pérez Castro, this new-generation winery creates rich wines made with 100% local grapes. With six labels under their barrel, their blends are sold to top restaurants and hotels in Mexico City, Riviera Maya, and Cabo. The preferred Sacro—a mix of Cabernet Sauvignon and Merlot—has hints of pomegranate, cherry, pepper, berries, and maple syrup, while the Tinto de la Hacienda has characteristics of compote and jam. For something unique, try Pagano, their rebel baby Grenache that comes in a square bottle. The circular tasting room overlooks a pit of shiny wine tanks where vines dangle from above. It's the place where cool people sip, especially San Diego day-trippers who Instagram their pours in front of murals by Mexican artist Jorge Tellaeche. Tastings are by appointment. ⊠ *Plot 13, San Marcos Village, San Antonio de las Minas* ☎ *646/156–8466* ⊕ *www.lomita. mx* ⊒ *Tastings $35* ⊙ *Closed Mon. and Tues.*

Liceaga

WINERY | This winery produces a variety of Merlot- and Cabernet-heavy blends. Try Liceaga's "L," a complex and elegant wine with hints of cherry, blackberry, cassis, plum and pepper. The tasting room is open most days 9–4. ⊠ *Carretera Tecate–Ensenada, Km 93, San Antonio de las Minas* ☎ *646/188–5742* ⊕ *www. vinosliceaga.com* ⊒ *Four tastings, $20.*

Mogor Badan (*El Mogor*)

WINERY | One of the area's few vineyards to offer organic wines, this 1950s ranch has gained renown for whites such as their remarkably fragrant Chasselas del Mogor. Their newer Pirineo blends a contemporary Mexican Grenache with a French Syrah. Wine tastings are available by reservation only on weekends 11–5 in their underground cave. After wine tasting, dine at the neighboring garden restaurant, operated by the talented chef Drew Deckman. ⊠ *Rancho El Mogor, Carretera Tecate–Ensenada, Km 85.5, San Antonio de las Minas* ☎ *646/156–8156* ⊒ *3 tastings with appetizers, $25* ⊙ *Closed weekdays.*

Monte Xanic

WINERY | Tastings at Monte Xanic take place at the edge of a lovely pond and include three reds and two whites for $35. Most impressive is their consistency, right down to the cheapest table wines. Tastings and tours are available by appointment only. Be sure to check out the impressively styled cellar. ⊠ *Careterra Tecate–Ensenada, Km 70, Valle de Guadalupe* ☎ *646/155–2080* ⊕ *www. montexanic.com.mx.*

Paralelo

WINERY | In 2005, this underground bunker-style Paralelo was built by the Hugo d'Acosta clan as "parallel" to Casa de Piedra. The 25-acre vineyard produces two red blends—the excellent and balanced Arenal and the heavier, minerally Colina— as well as a Chenin Blanc Emblema. Although the winery is technically closed to the public, an advanced reservation is likely to land you a rooftop tasting with enologist and director, Thomas Egli. ⊠ *Carretera Tecate–Ensenada, Km 93.5, Valle de Guadalupe* ☎ *646/156–5268* ⊕ *www.vyva.mx/paralelo* ⊙ *Closed Sun.*

Vena Cava

WINERY | Even if you're not into wine, a visit to this award-winning winery is well worth a visit. Winemaker Phil Gregory blended his passion for sustainable practices and wine making into the architecture of this funky wine cave made from old fishing boats. Bursting with character, these 1930s vessels once sailed the waters off the coast of Ensenada. Today they serve as the domes that cap the wine cellar, housing Vena Cava's labels considered among the best blends in Mexico. Vena Cava is one of the few wineries to produce natural wines, free of sulfites and with no added yeast. The Big Blend Tempranillo is elegant, gentle, and fruit-forward, and the 2016 Cabernet Sauvignon is remarkably smooth. This fine balance of science and art have become an obsession for the talented winemaker who uses French barrels and organic grapes from local valleys. Tastings are offered 11–5 on the hour for $25. Stay awhile and enjoy a meal at the food truck out front, serving an urban take on Baja cuisine. ⊠ *Rancho San Marcos, Valle de Guadalupe* ☎ *646/162–6526* ⊕ *www. venacavawine.com.*

Vinisterra

WINERY | Within Vinisterra, expect to find Tempranillo and Cabernet-Merlot blends, which are big and juicy. Tastings are available 11–4. Four tastings will run you about $15 to $64 depending on your selection. For groups of 10 or more, call well in advance for reservations. ⊠ *Carretera Tecate–Ensenada, Km 94.5, San Antonio de las Minas* ☎ *646/178–3350, 646/178–3310* ⊕ *www.vinisterra.com* ☉ *Closed Tues.*

Wine Museum (*Museo de la Vid y el Vino*)
CULTURAL MUSEUM | For a better understanding of the wine-making process, the Museo de la Vid y el Vino in the heart of Valle de Guadalupe has exhibits on wine history, viticulture, and wine-inspired art. The museum showcases a vast collection of agricultural tools and more than 100 wines from the region. Don't miss the spectacular panoramic view of the valley and the outdoor amphitheater surrounded by vineyards. ⊠ *Carretera Tecate–Ensenada, Km 81.37, Valle de Guadalupe* ☎ *646/156–8165, 646/156–8166* ⊕ *www.museodelvinobc.com* 🖼 *$4* ☉ *Closed Mon.*

🍴 Restaurants

Animalón
$$$$ | **INTERNATIONAL** | Pull up an equipale barrel chair and savor lunch under the canopy of a 200-year-old oak tree at this open-air restaurant, chef Javier Plascencia's tribute to local producers and the Valle lifestyle. Featured dishes change almost weekly, but you might find duck confit, kanpachi tostadas, lobster tallarines, and rib eye with sweet corn. **Known for:** tasting menu with wine pairing; superlative hospitality and setting; creative appetizers. ⑤ *Average main: $157* ⊠ *Carretera Tecate–Ensenada, Ejido, Km 83, Valle de Guadalupe* ☎ *646/375–2658* ⊕ *www.animalonbaja.com* ☉ *Closed Mon. and Tues. and Nov.–Mar.*

★ Conchas de Piedra
$$ | **SEAFOOD** | Read the sign on wall that asks, "Do you oyster?" and then dive into a culinary journey that blends an alfresco shell bar with local sparkling wines. Bypass the à la carte options of poke, and shellfish tostadas (although equally delicious), and go straight for the seven-course tasting menu ($100) that makes this place one to brag about. **Known for:** presentation is on point; sparkling wines from on-site winery Casa de Piedra; fresh concept by chef Drew Deckman. ⑤ *Average main: $20* ⊠ *Casa de Piedra Winery, Carretera Ensenada Tecate, Km 93.5, Valle de Guadalupe* ☎ *646/162–8306* ⊕ *www.conchasdepiedra.com* ☉ *Closed Mon.–Wed. No dinner* ☞ *Groups of 6 or more must have a reservation.*

Deckman's En El Mogor
$$$ | **MEXICAN FUSION** | Dining at Deckman's is like stepping into the quintessential Pinterest photo, replete with an open-air kitchen, straw floor, and wooden tables adorned with wildflowers. As if the chirping birds, adobe structure, soft jazz, and vineyard views weren't enough, you'll find a revolving menu built around seasonable products from

the neighboring Mogor Ranch. **Known for:** one of best restaurants in Mexico; farm-to-table experience; artisanal-ranch menu. $ *Average main: $25* ✉ *Carretera Ensenada–Tecate, Km 85.5, San Antonio de Las Minas, Valle de Guadalupe* ☎ *646/188–3960* ⊕ *www.deckmans.com* ⊘ *Closed Tues. and Wed.*

★ Ensō Omakase

$$$$ | **SUSHI** | It's San Diego that connected chefs Robert Ruiz and Drew Deckman, but it's their commitment to sustainable seafood that turned it into a 15-course sushi collaboration like none other. More than a restaurant, it's a total dining experience that starts with a welcome drink in the vineyard as chef Ruiz prepares the sushi bar for a maximum of eight guests. **Known for:** sustainable seafood advocate; intimate dining experience with exclusive wines; local, seasonal ingredients. $ *Average main: $150* ✉ *Rancho Mogor, Carretera Ensenada–Tecate, Km 85.5, next to Deckman's, Valle de Guadalupe* ✛ *San Antonio de Las Minas* ☎ *646/210–8635* ⊕ *www.ensomakase.com* ⊘ *Closed Tues. and Wed.* ☞ *Two seatings at 3 and 7 pm.*

★ Fauna

$$$$ | **MEXICAN FUSION** | Imagine a restaurant where communal tables sit among sunflowers, where rosemary sprigs burn like incense, and where chefs are free to create an experimental menu. That's Fauna, tucked within the Bruma property and run by prodigy-chef David Castro Hussong, who consistently pours out culinary magic. **Known for:** ever-changing menu with highlights like tender lamb; summer garden setting and winter cozy dining room with sheepskin chairs; impressive presentation. $ *Average main: $50* ✉ *Bruma, Carretera Ensenada–Tecate, Km 73, Valle de Guadalupe* ☎ *646/103–6403* ⊕ *www.faunarestaurante.mx.*

Finca Altozano

$$ | **MODERN MEXICAN** | From the moment you see guests clinking glasses atop wine-barrel towers, you know you're in for a memorable dining experience. On the edge of sprawling vineyards, this rustic setting has a seasonal menu to match. **Known for:** regional ingredients; oak-grilled quail and octopus; famous wine-barrel towers. $ *Average main: $18* ✉ *Carretera Tecate–Ensenada, Km 83, Ejido Francisco Zarco, Valle de Guadalupe* ☎ *646/688–1016* ⊕ *www.fincaltozano.com* ⊘ *Closed Mon. between Nov. and Mar.*

Latitud 32

$$$ | **STEAK HOUSE** | Named for its location on the map, this upscale restaurant at El Cielo Vineyards specializes in grilled cuts and Baja-Yucatán cuisine. Suggested El Cielo wines are listed next to each menu item to assure a perfect pairing with dishes baked in annatto, sour orange, and other unique indigenous spices. **Known for:** Baja-Yucatán fusion; outstanding oysters; panoramic views. $ *Average main: $30* ✉ *Parcela 118, Km 7.5, at El Cielo, Valle de Guadalupe* ☎ *646/155–2220* ⊕ *www.vinoselcielo.com.*

Lunario

$$$$ | **MODERN MEXICAN** | **FAMILY** | This jaw-dropping restaurant at Lomita winery is your chance to try a six- or eight-course tasting menu with a wine pairing. Grab a table overlooking the vineyards or head indoors, where a glass-roofed dining room allows the stars to shine over your table. **Known for:** spectacular wines from Lomita and Carrodilla wineries; observatory-esque dining room; menu featuring local ingredients. $ *Average main: $65* ✉ *Ejido el Porvenir, at Lomita winery, Valle de Guadalupe* ☎ *646/156–8469* ⊕ *www.restaurantelunario.com* ⊘ *Closed Mon.–Wed.*

★ Malva

$$$$ | ECLECTIC | With sprawling views of vineyards, this restaurant and open-air kitchen is shaded by a thatched palapa and surrounded by acres of farmland where chef Roberto Alcocer gathers ingredients. Beer, wine, vegetables, fruit, cheese, bread, meat, eggs, honey—nearly everything served is from the on-site farm, making this a true farm-to-table experience. **Known for:** locally sourced food; tasting menu featuring Mexican flavors; Baja seafood and ranch-grown foods. $ *Average main: $70* ⊠ *Carretera Ensenada–Tecate, Km 96, at Mina Penelope Vinicola, San Antonio de las Minas* ☎ *646/155–3085* ⊕ *www.minapenelope.com* ⊘ *Closed Mon. and Tues.*

 # Hotels

Properties in Valle de Guadalupe range from ranch-style B&Bs amid orchards, to eco-lofts on boulder-strewn hillsides. A welcome drink is fairly standard at most hotels, and some even include breakfast and wine tasting in the room rate. Don't expect to find TVs or nightlife in these parts, since wine tasting and early nights are top priorities. Some hotels request that toilet paper not be flushed due to gray water systems and clogging drains. Depending on where you're staying, remote properties are at the end of long dusty roads pitted with potholes. Charging stations for electric cars are available at newer hotels and restaurants.

Adobe Guadalupe

$$$ | B&B/INN | As the grand dame of the valley, this magnificent country inn surrounded by vineyards welcomes you with brick archways, fountains, and a pasture with white horses. **Pros:** on-site food truck serves great tapas Thursday–Monday; electric car charging stations; rates include wine tasting and breakfast. **Cons:** weekends usually booked six months in advance; chilly pool; no children under 12. $ *Rooms from: $275* ⊠ *Off Hwy. 3 through Guadalupe village, Valle de Guadalupe* ✥ *6 km (4 miles) along same road, right turn at town of Porvenir* ☎ *646/155–2094* ⊕ *www.adobeguadalupe.com* ⊅ *6 rooms* ❖ *Free Breakfast.*

Bruma (*Casa 8*)

$$$$ | B&B/INN | Inside the luxury compound at Bruma, you'll find a winery, the top-notch Fauna restaurant, villas, a market, and the architectural masterpiece, Casa 8; its eight suites are joined by a main house complete with a common living room, kitchen, pool, and sundeck. **Pros:** contemporary design; excellent restaurant; luxurious property. **Cons:** pricey hotel with two-night minimum on weekends; noise carries between rooms; booking process could use improvement. $ *Rooms from: $440* ⊠ *Otro Carretera Tecate–Ensenada, Km 74, Valle de Guadalupe* ☎ *646/116–8031* ⊕ *www.bruma.mx* ⊅ *16 rooms* ❖ *Free Breakfast.*

Casa Mayoral

$$ | B&B/INN | This road less traveled leads to four cozy cabins in a farmy setting with donkeys, vegetable gardens, and hammocks swaying under the shade of an orange grove. **Pros:** in-room massages by request; gated property; sustainable cabins with breakfast and valley views. **Cons:** low water pressure; bumpy road and remote; nothing fancy. $ *Rooms from: $176* ⊠ *Carretera Tecate–Ensenada, Km 88.24, Valle de Guadalupe* ☎ *664/257–2410* ⊕ *www.casamayoral.com* ⊅ *6 rooms, 1 house* ❖ *Free Breakfast.*

★ Contemplación Hotel Boutique

$$ | HOTEL | At the push of a button, remote-controlled blackout curtains unveil vineyard views from this property's freestanding villas with floor-to-ceiling windows. **Pros:** gourmet cuisine at Salvia Blanca; community fire pit, gym, spa, pool, and Jacuzzi; kindhearted staff. **Cons:** super pet-friendly can mean a lot of dogs; rooms could use a deep clean; minibars aren't always stocked. $ *Rooms from: $250* ⊠ *Parcela 325 Calle Merlot, Ejido el Porvenir, Valle de Guadalupe*

Did You Know?

Baja California produces about 70% of Mexico's wine; its main wine region, Valle de Guadalupe, is home to more than 100 wineries.

☎ *646/311–0995* ⊕ *www.contempla-cionhotel.com* ⤳ *12 rooms* ⫯❙ *Free Breakfast.*

★ El Cielo Winery & Resort by Karisma

$$$$ | **RESORT** | As the largest hotel in the area, "Heaven" is the closest thing the Valle has to the big resort experience common in Riviera Maya, but without all the traffic or all-inclusive magnitude. **Pros:** gated property with 24-hour security; blend-your-own-wine experience workshop; eco-responsible practices. **Cons:** $70 pet fee; restaurant is pricey; breakfast not included. ⑤ *Rooms from: $400* ✉ *Carretera El Tigre–El Porvenir, Km 7.5, Parcela 117 El Porvenir, Valle de Guadalupe* ⊕ *www.elcielovalledeguadalupe.com* ⤳ *91 rooms* ⫯❙ *No Meals.*

Encuentro Guadalupe

$$$$ | **HOTEL** | With freestanding steel box-cabins perched on a boulder-strewn hill, this property has architect Jorge Gracia to thank for its innovative design. **Pros:** pet-friendly; unique design; hiking trails. **Cons:** no kids under 13; must sign liability waivers at check-in; room rates don't match quality of service. ⑤ *Rooms from: $498* ✉ *Carretera Tecate–Ensenada, Km 75, San Antonio de las Minas* ☎ *646/155–2775* ⊕ *www.encuentrocollection.com* ⤳ *20 rooms* ⫯❙ *No Meals.*

Hacienda Guadalupe

$$$ | **HOTEL** | Privacy, comfort, and quality are the pillars of this hacienda-style property that draws a loyal clientele for the central location and reasonable rates. **Pros:** great value and spotless property; gorgeous waterfall pool; hospitality at its best. **Cons:** winery and restaurant closed Tuesday; no TVs; low water pressure. ⑤ *Rooms from: $264* ✉ *Carretera Tecate–Ensenada, Km 81.5, Valle de Guadalupe* ☎ *646/155–2859* ⊕ *www.haciendaguadalupe.com* ⤳ *16 rooms* ⫯❙ *No Meals.*

Hotel Partana

$$$ | **HOTEL** | In the heart of Baja's wine country sits this modern 10-room boutique hotel within walking distance of Valle's top restaurants. **Pros:** rooms are built in between vines; modern amenities and artisanal toiletries; private accommodations each have a rooftop terrace. **Cons:** not a full-service hotel; loose gravel pathway to room; patchy Wi-Fi. ⑤ *Rooms from: $268* ✉ *Next to Finca Altozano, Carretera Tecate–Ensenada, Km 83, Valle de Guadalupe* ☎ *646/668–1970* ⊕ *www.hotelpartana.com* ⤳ *10 rooms* ⫯❙ *No Meals.*

La Villa del Valle

$$$$ | **B&B/INN** | Perched on a hilltop overlooking Vena Cava winery, this luxury inn is reminiscent of a Tuscan villa. **Pros:** convenient on-site food truck; wine tasting, teatime, snacks included in rate; excellent breakfasts. **Cons:** no kids under 13; guests are not given keys to lock rooms; two-night minimum stay. ⑤ *Rooms from: $315* ✉ *Off Carretera Tecate-Ensenada, Km 88, Valle de Guadalupe* ✛ *Between San Antonio de las Minas and Francisco Zarco. Exit at Rancho Sicomoro and follow signs* ☎ *646/156–8007, 818/207–7130 in U.S.* ⊕ *www.lavilladelvalle.com* ⤳ *6 rooms* ⫯❙ *Free Breakfast.*

Lumi

$$ | **HOTEL** | **FAMILY** | It's love that launched this stunning Nordic-inspired container hotel, starting with a romance between a Finnish woman and a Mexican man who turned their marriage into a passion project that beautifully blended both cultures. **Pros:** pets stay free; sauna great on cold nights; bikes for use. **Cons:** no walk-ins; must reserve sauna; remote property. ⑤ *Rooms from: $229* ✉ *Camino Vecinal, Ejido El Porvenir, Valle de Guadalupe* ☎ *686/261–8030* ⊕ *www.lumi.mx* ⤳ *11 units* ⫯❙ *Free Breakfast.*

Terra del Valle

$ | B&B/INN | Beyond the lavender fields and orange groves of this 12-acre property are ranch-style adobe suites insulated with bales of hay and equipped with surprising amenities like organic bath products, plush robes, and private terraces. **Pros:** excellent value; swimming pool; Jacuzzi and bikes for use. **Cons:** soft mattresses; usually booked; remote location on dirt road. ⓢ *Rooms from: $140* ✉ *Rancho La Concha, Camino San José de la Zorra s/n, Ejido El Porvenir, Valle de Guadalupe* ☎ *646/117–3645* ⊕ *www.terradelvalle.com* ⇱ *5 rooms* ⦿*| Free Breakfast.*

 Shopping

La Casa de Doña Lupe

LOCAL GOODS | Near L.A. Cetto, Dona Lupe's store-meets-restaurant sells organic jams, chili marmalades, olive spreads, cheeses, salsas, oils, wines, breads, and other local delicacies. Products can be shipped to the United States. ✉ *Valle de Guadalupe* ✛ *Off Carretera Tecate–Ensenada, turn left and follow road past L.A. Cetto to yellow building* ☎ *646/193–6291* ⊕ *www.lacasadonalupe.com.*

 Activities

Quinta Monasterio Spa

SPA | The creative makers of Quinta Monasterio wine combine tastings with spa treatments, which incorporate grapes, lavender, citrus, and olive oil directly from their property. Housed in an innovative two-story container, the small spa accommodates one to four guests and includes massages, facials, exfoliations, manicures, pedicures, and aromatherapy in the sauna created from old wine barrels. Spa packages include lunch and a glass of wine; appointments are by reservation only. ✉ *Quinta Monasterio 12, San Antonio de las Minas* ✛ *Take Hwy. 3 to el Ejido Porvenir, turn right and follow signs* ☎ *646/156–8023* ⊕ *www.quintamonasterio.com.mx/spa.*

7

Baja California VALLE DE GUADALUPE

Index

Photo Credits

Front Cover: Frederick Millett/Alamy Stock Photo[Aerial view looking west of Lands End, Cabo San Lucas, Mexico, Baja California Sur, where the Sea of Cortez meets the Pacific Ocean]. **Back cover, from left to right:** LindaYG/iStockphoto. Larry Dignan/iStockphoto. Andreygudkov/iStockphoto. **Spine:** Kirk Fisher/iStockphoto. **Interior, from left to right:** DavidWitthaus/iStockphoto (1). Sarah_Robson/Dreamstime (2-3). Cavan Images/GettyImages (5). **Chapter 1: Experience Los Cabos:** Frederick Millett/Shutterstock (6-7). Los Cabos Tourism Board (8-9). Los Cabos Tourism Board (9). Niknikon/iStockphoto (9). Douglas Peebles Photography/Alamy Stock Photo (10). Toddtaulman/iStockphoto (10). Ferrantraite/iStockphoto (10). El Squid Roe (10). Los Cabos Tourism Board (11). Los Cabos Tourism Board (11). Hasselblad H4D (11). Ed-Ni-Photo/iStockphoto (11). Leswrona/Dreamstime (12). Michael Seidl (12). Francisco Estrada PhotoMexico (12). Kartinkin77/Shutterstock (12). Barbara Kraft (13). Huerta Los Tamarindos/Los Cabos Tourism Board (13). Grey82/Shutterstock (16). Los Cabos Tourism Board (16). Lupe Amador/Shutterstock (16). ChavezEd/Shutterstock (17). One&Only Palmilla (17). Tamarindos Mexican Farm to Table (18). Pueblo Bonito (18). Carlosrojas20/iStockphoto (18). Jacopo Ventura/Shutterstock (18). MielPhotos2008/iStockphoto (19). TTSeng/Wikimedia Commons (19). Paul Camhi/La Lupita (19). Restaurante Los Tres Gallos (19). San Miguel Glass blowing (20). Dianeta8/Shutterstock (21). **Chapter 3: Cabo San Lucas:** Emperorcosar/Shutterstock (59). Marcos Botelho Jr/Shutterstock (67). Kartinkin77/Shutterstock (80). Wildestanimal/GettyImages (83). Wildestanimal 2019/GettyImages (86). Michael Braun/GettyImages (87). Grandriver/GettyImages (88). **Chapter 4: The Corridor:** Dbsocal/Shutterstock (91). Odor Zsolt/Shutterstock (100). Tatiana Koshkina/iStockphoto (102-103). The Esperanza (105). OneandOnly Palmilla (107). National Geographic Creative/Alamy Stock Photo (113). Damian Davila/iStockphoto (114). Geoffrey von Zastrow/Shutterstock (114). VG Foto/Shutterstock (114). Stuart Westmorland/GettyImages (115). Cavan Images/GettyImages (116). Javier Garcia/Shutterstock (118). Anthony J Rayburn/GettyImages (118). **Chapter 5: San José del Cabo:** Karamysh/Shutterstock (121). Gerasimovvv/Dreamstime (128-129). FloraFarms/ Los Cabos Tourism Board (131). Khamsai Vang/Flickr (134). Galina Savina/Shutterstock 138). John Mitchell/Alamy (140). Patricia Chumillas/Shutterstock (141). Ken Ross/Viesti Associates Inc (143). Ken Ross/Viesti Associates Inc 143). Jane Onstott/Huichol Art (143). Ken Ross/Viesti Associates Inc. (143). Ken Ross/Viesti Associates Inc (143). Wonderlane/Flickr (144). Patti Haskins/Flickr (144). Jose Zelaya/Huichol Prayer Arrow (144). Fontplaydotcom/Dennis Hill/Flickr (144). Jane Onstott/Huichol Bag (144). Csp/Shutterstock (145). **Chapter 6: Los Cabos Side Trips:** Ryan C Slimak/Shutterstock (149). Shawn Goldberg/Shutterstock (164). Matt Gush/Shutterstock (176-177). Joost van Uffelen/Shutterstock (180). Michael S. Nolan/Alamy Stock Photo (183). Renacal1/iStockphoto (184). Michael Nolan/GettyImages (184). Jan-Dirk Hansen/iStockphoto (185). Leonardo Gonzalez/Shutterstock (187). **Chapter 7: Baja California:** Priscilia Salinas/Shutterstock (195). VG Foto/Shutterstock (201). Sherry V Smith/Shutterstock (215). Leon Felipe Chargoy/Shutterstock (216) Adeliepenguin/Dreamstime (216). Diabetestijuana/Dreamstime (216). Jebarahona/WikimediaCommons (217). Sherry V Smith/Shutterstock 218). Mikel Dabbah/Shutterstock (218). Sherry V Smith/Shutterstock (223). **About Our Writers:** All photos are courtesy of the writers except for the following: Marlise Kast-Myers courtesy of Unscripted Photos. Jenny Hart courtesy of Pablo Seijo.

Every effort has been made to trace the copyright holders, and we apologize in advance for any accidental errors. We would be happy to apply the corrections in the following edition of this publication.

Notes

Notes

Notes

Notes

Notes

Notes

Notes

Fodor's LOS CABOS

Publisher: Stephen Horowitz, *General Manager*

Editorial: Douglas Stallings, *Editorial Director;* Jill Fergus, Amanda Sadlowski, *Senior Editors;* Brian Eschrich, Alexis Kelly, *Editors;* Angelique Kennedy-Chavannes, Yoojin Shin, *Associate Editors*

Design: Tina Malaney, *Director of Design and Production;* Jessica Gonzalez, *Senior Designer;* Jaimee Shaye, *Graphic Design Associate*

Production: Jennifer DePrima, *Editorial Production Manager;* Elyse Rozelle, *Senior Production Editor;* Monica White, *Production Editor*

Maps: Rebecca Baer, *Map Director;* David Lindroth, Mark Stroud (Moon Street Cartography), *Cartographers*

Photography: Viviane Teles, *Director of Photography;* Namrata Aggarwal, Neha Gupta, Payal Gupta, Ashok Kumar, *Photo Editors;* Jade Rodgers, Shanelle Jacobs, *Photo Production Interns*

Business and Operations: Chuck Hoover, *Chief Marketing Officer;* Robert Ames, *Group General Manager*

Public Relations and Marketing: Joe Ewaskiw, *Senior Director of Communications and Public Relations*

Fodors.com: Jeremy Tarr, *Editorial Director;* Rachael Levitt, *Managing Editor*

Technology: Jon Atkinson, *Executive Director of Technology;* Rudresh Teotia, *Associate Director of Technology;* Alison Lieu, *Project Manager*

Writers: Luis Domínguez, Jenny Hart, Marlise Kast-Myers

Editor: Alexis Kelly

Production Editor: Jennifer DePrima

th Edition

ISBN 978-1-64097-740-2

ISSN 2326-4152

SPECIAL SALES

This book is available at special discounts for bulk purchases for sales promotions or premiums. For more information, e-mail SpecialMarkets@fodors.com.

PRINTED IN CANADA

10 9 8 7 6 5 4 3 2 1

About Our Writers

Luis Domínguez is a Riviera Maya-based freelance writer and independent journalist interested in travel, languages, art, books, history, philosophy, politics, and sports. He has written for Fodor's, DK, Yahoo!, Telemundo, and Odigoo Travel, among other digital and print publications in North America and Europe. Luis updated the San José del Cabo and Corridor chapters of this guide. You can follow him on X @luisf_dominguez or check out his website ⊕ *luisfdominguez.com.*

Jenny Hart is an American travel writer and advisor based in Mexico. She specializes in covering Mexico, Latin America, and the Caribbean for English-language audiences and is particularly passionate about promoting tourism to her adopted country. Read more of her expert tips and insights on Mexico travel at ⊕ *mexpat. co*and follow her adventures around Los Cabos and beyond on Instagram at @jennyjhart. She updated the Cabo San Lucas and the Los Cabos Side Trips chapters.

Journalist and author **Marlise Kast-Myers** has traveled to more than 80 countries and has lived in Switzerland, Dominican Republic, Spain, and Costa Rica. Before settling in Southern California, she completed a surfing and snowboarding expedition across the world. Following the release of her memoir, *Tabloid Prodigy*, Marlise co-authored over 40 Fodor's Travel Guides including books on Cancun, San Diego, Panama, Puerto Rico, Peru, Los Cabos, Corsica, Riviera Maya, Sardinia, Switzerland, Vietnam, and Costa Rica. She served as a photojournalist for *Surf Guide to Costa Rica* and authored *Day and Overnight Hikes on the Pacific Crest Trail.* Based in San Diego County, she writes travel features for *The San Diego Union Tribune* and other publications. She currently lives at the historic Betty Crocker Estate where she and her husband, Benjamin operate an antique business, Brick n Barn. Her website is ⊕ *www.marlisekast.com.* She updated the Experience, Travel Smart, and Baja California chapters.